General
Stephen D. Lee

General
Stephen D. Lee

by
Herman Hattaway

University Press of Mississippi

JACKSON

1976

To

Norman Lederer

Copyright © 1976 by the
University Press of Mississippi
Library of Congress Catalog Card Number 75–42612
ISBN 0–87805–071–X
Manufactured in the United States of America
Printed by Kingsport Press, Kingsport, Tennessee

THIS VOLUME IS AUTHORIZED
AND SPONSORED BY
MISSISSIPPI STATE UNIVERSITY
STARKVILLE, MISSISSIPPI

Contents

List of Maps

Acknowledgments

T. Harry Williams suggested a work on Stephen D. Lee, and he aided the project immensely with both guidance and encouragement. Other teachers at Louisiana State University who gave beneficial evaluations include Walter C. Richardson, John Loos, Burl Noggle, E. Ramon Arango, and James D. Hardy, Jr.—who has been a special friend.

Various scholars around the country gave me their opinions of Lee, and several aided me in gathering material. They include John K. Bettersworth and Glover Moore of Mississippi State University; Clement Eaton, University of Kentucky; John K. Mahon, University of Florida; R. A. McLemore of Clinton, Mississippi; and, the most helpful of all, Archer Jones of North Dakota State University.

My colleagues at the University of Missouri—Kansas City kindly listened to readings of all or a part of the manuscript in its several revisions. These include Robert L. Branyan, Lawrence H. Larsen, Jesse V. Clardy, Stanley B. Parsons, Jr., Richard D. McKinzie, James S. Falls, Donald DeB. Beaver, and Theodore Freidell.

Other historians also gave me assistance and advice, especially Mrs. George S. Hazard and the late William J. Love, both of Columbus, Mississippi; Edwin C. Bearss, National Park Service—who has begun work on an administrative history of the Vicksburg Military Park and obligingly loaned me his notes and drafts; John D. Thompson, Seminole, Texas—who compiled a commendable Master's thesis on Lee at the University of Texas in 1950; Thomas C. Read, Charleston, South Carolina; the late Ray D. Smith, Chicago,

Illinois; Kendon Stubbs, Alderman Library, University of Virginia; Miss Lucille Peacock, Evans Memorial Library, Aberdeen, Mississippi; Elmer O. Parker, the National Archives; Larry Pursley, Abbeville, South Carolina; Steve Herman, Curtis, Nebraska, and John G. Lee, Farmington, Connecticut.

I cannot close without a word of appreciation to my parents—and of love to Margaret, my wife, whose encouragement and assistance were beyond estimation.

Introduction

STEPHEN DILL LEE has been hardly noticed in history, even by specialists dedicated to the study of the South or the Civil War; and it is unfortunate for both the South and the nation that men like Lee have been ignored while southern fireaters and other eccentrics received attention. This bias has affected interpretations of the southern people and obscured insights into the nature of the South. Without men like Lee to lead and build the region after the Civil War, the United States might now be as chaotic as Ireland.

Lee lived through a period of traumatic change. He served both as a valuable soldier and as an exemplary civilian. Important in the Confederacy and the New South, he at first fought to preserve an old way of life and then helped lead the way into a new social order. He was not one of the plain folk of the Confederacy; neither was he of the aristocracy. Lee attained wide reputation and prominence, but his fame never approached that of the more noted figures of the period. Men like Nathan Bedford Forrest and Pierre G. T. Beauregard fought the war with a passion; Lee fought as a professional soldier.

Lee impressed people with his fine physical appearance. In the 1850s and 1860s, he was a handsome man, gray-eyed and fair complexioned. He stood six feet tall and seemed taller than he was. One of his enthusiastic friends declared that "by nature's endowment, he stands like Saul of Kish, higher than the masses. . . ." Lee when young began wearing a thick beard that made him look older, wiser, and more distinguished than a man of his age. In later years, white hair and beard gave him a noble and majestic appearance. Acquaintances said that he had a gentle, kindly voice, but his grandson remembered that everyone seemed to hold him in awe.

Although Lee's military career occupied but fifteen of his seventy-five years, this period had the most influence and impact upon his development. It shaped and molded everything that he did later. Every activity in which he participated, every organization he joined, and every cause that he championed was influenced by his military experiences and education.

His daily contact with troops developed in him a profound compassion. At every opportunity after the Civil War, he did all in his power for the kind of people who had fought with him. A Bourbon in practice, he had the soul of a populist. He literally created a college for the war's survivors and their children, with a curriculum designed for the common man, not the wealthy. Obsessed with the necessity of having coursework of immediate use, he organized Mississippi A. & M. College to resemble West Point—reasoning that, if good soldiers should study all subjects that pertain to the military, good farmers should study all subjects pertinent to agriculture.

The United States Army was good for Lee. It gave him a sound education, social grace, and a respectable place in society. The training taught him discipline and honed his physical and mental abilities. Throughout most of his long life, spanning two-thirds of the nineteenth century and continuing into the twentieth, from 22 September 1833 to 28 May 1908, he consistently revealed administrative competence, steadfastness, a remarkable capacity for growth, and the ability to make the best of a situation.

Almost nothing distracted Lee. At times revealing even a degree of fanaticism, if Stephen Lee set himself to a job, it was sure to be with a stronger zeal than most other men had. Pragmatic and persistent, he never attempted to do too many things at once; but he never indulged in idleness. He achieved his successes, in war and in peace, because he had tenacity, resolution, and abundant managerial ability. Supremely honest, straightforward, and devoted to his chosen tasks, yet he is somewhat difficult to characterize. An eccentric personality would have been easier to depict. Lee possessed the rare capability of suppressing extraneous interests and devoting himself to the work at hand.

When Lee died in 1908, the newspapers in more than sixty cities paid him tribute. Many plaudits came from outside the South, and some came from foreign newspapers. The Memphis *Commercial Appeal* touched a recurrent note in dubbing Lee a "knightly gentleman and chivalrous soldier, beloved by every man, woman, and child in Dixie Land." The Richmond *Times-Dispatch* carried perhaps the most judicious of all the editorial eulogies. Avoiding false statements and effusive praise, the Richmond paper concluded: "He was a splendid soldier and a fine citizen, and the entire South joins with his mates in the UCV to mourn his death."

A year later, the President of the United States had occasion to give his sentiments about Lee. William Howard Taft visited Columbus, Mississippi, Lee's home town; and in the course of his official speech, the President recalled Lee, saying, "I am indeed sorry that it was not given to me to meet him in person and receive that kindly, gentle influence that he shed wherever he moved. . . . In regard to the relations in the South to the rest of the union . . . , he represented that spirit which I would invoke on the part of every Southerner." Taft's tribute captured the spirit of the ideal for which Lee had made himself a symbol.

General
Stephen D. Lee

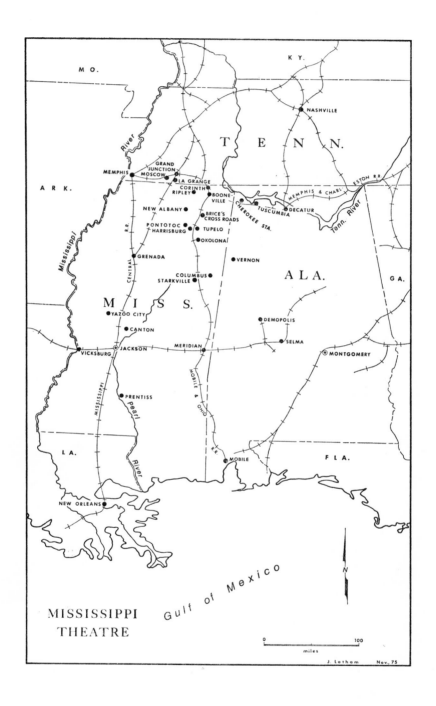

MISSISSIPPI
THEATRE

1

Young Warrior

STEPHEN DILL LEE was born in Charleston, South Carolina, into the fifth generation of a proud southern family. His ancestor Thomas Lee founded the family's American branch by immigrating from Saint Michaels, Barbados sometime before 1738. Stephen's paternal grandfather, also named Thomas, was a gifted and prominent judge. Thomas junior, the eighth of the judge's ten children, graduated as a doctor of medicine from the medical school of South Carolina in 1830. He married Caroline Allison, and their first child, a son, arrived on 22 September 1833. Dr. Lee honored one of his older brothers and named the child Stephen.[1]

The family was distantly related to the Lees of Virginia, but for a long time they knew nothing of this connection. Years later, when asked if he were related to the great Gen. Robert E. Lee, Stephen replied that he was not but that he "would consider it quite an honor to be." Much later in his life, Stephen became interested in genealogy and helped to prepare a family tree, a study which revealed a kinship between Francis Lee, Stephen's great-great-great-grandfather and Robert Lee, Lord Mayor of London in 1602, and an ancestor of Virginia's Robert E. Lee.[2]

The South Carolina Lees lived comfortably; and two years after Stephen's birth, his sister Caroline Kezia Rachel was born. This happy event unfortunately was followed shortly afterwards by tragedy—Mrs. Lee died. Stephen was not old enough to have formed a permanent memory of her, and as an adult the only recollection he had of his mother was being led by the hand to her funeral.[3]

Soon after his wife's death, Dr. Lee's health was severely damaged by a fever epidemic, and he moved with his children to Rock Mills in Anderson County, Abbeville District, where he hoped to recover. Here he built a new house, where he spent the rest of his life. He married Elizabeth Cummings Humphreys in September 1839, the same month that Stephen celebrated his sixth birthday. Elizabeth bore Dr. Lee five children, three sons and two daughters.[4] The presence of a new mother and many brothers and sisters contributed to a happy but uneventful childhood for Stephen. His father remained sickly and unable to earn more than a meagre living.[5]

Largely because of these economic conditions, Stephen received little formal schooling during his early years. Stephen began his education in 1846, at the age of eleven, when he went off to a boarding school run by his namesake uncle in Asheville, North Carolina. Born in 1801, Dr. Thomas Lee's brother, Stephen, attended West Point for two years, from 1819 to 1821, resigned for unrecorded reasons, and later attended the aristocratic College of Charleston, where he received a bachelor's degree in 1828.[6] Possibly because of this uncle's influence, and probably in order to get a free college education which he could not afford otherwise, young Lee decided to apply for an appointment to the military academy at West Point.

Stephen made his request to James L. Orr, at that time only a candidate for Congress from the second congressional district in South Carolina. Lee showed early that he had some audacity. Orr promised that if elected he would try to secure the coveted appointment for Stephen. And Orr did win. He wrote out the recommendation in April 1849, though the appointment was processed too late for Stephen to begin studies that year, and the eager young man had to wait another fifteen months. He reported to West Point on 1 July 1850 and commenced his career as a soldier.[7]

As Stephen Lee and his classmates soon discovered, the United States Military Academy had high standards and a rigorous program. Only a fraction of the young men who began study with Lee achieved success and became officers. Not quite half of the group, 46 of 106, received a commission. By the end of his years as a cadet, Lee, perhaps more than most of the others, learned to perform at the very best of his capability. The remainder of his military career was characterized by a similar devotion to duty. As early as 1867, one writer concluded that Lee the soldier "had no dormant powers—his were all awake, highly disciplined and ready for action."[8]

Seventy members of the entering class of 1854 received their first introduction to West Point life in a two-month summer encampment. The group moved into barracks by September 1850 and soon was joined by thirty-six late arrivals. The daily routine, one cadet wrote, consisted of "recitations, horse-riding, drills, and out-door and in-door instruction." Every new class member suffered some annoyance, but there was no serious hazing.[9]

When Lee first arrived, the academy had changed a great deal since its establishment nearly a half-century earlier. West Point, the country's major source of college-trained engineers in the nineteenth century, had become a very respectable school. Scarcely any of the original buildings remained; and as the physical plant improved, so did the quality of instruction.[10] Capt. Henry Brewerton served as superintendent of West Point during the first half of Lee's cadetship. The capable Dennis Hart Mahan was professor of civil and military engineering. And several others were present who distinguished themselves later in the Civil War. These included Mahan's assistant, Bvt. Capt. Gustavus W. Smith, later a Confederate major general and briefly the secretary of war; Bvt. Maj. Fitz John Porter, then assistant professor of mathematics, Bvt. Capt. Edmund Kirby Smith, destined to be the last Confederate general to surrender a force of significant size.[11]

George H. Thomas, the professor who had the greatest impact upon Lee, famous as "the Rock of Chickamauga," and whom Lee would fight at the Battle of Nashville, instructed the cadets in both artillery and cavalry. "A cold, phlematic, unimpressionable man he always seemed," remembered one of Lee's chums, "but a born soldier." Some of Thomas's critics believed that he gave high marks for indifferent recitations, and perhaps he did; but if a teacher's success is measured by the future performance of his students, Thomas was remarkable. In addition to Stephen Lee, Thomas alumni included Philip Sheridan, one of the three most famed union generals in the Civil War, and James E. B. ("Jeb") Stuart, the "eyes" of R. E. Lee's army. Stephen Lee received superior grades from Thomas, particularly in cavalry, but the ratings stood second in importance to the real knowledge he gained.[12] Conspicuously good service with artillery contributed toward all of Lee's Civil War promotions between captain and brigadier general, and his ability in cavalry later proved very helpful to the Confederacy on more than one occasion.

Lee formed warm relationships with several of the cadets who later achieved high rank in the Civil War armies. William D. Pender was his dearest friend. One year Lee's junior, Pender escaped Lee's initial handicap of low rank in the Confederate Army and began the Civil War as a colonel. He died a major general, suffering from a wound received at Gettysburg, leaving his pregnant twenty-three-year-old widow to name their posthumously born son Stephen Lee Pender.[13]

Nine of the gradautes in Lee's class became Civil War generals. Lee and Pender both did and were close friends with several of the others, including James Stuart (who was called "Beaut" or "Beauty" at this time rather than the later "Jeb"), Custis Lee, John Pegram, and Oliver Otis Howard. All of these men served with the Confederacy except Howard, one of the only two in the class who became Union generals.[14]

Lee and his classmates did not suffer from economic difficulties once they entered the Point. Some of the cadets came from humble origins, others were wealthy, and a number like Lee had experienced moderate circumstances. Cadets needed very little money, and Lee's father was able to send him a sufficient amount from time to time. Actually, to aid the spirit of democracy within cadet ranks and to foster the military training, West Point officials carefully limited the amount of money that any student could have at his disposal.

Lee spent his entire adolescence and young manhood in a military environment. His social contacts were with people from all over the United States, and this experience contributed to his ability to get along with people from diverse backgrounds as well as to gain their support and cooperation. Lee never took the "grand tour" that some wealthy southern males considered essential to complete an education; he never managed slaves, nor ran a business, and was at home only a very little. When Civil War came he did not immediately join the southern side; he took time to consider the alternatives. But his experience made him a very valuable man to the side that he chose.

As a cadet in 1850 Lee possessed only potential, not innate generalship, and he should have worried more in the beginning about his academic pursuits. It probably shocked him to learn during the first few months that the art of soldiering required substantial effort in seemingly nonrelated subjects. After twelve weeks of schooling, his instructors rated him last in a mathematics section of fourteen cadets, and he fared little better in English studies, finishing thirteenth out of fourteen.[15]

In later life, Lee recalled that he had a terriffc struggle getting through West Point, but in truth he never was in danger of completely failing in his studies. He had to work hard, but he did finally buckle down and perform well. On the first semiannual examinations in January 1851, Lee placed forty-first out of ninety-three plebes in mathematics and twenty-ninth in English studies. He ranked thirty-seventh in overall class standing. The class thinned by the end of the academic year; and among the sixty-three veterans who remained, Lee stood twenty-eighth.[16]

Apparently Lee initially found the physical aspects of the training easier to cope with than the academic. Several times in 1850 and 1851 he was "distinguished for correct deportment." Two hundred demerits in a single year could bring a cadet's dismissal, but Lee safely accumulated only forty-five during his first twelve months.[17] All of his offenses were minor, and he did not appear on the punishment rolls.

He followed this superb beginning with a sharp change for the worse in the ensuing year, when he had well over one hundred demerits. His "trifling and inattentive behavior in Mathematical Academy" brought him his first serious punishment. Then in April 1852, he received a citation for "trifling in French class." The nadir came in May, when he went on report for "highly insubordinate conduct," along with six other cadets. A garrison court martial found them guilty. Lee's sentence restricted him from privileges and assigned him extra duties until the end of June.[18]

Lee trifled very little after this time. This episode was the most serious trouble that he ever got into at the academy, and he learned his lesson. During his punishment period he strictly toed the line; and by the end of June, a chastened cadet, he was noted for his "outstanding deportment." The new superintendent who took office the following fall had no disciplinary problem with Stephen Lee during the remaining two years of his cadetship.

This significant change in superintendents brought to the office forty-five-year-old Capt. and Bvt. Col. Robert E. Lee, a real inspiration to the cadets. He immediately stiffened discipline and upgraded academic standards, but he also understood boys. The colonel's own son, Custis, was a member of Stephen Lee's class, and he consistently ranked near the top, ultimately finishing in first position. He usually visited his parents' home on Saturday afternoons, often accompanied by one or more of the other cadets.[19] Owing to his friendship with Stephen, the two enjoyed R. E. Lee's hospitality from time to time.

Superintendent Lee occasionally held parties at his residence, inviting some of the cadets to associate with the unattached young ladies who always were present. Stephen recalled attending one such gathering and admitted he had been extremely bashful and too timid to mingle with the female guests. Robert E. Lee won Stephen's everlasting adulation by devoting the greater part of the evening to the "wall flowers," trying to draw them out and make them feel at ease.[20]

Social affairs with desirable members of the opposite sex were a pleasant diversion for most of the cadets, including Lee, once he overcame his shyness. They highly prized an invitation to Superintendent Lee's because the academic year did not feature many opportunities for mixed social intercourse. And even though the summer season saw quite a few "city belles and other fair harpies" besieging the Point, as one cadet complained, they only "congregate to whet their beaks on unsophisticated squabs simply to retain normal appetites, cultivate the lure and wiles, and keep their hands in for the winter campaign." During slack times the cadets occasionally compensated for the lack of girls by holding a "stag dance"—only boys present.[21] Lee profited from both his unofficial social training sessions and encouragement from his colonel, ultimately developing a social grace and personality that charmed several fair ladies until he married, late in the Civil War. Not surprisingly, then, a newspaper reporter observed Lee during the conflict as "a man of commanding presence, exquisite courtesy, and superior intelligence . . . , the centre of every circle."[22]

Girls and parties occupied a large portion of the cadets' slight free time, but they also were aware of national political events. Lee's years at the Point covered an exciting and critical period in U. S. history. Sectional strains were plainly evident, even to the budding young soldiers who led something of a sheltered life. One later wrote that "It looked as if grim-visaged war was about to cry havoc, and let loose, eight or nine years before the summons came." But the cadets, although coming from every part of the country, avoided open hostility among themselves over the problems that divided the land and forced them into armed conflict with one another less than a decade later. As a member of the class declared, "the thought with all seemed to be, the dread inevitable is near at hand, but why dissever friendly relations before it comes?"[23]

So Lee continued his studies in relative calm. As a member of the Second Class in 1852–53, he accumulated only forty-five demerits, receiving punishment for "making improper use of the barracks" (probably horseplay), "carrying his musket improperly" while on sentinel duty, "quitting hold of his gun in duty box," and for "laughing at artillery drill."[24] Such offenses merely marked him as being like other young men, capable of engaging in occasional frivolity. In academic studies, he continued to rate somewhat *above* the middle of his class. An occasional exceptionally high standing in one subject, such as ninth in the class for drawing in February 1853, only preceded a low mark in that subject the following month. He finished the year fifteenth out of fifty-two, getting outstanding marks in philosophy and conduct.[25] It was his best showing. He got into minor trouble as a First Class cadet, but he avoided serious breaches of regulations and maintained his studies at his usual level. He made the list of thirteen cadets "distinguished for correct deportment" during the month of December 1853, but otherwise he received neither honors nor punishment. He collected a total of 139 demerits for the year.[26]

Midpoint of the last year of the Class of 1854 approached, and the cadets steeled themselves for the final rounds of examinations. Among the forty-six First Classmen completing the January 1854, semiannual examinations, Lee ranked twenty-sixth in engineering, twenty-second in ethics, and twenty-fourth in mineralogy. Four months later, on the last tests, he rated twenty-third in engineering, eighteenth in ethics, nineteenth in mineralogy and geology, eighteenth in infantry tactics, nineteenth in artillery tactics, and fourth in cavalry tactics. He stood seventh among the fifteen in the class recommended as best qualified for the mounted service.

In the final class standing for the entire four years, he was seventeenth—near the top of the middle third of the forty-six graduates —four points above the next lowest cadet and eleven above his friend, Pender, but seventy-nine below the next highest man and 567 points behind the class leader, Custis Lee.[27]

Lee and his comrades graduated, went on leave, and then returned for their new assignments. The class proudly displayed their rings with the emblem they had selected, a mailed hand holding a sword and the prophetic motto, "When Our Country Calls." Time proved it an appropriate choice. Thirty-seven of the forty-six fought later in the Civil War, twenty-three as Federals and fourteen with the Confederacy.[28]

Gradautes from the military academy received assignments to corps and regiments on a merit and choice basis. The academic board recommended one or more corps to which a man might be assigned, those cadets with the higher ratings being eligible for more of the "elite" duty slots. For example, the top three cadets in Lee's class might choose any corps they wished, and they were the only ones who could select the engineer corps. The next group, four in number, had for their best choice the topographical engineers, a separate corps. Lee fell into the third group, seventeen cadets who were offered ordnance, artillery, infantry, dragoons, or mounted riflemen, in that order. Lee chose to join the Fourth Regiment of Artillery.[29] More than five months passed before Lee reported for active duty. Illness caused his absence, and he was in poor health after arriving at his first post. His commission, signed by Secretary of War Jefferson Davis, indicated his rank as second lieutenant dating from the first of July and assigned him to Company D, Fourth Artillery.[30]

The United States was then following a policy of scattering the units of a regiment all over the country, some serving as foot troops, others as cavalry, mounted riflemen, or foot garrisons. Company D helped man Ringgold Barracks, far down in the southern tip of Texas near the Rio Grande and the Mexican border. Lee had permission to delay joining his company; and upon reaching New Orleans, he secured another extension of leave.[31]

On 6 December 1854, the twenty-one-year-old second lieutenant reached Ringgold Barracks. Stationed there were five companies of the Fifth Infantry and their chief, Col. Gustavus Loomis, who also served as post commander, as well as two companies of mounted riflemen and Company D, Fourth Artillery; in all, twenty officers and 507 men. Company D had fifty-five men, thirteen more troopers than its authorized forty-two. So Lee and his captain, Joseph Roberts, the only two officers in the company, had to perform the duties that normally would be done by five or six officers.[32]

Lee spent nearly two years here getting valuable lessons in his profession. He had lingering troubles with his health, intermittent fever, and went on a convalescent leave to Brazos, Santiago in March. A minor complication arose when he could not get a steamboat to return him on time, and he was carried on the rolls as "Absent Without Official Leave"; but on returning he cleared up the matter with no difficulty. Captain Roberts meanwhile transferred from the post and shortly afterwards was succeeded by 1st Lt. William A. Nimmo. Lee gained temporary command experience when Nimmo went on sick leave in May.[33] This was Lee's first opportunity to command troops; and as the months slipped by, he gained experience and began to season and mature.

A new adventure began in the fall of 1856. The United States previously had fought two wars against the Seminole Indians in Florida, and a third was then imminent. A small part of the tribe had refused to relocate in the West and had hidden in the Everglades and the big cypress swamps. They raided white settlements, ran off cattle and horses, robbed wagon trains and stage lines, and occasionally shot a settler. The Indians numbered only about five hundred in all; but under the leadership of Chief "Billy Bowlegs," they were effective in harassing the settlers, who had for many months been apprehensive and fearful of new Indian attacks. Their constant panic led to frequent calls for aid from the government. U. S. officials finally yielded to pressure, and on 2 November Lee and most of the garrison from Ringgold departed the post, traveled via Fort Brown to the Gulf of Mexico, and boarded the steamer *Ranchero* bound for Florida.[34]

The regular troops disliked any thought of slaughtering the Indians, preferring to capture them instead. Regular officers often would rankle the exuberant and numerous volunteer companies and militia units by expressing pleasure with the outcome of engagements relatively free from bloodletting, saying "We haven't lost any Indians."[35] But the government desired to maintain federal control of military actions in Florida as well as to placate the settlers, and therefore many more regular officers and men moved into the area.

Lee's company located at Fort Myers on the west coast of Florida, about one hundred miles south of Tampa. A number of Seminoles who had been captured were kept there in camp, and of course they had to be guarded. The artillery units, without their guns, served here in the capacity of foot troops. Because they continued to wear the identifying color of their corps, they were called "Red-legged infantry."[36]

On 24 January 1857, after only two and a half years in grade— quite a short time in this era—Lee's promotion to first lieutenant arrived, a tangible recognition of his capability. It had been signed by President Franklin Pierce and Secretary of War Jefferson Davis on 27 November and gave Lee the higher rank dating from 31 October 1856. The commission also reassigned Lee to Company F, then commanded by Capt. John C. Pemberton, the ill-fated future "defender of Vicksburg," whom Lee came to know intimately and to admire very much.[37]

Several officers who were present in the area later became Union generals. Lee's friend and classmate, Oliver O. Howard, was chief of ordnance; Capt. Winfield Scott Hancock was depot quarter-master. Hancock was destined to become a Union major general and would distinguish himself at Chancellorsville, employing what came to be regarded as a classic maneuver of defensive warfare, and at Gettysburg in securing Culp's Hill, an action crucial to the out-come. Rightly called "Hancock the superb" he would be the Democratic Party's presidential nominee in 1880. The others in-cluded Captains William W. Burns, Randolph B. Marcy, and the future Federal cavalry commander at Gettysburg, Alfred Pleasan-ton.[38]

Col. Gustavus Loomis, Lee's former post commander at Ring-gold, had charge of the Department of Florida headquarters. By summer 1857, he was impatient with the overzealous campaigning of the volunteer units and determined to make a peace with the Indians without waiting for them to make the first move. He named O. O. Howard a "peace commissioner" and sent him with some of the captured Indians, including women and children, with a sixty-man escort to find Chief "Billy Bowlegs" and try to make a bargain. Capt. J. A. Brown assumed charge of the escort detachment and commanded one of its two sections; Lee commanded the other.[39]

The expedition got underway in late June and proceeded toward Lake Okeechobee. Part of the route went through swamps and difficult terrain, but the group took easy marches and frequent rests. Howard grabbed a few minutes of sleep during so many halts that Lee joked he thought "a nap better than a toddy." They met no hostile Indians, and the two friends enjoyed the trip together. But unfortunately by meeting no hostile Indians, they also were unable to talk with any rebelling chiefs and could not accomplish their mission. After reaching Lake Okeechobee, they released a captive Indian woman and a child to return to their tribe, whereupon the soldiers started back.[40]

During the return trip, while crossing a meadow, Lee and Howard saw a strange apparition. Such meadows, or prairies, as these fields were then called in Florida, about a quarter of a mile square and covered with long yellow grass, usually surrounded a pond. Many of them flooded during the wet season; and already at this early time of year, daily showers fell. Lee and Howard were riding a short distance ahead of the main body. Suddenly, high in the air, they saw a striking scene: a distinct image of soldiers, ambulances, and army wagons moving amid the clouds. In later years when writing his autobiography, Howard reflected that the mirage was a portent of the coming civil war in which they would fight on opposite sides.[41]

Back at Fort Brooke, near Tampa, Lee—already recognized as a good administrator—performed the duty of mustering into service more of the anxious volunteer troops. He journeyed to Ocala, Florida, well to the north, and there helped to organize five companies of mounted men. He saw to their immediate subsistence, issued them their first equipment, and then ordered them to march toward Fort Brooke. The task took about a month, from mid-July to mid-August.[42]

Lee saw no more field action in Florida, for on 22 August 1857, he became acting assistant adjutant general of the department. Soon the Seminoles made another peace, and all but a small remnant of the tribes removed to the Indian Territory west of the Mississippi River. Lee served at his desk job until 18 September and then left with his regiment. The Fourth Artillery now drew duty in another turbulent and troubled area, the Kansas Territory.[43]

Some persons spoke of the periodic guerilla disturbances in Kansas as a "civil war," and the federal government finally decided to station troops in the Territory. The Fourth Artillery arrived in October 1857, and occupied posts in the region that became Kansas, Utah, and Nebraska.[44] Lee located at Fort Leavenworth, a post with seventy officers commanded by Brig. Gen. William S. Harney, one of the four officers of the line in the Regular Army of the United States when the Civil War began, but whose significant military contributions all occurred earlier, on the frontier and in Mexico. Lee did not join in the police actions then being conducted in Kansas. Appointed regimental quartermaster upon leaving Florida, he occupied that position for the rest of his tour in the U. S. Army. When his company left Leavenworth after a few months, he remained on detached service and attended to commissary and supply problems.[45]

Apparently Lee functioned very effectively at desk duties. The possibility exists, of course, that his supervisors felt he should be given paperwork jobs because he was inferior when working with line troops. While this does not seem to have been the case, Lee continued to receive more and more administrative tasks. He developed an image as a staff officer. Perhaps he encouraged the development, believing that he could achieve higher rank more rapidly in this way. But he later claimed that he preferred field work. The most likely explanation for Lee's frequent staff assignments is that he was a "good soldier," who agreeably accepted any task and attempted to do it well. If Lee drew more than his share of desk work, he gained valuable administrative experience.

On 16 May 1858, Lee departed Leavenworth, and by 2 August he joined the garrison of Fort Laramie, Nebraska Territory. There he became post treasurer and had considerably greater responsibility as regimental quartermaster. One hundred twenty-seven civilians, clerks, wagon masters, carpenters, blacksmiths, and teamsters worked in Lee's department. Their payroll amounted to as much as $5,404 per month, a large sum for that time.[46] This complex and diverse work provided yet more experience for Lee.

On 9 November 1858, Lee took a seven-month leave. He reported back to Fort Leavenworth on 5 June 1859, with a group of recruits he had been assigned to conduct. Then he transferred to Fort Randall, Dakota Territory,[47] a fort that had been built in 1856 in the southeastern part of present-day South Dakota. Although Fort Randall was small, with hostile Indians on all sides, the duty remained rather humdrum, and the months crept by while he served as quartermaster, commissary, and ordnance officer.[48] The routine enlivened as 1860 ended and news began arriving of Abraham Lincoln's election to the Presidency and of impending secession by the South.

Almost two months after South Carolina left the Union, Lee resigned from the army. Did he delay, not wanting to make the decision, or was the news just slow in arriving? A man who knew him said Lee took the step with regret and that "he was never sanguine of the success of the Southern movement for independence."[49] But Lee did take the step; and if he truly feared that the South had no chance, he never showed it in his later actions.

Lee received permission to return to his home to await the decision upon his letter of resignation.[50] He left Fort Randall on 17 February 1861, and rode in an army wagon, with a small escort, to Sioux City. From there he caught a stage to Saint Joseph, Missouri; and then by rail and horseback, he hurried on his journey to Charleston, there to encounter the most fateful moment of his life, the crossing of a veritable "Rubicon."

2

Across the Rubicon

THE UNITED STATES accepted Stephen Lee's resignation of his commission, effective 20 February 1861. Lee's home state, South Carolina, had withdrawn from its union with the United States; and until formation of the Confederacy on 4 February 1861, the Palmetto State functioned as a separate nation. During that time, and briefly thereafter, South Carolina maintained its own army. Upon returning home, Lee at once reported to Gov. Francis Pickens, who made him a captain in the state's Regular Artillery Service.[1] In Charleston, Lee and other professional soldiers assumed various duties, relieving cadets of the Citadel and numerous other volunteers.

The chief duty of these state troops was to remove the United States Army garrison at Charleston. The Federal commander was Maj. Richard H. Anderson, a competent officer and firm Unionist but ironically a Kentucky-born pro-slavery man whose wife was a Georgian. After South Carolina seceded, Anderson moved his force of eighty-five soldiers and forty-three civilians into Fort Sumter, the strongest of several installations in the harbor. South Carolina demanded that Anderson evacuate his command of "foreign troops," but he refused. Then, on 9 January 1861, Citadel cadets fired upon and drove back the merchant ship *Star of the West,* loaded with reinforcements and supplies. An impasse developed: the South Carolinans could not get Anderson out, and Anderson could not get help in.

The mood in Charleston varied from excitement to rage. Crowds collected in the streets; official and unofficial military organizations

16

paraded; hotheads shouted for action. Enthusiasm grew, and so did tension. Both Anderson's garrison and the South Carolinians became more determined and resigned. A slow but gradual militarization took over the city.

Thus events and moods set the stage for civil war, but neither side quite knew what to do next. Actions proceeded in a curious and gentlemanly way. South Carolina officials allowed Anderson to receive a daily mail and fresh beef and vegetables from Charleston. Anderson meanwhile methodically strengthened Sumter's defenses. At the same time the state military authorities took possession of Fort Moultrie, Castle Pinckney, the arsenal in Charleston, and other former U. S. property. The Southerners also mounted guns at Fort Moultrie and constructed batteries at other nearby places.[2] Lee played a responsible role in some of these activities.

Meanwhile, other states seceded; and soon all joined together, forming the Confederate government. Most of South Carolina's army integrated into the armed forces of the new nation. So the Confederacy sent a new commander to take charge of operations at Charleston and to assume control of the former state troops. It sent the Creole general, thought by many to look like Napoleon in a grey uniform, Pierre Gustave Toutant Beauregard.

He arrived on 3 March 1861, and three days later appointed Lee to his personal staff. This staff contained a number of high luminaries, ex-governors, and senators, but Lee got his position by impressing Beauregard with crispness and effective performance of duty. A worthy officer like Lee stood out and caught the eye. The Creole generally felt displeasure with the soldiers at Charleston, and he wrote on 11 March, "I find a great deal in the way of zeal and energy around me, but little professional knowledge and experience."[3] Beauregard realized more acutely than most officers the importance of good staff work. He himself had functioned as a staff officer during the Mexican War and had received considerable recognition for his service. Now he desired that Lee follow a similar path. Lee demonstrated obvious administrative ability, and Beauregard determined to utilize it.

The twenty-seven-year-old captain became acting assistant commissary general and acting assistant quartermaster general. It marked the beginning of a dilemma for Lee, for now he had decided to apply for a commission in the Confederate States Army.

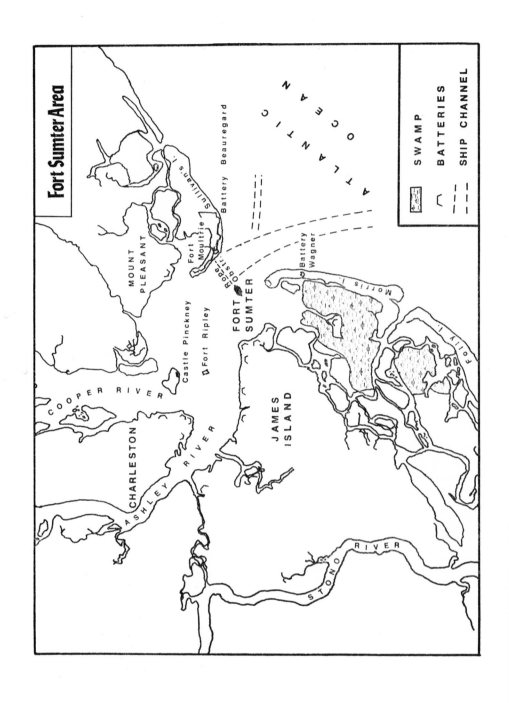

Fort Sumter Area

MOUNT PLEASANT

Sullivan's I.

Fort Moultrie

Battery Beauregard

ATLANTIC OCEAN

Battery Wagner

Morris I.

Folly I.

FORT SUMTER

Ripley's I.

Obstr.

Castle Pinckney

Fort Ripley

COOPER RIVER

CHARLESTON

ASHLEY RIVER

JAMES ISLAND

STONO RIVER

SWAMP

BATTERIES

SHIP CHANNEL

He consistently claimed that he longed for field duty, but already in the old United States Army he had become marked as a desk soldier. Again circumstances channeled him into paperwork and coordinating activity. Which course should he take? Should he seek future staff assignments, or should he apply for a commission in a combat arm? Which was best for his career? Which was best for the Confederacy?

Finally Lee made up his mind and wrote the Confederate secretary of war, "I wish a commission in the arm of service which will give me the most rank." Consequently, he listed as first preference the adjutant general's corps, then artillery, dragoons, and infantry. Beauregard urged him to follow this course and personally penned a recommendation for approval, with no comment about which arm Lee seemed best suited to serve.[4] But the Confederate authorities wisely decided to commission Lee in the regular corps of artillery.

In the meantime Beauregard gave Lee the additional task of acting as assistant adjutant general; and until his new commission arrived, sometime during the fourth week of April, Lee continued to function as a member of the South Carolina army on detached service to Beauregard's headquarters. He still wore his blue uniform of the United States Army, as was the practice of most recently resigned officers. Naturally he removed the U. S. insignia, and probably he wore some special regalia, as did others on Beauregard's staff. One female observer described their costume as "the bravest of aide-de-camp toggery, sword and red sash."[5] Beauregard obviously felt that the holders of such assignments deserved recognition.

During the five weeks after Lee joined Beauregard's staff, both Confederate and Union authorities moved closer to war. Attitudes hardened; and in the first week of April, Beauregard stopped allowing provisions and mail to enter Sumter. Washington officials decided at the same time both to hold the fort by force if necessary and to send a naval relief expedition with supplies. The Confederates ultimately decided to take action and to capture the place before the Unionists made it any stronger. Beauregard prepared for possible infantry action as well as an artillery bombardment, and on 9 April Lee checked to see that each man had a basic load for small arms.[6]

On Thursday, 11 April, Beauregard felt ready to make his move. A heavy swell out at sea kept the Federal steamer *Baltic* from approaching Fort Sumter with a load of provisions. The Confederate general drafted a formal demand that Anderson surrender, finished it by noon, and called several aides, including Lee, to his office. Beauregard entrusted his order to two aides, Lee and Col. James Chesnut, a U. S. Senator from South Carolina until the preceding December. An aide-de-camp to Gov. Pickens joined them, and the three shoved off from Charleston wharf at 2:20 P.M., headed for Fort Sumter in a small rowboat flying a white flag.[7] When the aides reached Sumter, the Federal officer of the day met the boat at the wharf and escorted the three into the guardroom, where Major Anderson met them. "We were welcomed by the major with great courtesy," Lee and the other aides wrote in their report; and "after receiving and reading our communication, he left us to consult with his officers. About 4:30 he again joined us."[8]

While Anderson was gone, Lee and Chesnut snooped a little. They had sufficient time and freedom surreptitiously to inspect various aspects of Sumter's defenses. When they returned to Charleston, they exuberantly proclaimed that "the Federals would have to give up that fort, or be burned alive in it," because there was so much exposed wood and debris that hot shot could ignite.[9]

Anderson finally returned with a written reply. He would not surrender. The aides accepted the answer and spent a few brief moments in courteous conversation with Anderson as they all walked together toward the wharf. There Anderson threw a whole new light upon the matter when he asked whether Beauregard would open fire at once, without giving further notice. Colonel Chesnut, after hesitating because he really did not know, replied that there would be further warning before the Confederates commenced fire. The major concluded their meeting with the remark that "If not hacked to pieces by our batteries he would be starved out in a few days."[10] Then as the Confederates entered their boat, Chesnut realized that Anderson had indicated the fort might be taken without a fight, asked the major to repeat the remark and, oddly, requested permission to include it in his report to Beauregard. After Anderson reluctantly assented, the aides hurried back to Charleston to present their significant report.

On learning Anderson's words, Beauregard telegraphed the Confederate war department and received orders to ask Anderson to state a specific time when he would evacuate the fort. If Anderson replied unsatisfactorily, Beauregard was authorized to take Sumter by force. Lee and his associates made ready for another boat trip. It would be a long night.[11]

Word went out along the string of Confederate batteries to get everything ready for action. Meanwhile, the governor's aide secured better transportation for the group, a barge manned by six Negro oarsmen.[12] Beauregard carefully instructed them to deliver the ultimatum to Anderson and to decide themselves whether or not the Union commander's answer was satisfactory. If not, by Beauregard's orders they were to go at once to Fort Johnson on James Island, and command that a signal gun be fired. That would be the indication for all the Confederate guns to begin. Lee and Chesnut thus became official representatives of their government, with authority to commit it to war. They fully understood Beauregard's conditions, and they had sufficient insight and experience to warrant being entrusted to evaluate Anderson's reply and act accordingly. Beauregard gave them a grave and weighty responsibility but one which they were qualified to handle. They left the general; and, on the way to their boat, Roger Pryor joined them. A hot-tempered and loose-tongued Virginia congressman, Pryor had come to Charleston with one purpose—to help prod the South into striking a blow. The boat slipped off silently into the rather foggy night and reached Sumter forty-five minutes after midnight.[13]

Major Anderson received the message and again called his officers into a private conference while the Confederates waited. The three aides went inside the fort; Pryor waited in the boat because he suddenly grew apprehensive at the last minute and remembered that his home state, Virginia, still remained in the Union. He had no business at all being where he was and might even be accused of treason.

The Federals debated so long that the Southerners grew impatient. "Major Anderson made every possible effort to retain the aides till daylight," Lee recalled, "making one excuse and then another for not replying." Time crept by and nerves grew thin. At one point Anderson appeared and snapped, "You have twice fired on my flag, and if you do so again, I will open fire on your batteries." Several shots already had been exchanged—all hastily apologized for as "target practice," and "terrible carelessness of inexperienced gunners." On 8 March, one shot actually had hit the fort.[14] Finally at 3:15 A.M., Anderson gave his answer. He would evacuate on 15 April, four days away. But Anderson added so many "ifs" to his agreement to evacuate that his answer became no answer at all—if he were not fired upon, if he were not resupplied, and if he received no orders to the contrary. The Confederate officers took only five minutes to declare the reply unsatisfactory. And the decision later met with Beauregard's complete approval. The general undoubtedly would have decided the same thing had he been present. Yet, it was perhaps the most important decision any of them ever made. For a brief moment the aides held the course of history in the palms of their hands. After the decision, their lives—and the lives of millions of others—never again would be the same.

Sitting in one of the casemates of the fort, Colonel Chesnut dictated the wording of a note; Captain Lee wrote it down, while the governor's aide made a copy. The Confederacy would open fire upon Fort Sumter one hour from that moment. It was then exactly 3:20 A.M. Lee noticed that Anderson studied the announcement and seemed to be profoundly moved. "He seemed to realize the full import of the consequences, and the great responsibility of his position. Escorting us to the boat at the wharf, he cordially pressed our hands in farewell, remarking, 'if we never meet in this world again, God grant that we may meet in the next.' "[15]

The Confederates rowed over to Fort Johnson in the thickening haze and fog, and the aides immediately informed the commander to open fire at the appointed time. After a brief discussion, the aides left and traveled in the boat until they were about one-third the distance between Fort Johnson and Fort Sumter. The fog grew spotty by this time, and the men in the boat could see both forts. Someone ordered the oarsmen to stop rowing, and the craft drifted in silence for several minutes.[16]

Finally the suspense ended. There was a flash of light and a dull explosion. Arching high in the air, a burning fuse traced the path of the mortar round. Lee wrote that "the firing of the shell was a success. It burst immediately over the fort, apparently about one hundred feet above." The shot was a signal, a special shell designed to give off a lot of light. Lee also wrote: "The firing of the mortar woke the echoes from every nook and corner of the harbor, and in this the dead hour of night, before dawn, that shot was a sound of alarm that brought every soldier in the harbor to his feet, and every man, woman, and child in the city of Charleston from their beds. A thrill went through the whole city. It was felt that the Rubicon was passed. No one thought of going home; unused as their ears were to the appalling sounds, or the vivid flashes from the batteries, they stood for hours fascinated with horror." Two more batteries opened up within ten minutes of the first firing, and by 4:45 A.M. the Confederate installations all were shooting. Anderson chose to return no fire until daylight, about the same moment that the aides walked into Beauregard's office.[17]

The bombardment continued all day on 12 April. "Tolerable good firing on our side," Lee noted; "rather wild from Sumter." Actually neither side did any real damage to the other. There was much noise, but it was a bloodless conflict. All of Anderson's operative guns were smoothbores, out of effective range. Beauregard's guns too, with one exception, were of the same type and unable to hurt the fort any more seriously than to batter the walls and leave pock marks. A dull drizzle of rain that fell all day added the only touch of gloom to the scene.[18]

Strong winds and a cold, driving rain came on the night of 12–13 April, but the next morning dawned bright and sunny. The Federal naval relief expedition dropped anchors just outside the harbor, afraid to enter the area of fire. Anxious Confederates hoped to bring matters to a climax soon, and superstitious Charleston observers interpreted the beautiful day as a good omen.[19]

Hot shot fired from Fort Moultrie landed within the walls of Sumter and caused the barracks to burst into flames. The Confederates redoubled their firing in an attempt to keep the Federals too busy to extinguish the fire. Meanwhile Major Anderson's men continued discharging their guns, but at longer intervals, taking time in between to fight the flames. Lee said that "this brave action, under such a trying ordeal, aroused great sympathy and admiration on the part of the Confederates for Major Anderson and his gallant garrison." The Southerners gave a cheer whenever the Federals fired, and they jeered the Union vessels that elected to remain in safety outside the harbor instead of coming to Sumter's aid.[20]

Lee noted in his diary, "terrible cannonading from all the batteries—during the fire shells fall thick and fast in and around the doomed fortress—but still their Flag bids defiance."[21] But suddenly, near midday, that flag went down. Beauregard dispatched Lee,

Roger Pryor, and William Porcher Miles, a Charlestonian and member of the Confederate congress for the war's duration, to go ask Anderson if the Federals wanted any help. Of course this was also a subtle way of checking to see if Anderson was ready to surrender. Beauregard referred to Pryor and Miles as colonels, though they were still civilians; Lee with his cooler head and businesslike efficiency more or less had charge of the expedition. Before the boat could get to Fort Sumter, Lee noticed the United States flag back up, and he therefore decided to return to Charleston. They went a little way toward the city and then glanced back. The Union flag had disappeared, and a white one was flying in its place. Lee had the boat turned around once more, and they rowed quickly to the fort.[22]

The flag had come down the first time because it was shot down. The Federals improvised a new pole and remounted their colors. Before Lee and his companions finished all their turnings around and got to Sumter, the colorful and eccentric Confederate Col. Louis T. Wigfall, who had been on Morris Island, reached the fort in a small rented boat, announced that he was from Beauregard's headquarters, and requested that Anderson surrender to him. Wigfall had been a United States senator from Texas and was one of Beauregard's aides, but he had no authority whatever to make this visit. He had not even seen Beauregard since 12 April, when he had been sent off on another mission. Wigfall promised very generous surrender terms to Anderson; they reached an agreement, and the white flag was hoisted. Soon after Wigfall left, Lee, Pryor, and Miles arrived.[23]

As they approached the fort, the aides heard a call from one of the fort's embrasures. The wharf was mined and the fire was near it, the voice explained, so the aides had to enter the fort through an embrasure. When they announced their mission to Anderson, he told them about Wigfall's visit. The aides explained that Wigfall's action was unofficial and that even they were not authorized to offer terms, so Anderson replied, "There is a misunderstanding on my part, and I will at once run up my flag and open fire again." Lee and the other Confederate emissaries urged that such action would be useless, and they all went into a casemate to talk things over.[24]

While negotiations progressed, Pryor helped himself to a drink which he thought was whiskey but which actually was iodide of potassium. The mixture was a medicine, extremely poisonous in anything but very small doses. Pryor had to have his stomach pumped out by his enemy, and this incident surely ended his war-like feelings for the moment. Some of the Union soldiers objected to their doctor helping Pryor, for if a rebel leader was stupid enough to come to Fort Sumter and poison himself he deserved no help. But the good-natured doctor replied that he was responsible to the United States for all the medicine in his hospital and therefore could not allow Pryor to carry any of it away.[25]

Lee and Miles reached an agreement with Anderson that the aides would return to Beauregard with a written statement explaining the arrangement with Wigfall. Anderson would not fire in the meantime and would surrender if Beauregard agreed to the stated terms. (But when Beauregard had seen the white flag go up, he had immediately dispatched two more aides to demand Sumter's capitulation.) Before Lee, Pryor, and Miles left the fort, these other aides arrived. Major Anderson undoubtedly grew flustered—how many times did he have to surrender?

These new aides offered the same terms as Wigfall had promised, except for allowing Anderson to salute his flag in an evacuation ceremony. The Confederates believed that Beauregard would grant even that if Anderson surrendered immediately. This he promised to do, and thus fell Fort Sumter—at a timely moment, because the wooden portions of Sumter were still on fire; and Lee observed that "wind was driving the heat and smoke down into the fort and into the casemates, almost causing suffocation." He remembered that "Major Anderson, his officers, and men were blackened by smoke and cinders, and showed signs of fatigue and exhaustion." The officers engaged in a little friendly conversation, and each side revealed to the other that they had sustained no personnel casualties whatever during the entire bombardment of nearly forty hours. Lee recalled that "congratulations were exchanged on so happy a result."[26] It was war, but many of the opposing soldiers still liked each other.

The only death of the entire episode took place during the surrender ceremonies the next day: Sunday, 14 April was a Sabbath marked with both pageantry and tragedy. Major Anderson had his guns fire a salute to the Union flag. Some shells behind one of the pieces accidentally exploded, instantly killing a Yankee private standing nearby. Several other persons sustained serious wounds.

Later Lee accompanied Beauregard, Governor Pickens, and other southern notables into the fort. Anderson should have been gone by this time, but he had stayed to bury the dead soldier inside the fort with full military honors. The Confederates witnessed what Lee described as the "very impressive scene" and "impressive prayer by the sailors' chaplain from the city." While Anderson's men marched out, in full dress uniform, carrying their arms, the Federal band played "Yankee Doodle." The Southerners hoisted the Confederate and Palmetto flags, and all batteries in the harbor fired salutes.[27] The South had itself a new fort and celebrated the victory.

The more serious minded, like Lee, took advantage of the opportunity to inspect the fort closely and to evaluate its potential as a Confederate asset. Lee cast a keen eye over the place and wrote in his diary on one page that there was "very little damage done to the walls of Sumter, but the quarters [were] completely gutted." On the next page he penned, "Fort Sumter in very bad condition, dreadfully injured by our fire, estimated cost for repairs about $350,000." He quickly realized that forts such as this, constructed of brick and mortar, were useless against the powerful new artillery coming into use.[28]

Lee concluded his inspection and returned to the city about dark. A new crisis had arisen. Reports indicated that the Federals were coming up Wapoo Cut, which connected the Stono and Ashley Rivers. Beauregard quickly sent Lee to put troops at Long Bridge over the Ashley River to intercept the enemy. Lee took a company of one hundred men and rushed to meet a foe who was not there. On finally learning that the whole thing was a false alarm, he brought the company back and dismissed them at 4:00 A.M.[29] At last he got some sleep.

Nothing happened the next day, but, in the evening, reports circulated that the Federal fleet, still just off the bar, had engaged the Confederate batteries. Lee accompanied Beauregard and other staff members to Morris Island, but nothing serious occurred and they returned to the city.[30] The rest of April went by quietly. Long roads stretched ahead, but at this point Lee saw them only dimly. In the next sixteen months he would receive many different assignments, find the adventure he thought lacking at Charleston, and demonstrate abilities that won him widespread recognition and three promotions.

3

Long Roads

TWO WEEKS AFTER the surrender ceremonies at Sumter, Beauregard gave written commendation to those who had served him during the affair. He cited Lee and others for their "indefatigable and valuable assistance night and day . . . in open boats . . . amidst falling balls and bursting shells." But Lee got no promotion, and he resumed his desk duties as quartermaster, commissary, ordnance, and engineer officer. On 22 April, he received the additional duty of acting as recruiting officer for the Charleston area.[1] For a time he would have to serve the Confederacy as a desk soldier.

Lee, with a number of junior lieutenants, mustered new recruits into service as fast as possible. Naturally this duty involved a large amount of paperwork; and with all the excitement centered on the build-up in Virginia, Lee grew tired of his tasks. He longed for a more active assignment and requested the Confederate authorities to relieve him of his assignment; but they refused, saying that his services were more important where he was.[2]

Meanwhile Lee received a short leave to visit his family in South Carolina, a trip that took about a day and a half each way. He stayed for several days, relating exciting tales about the adventure at Sumter. Doctor Lee, his fifty-two year old father, decided to join the army too, as a surgeon. The son agreed to see what he could do to help; and as soon as he returned to Charleston, he wrote his acquaintance, Congressman William Porcher Miles.[3] Apparently, however, the commission could not be secured, and Dr. Lee practiced medicine at home throughout the war.

Back at Charleston, Lee read an enticing newspaper advertisement for volunteers. Wade Hampton, the colorful and rich aristocrat, had secured permission to raise, partly at his own expense, a thousand-man "Legion" made up of combined arms—infantry, artillery, and cavalry. As Hampton sought recruits, many young men from South Carolina's best families responded, filling the ranks within less than a week.[4] Each company in the Legion enjoyed the privilege of electing its own officers. Lee let it be known that he was interested in being selected by dropping, at the right time and place, an "accidental remark that he would like to get into active service." Members of the Legion's artillery battery were only too glad to hear it, because none of them had any military knowledge. They wanted to fight but not to be killed as a result of blunders by incompetent leaders. In fact, they already had offered the honor of their command to several experienced officers who had declined. The battery held a brief meeting, elected Lee, and notified Colonel Hampton of the choice.[5]

Hampton used his personal influence to secure Lee's release from staff work. There may have been some serious objection to Lee getting the new assignment, for he wrote in his diary on 21 June that "the enemy are attacking my position." (He could not have meant Yankees; he was not then in the field.) Finally, however, Lee secured the promise of his desired release. Even so, he could not leave right away because some officials felt that his quartermaster duties were still vital. So, for the rest of June and well into July, Lee stayed in Charleston, administering great sums of money, paying Confederate troops and state units called into national service.[6] The Hampton Legion began moving to Virginia on 24 June 1861, and the entire outfit encamped there on 1 July, at Rockett's, in the suburbs of Richmond. Three weeks later the cavalry and infantry sections joined in the fight at First Manassas, but Lee's artillery battery did not receive its armament in time and remained in Richmond.

Since many battery members had been in the Charleston Washington Artillery, the unit took that name at first. Most of the men, all well off financially, took their personal Negro valets with them. Since almost everyone had a horse, Lee called them the "Washington Mounted Artillery." He finally left Charleston, one day after the battle at Manassas, and journeyed to Richmond to assume command.[7] The next twelve months constituted a critical period in Lee's military career.

In that year, Lee grew enormously as a commander. The period was the highpoint of his on-the-job military education. Distinguished from the mass of other junior officers, Lee became a "Can-do" commander: his guns were always operative, his men moved well, frequently under great difficulty, and he infused professionalism into his subordinates. Lee often had to work with new men—some of his units were green—but he never had *raw* troops because he never let them remain raw even for a single day.

As Jefferson Davis said, "Stephen D. Lee was one of the best all-round soldiers which the war produced."[8] Lee developed the talent of being able to win admiration, confidence, and cooperation. His men always liked him and served well under his leadership. With Lee as a commander, any organization turned into a better outfit. Going about his job methodically and quietly, often unobtrusively, Lee made remarkable contributions to the Confederate war effort. As a trainer he was different from other trainers. He was better and more thorough—and always active. Some officers did little or nothing when they should have been training. Lee showed initiative, even in the absence of orders. But he never displayed much dashing élan. Much of what he did was low key—though always in tune. His men secured ammunition, they located on high advantageous ground, and as a unit they never became incapacitated. Lee began this important year of growth by taking charge of his first field command, a full-strength and a well-equipped artillery battery. For many scarce items he could thank Col. Wade Hampton's influence and money. The Tredegar Ironworks in Richmond provided the battery with its first outfitting of guns—four twelve-pound howitzer smoothbores and two rifled pieces with bores three inches in diameter. The howitzers had a range of approximately nine hundred yards, and the rifled pieces could fire nearly one mile.[9]

Hampton also ordered a field battery of the new and famous Blakely rifled ordnance from England. These iron and steel guns, somewhat stronger than the bronze and iron Tredegar pieces, could fire at longer range with greater accuracy. The Federal naval blockade prevented some of the Blakely guns from reaching the Confederacy, but four pieces slipped in at Savannah, Georgia, and reached Lee's battery by November.[10]

Lee met his men and guns in Richmond. After taking time to serve as pallbearer at the funeral of Hampton's second in command who had been killed at Manassas, Lee began training his troops. Two days later, on 26 July 1861, he had the men putting harness together and hitching horses to the guns. He described the event in his diary as an "awkward scene—no drivers—wild horses." But in spite of the difficulties, the battery began marching on the next day to join the Confederate army at Manassas.

The hundred-mile march in very hot weather proved quite difficult for the green soldiers, and undoubtedly the men welcomed Lee's order to remain in camp all day on 1 August, because of the heavy rain. But the trek resumed on the next day, which was even hotter, and two horses died on the road. Finally, on 3 August, the battery reached Brentsville, about fifteen miles east of Warrenton and five miles south of Manassas. Here they joined the rest of the Hampton Legion, and Lee reported to Colonel Hampton. Together they went into Manassas for conferences with Gen. Joseph E. Johnston, the army commander, and his associate, General Beauregard. The Legion drew the task of anchoring the right flank of Johnston's command, at Freestone Point—the southern bank of the Occaquan's mouth.

Theoretically Lee's battery was the only artillery under Hampton, but the Legion soon acquired more than one battery of guns. Lee exercised general charge over all this artillery, even though he remained until early November officially only a battery captain. During August and September, the Legion constructed several campsites near Freestone Point, the principal one at Bacon Race Church, about twelve miles from Brentsville. In the surrounding Maple Valley, Lee conducted maneuvers with his artillerymen.[11]

Lee required daily drills with the pieces and a rigid schedule of soldierly duties, which was unusual. Believing that the war would not last very long, many commanders, especially at the junior level, preferred to be comfortable and lazy in camp. Greatly exceeding Hampton's requirements and Johnston's guidelines, Lee insisted upon frequent target practice and an occasional sham battle against cavalry. Many volunteers chafed at what they considered an unnecessarily rigorous routine, and indeed Lee was a harsh master; one of the men suffered a broken leg during the second day's drill. But Lee knew his business; he had absorbed a lot at West Point, and his considerable subsequent experience with small units helped immensely. His unit soon began to shape up, and its esprit de corps

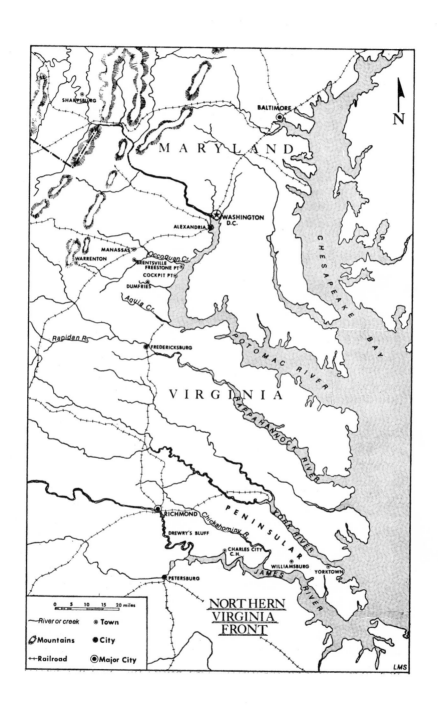

N

SHARPSBURG

M A R Y L A N D

BALTIMORE

WASHINGTON
D.C.

ALEXANDRIA

MANASSAS
WARRENTON
BRENTSVILLE
FREESTONE PT
COCKPIT PT
DUMFRIES

Occoquan Cr.

Aquia Cr.

C H E S A P E A K E   B A Y

Rapidan R.

FREDERICKSBURG

V I R G I N I A

P O T O M A C   R I V E R

R A P P A H A N N O C K   R I V E R

RICHMOND   Chickahominy R.

DREWRY'S BLUFF

P E N I N S U L A R

Y O R K   R I V E R

CHARLES CITY
C.H.

WILLIAMSBURG   YORKTOWN

J A M E S   R I V E R

PETERSBURG

0   5   10   15   20 miles

River or creek   ⊕ Town

ᛜ Mountains   ● City

++ Railroad   ◉ Major City

NORTHERN
VIRGINIA
FRONT

LMS

grew strong. To push men hard, to make them better than they really want to be, and to make them like it is leadership in its highest form. He not only taught the men how to perform their jobs—he also infused them with high ideals in support of their cause and enjoined them to sell their lives as dearly as possible should this awful necessity ever arise.[12]

Sometimes when Lee's men drilled, the hills nearby would be dotted with spectators who came to see the superb unit go through its paces, directed by the notes of a bugle. Every man in the battery had a horse, and they were known as the "flying artillery." Lee's unit was a prototype for the five Horse Artillery batteries that the Army of Northern Virginia ultimately utilized in bold aggressive actions.[13] Really good battery commanders like Lee were rarer than most field and general officers dared to concede, even to themselves.

Early in September, in preparation for attempting to blockade the Potomac River, Lee received orders to unmask his position at Freestone Point gradually by cutting away the woods between it and the river. On 25 September a small gunboat spotted the works and ran in close to reconnoiter. She fired six shots, which the Confederates did not return, and then chugged up river. But in less than an hour she was back—with help. Six wooden side-wheel steamers, with four cannon mounted to each side, attacked Lee's fortification.[14]

Before replying to the naval bombardment, Lee spoke to his men. It was their first time in combat, and he tried to stiffen their courage. He gave them permission to dodge the enemy fire but told them not to forget to man their guns. Very soon, in the small, hot engagement which ensued, both sides slapped at each other and both did some damage. "They were getting our range," Lee wrote, and "one fragment struck in the pit of our little rifle, several shells went but a few feet over our heads."[15] The Confederates fired even more effectively; and after three hours of furious fighting, the flotilla steamed off, one gunboat disabled and in tow, another beached within sight of the Confederates (it sank during the night).

This baptism of fire gave Lee's men confidence in their artillery pieces, in their officers, and in one another. Lee's training demonstrably had paid off. But although the Confederates had inflicted real damage on the Union boats, they had come dangerously close to suffering disaster themselves; and worse, they had not succeeded in completely blocking the river. Lee withdrew his guns the next night and encamped his battery on Powell's Creek.[16]

Never again did Lee allow artillerymen under him to try dodging enemy fire, having decided it was an unwise and useless practice. In their next engagement, another artillery duel with gunboats—this time at Colchester—Lee caught a noncommissioned officer cringing from fire and reduced him to private.[17] A gunner under Lee learned to man a piece regardless of what happened, either until told to cease fire or until wounded or killed. And Lee exacted the same high standards of himself. One admiring journalist warmly praised Lee's personal conduct under fire as characterized by "courage, coolness, and obedience to orders no matter what the risk or danger."[18] He had a certain charisma that drew men to him despite his quiet manner.

Another battery of artillery from South Carolina joined the Hampton Legion sometime in October 1861. Hampton decided to reorganize his artillery into a two-battery battalion and made Lee the commander. Rumors spread by the end of October that Lee soon would be made a major; and they proved true, for on 8 November he got the promotion,[19] two and one-half months after his twenty-eighth birthday. So Lee started his way up the promotion ladder, proceeding on his own merit. He had earned his new position of battalion major. He was the senior artillerist in the Legion, and he had performed very well as a captain. The amount of artillery and its proposed organization dictated that the Legion now needed a major. Lee was the best man immediately available for the post.

Lee's artillerymen engaged in several more minor actions before 1861 ended. He and his men did battle with some Federal batteries across the Potomac on 9 November at Cockpit Point, but the range was too great for accuracy during the several hours of firing. At least the gunners got some beneficial drill with their new Blakely pieces.[20]

A week later, on 15 November Lee's men spent all day harassing Union boats on the Potomac, utilizing hit-and-run tactics. The Confederates advanced up to Cockpit Point and opened fire on a Federal schooner, which carried huge thick-walled mortars mounted on her decks. The Northerners quickly abandoned ship. Lee withdrew his guns. The sailors got back aboard. Lee returned and drove them off again. Then he sent out a small party which set the boat afire. Other vessels arrived with the heavier Dahlgren guns and engaged Lee's batteries. Firing continued until the Confederate ammunition ran out. Lee's unit suffered no losses, though, as Lee observed, the enemy guns had a commanding position. He returned to camp at 10 P.M. in a drenching rain, estimating that at least two of the Union vessels were "too much injured to save."[21]

In these and other small actions, Lee's use of artillery was exemplary. Actually he inflicted only slight damage, and in every engagement he risked valuable guns which would be sorely missed if lost. But he produced beneficial results. Inactivity has a detrimental effect upon soldiers, and Lee knew it. When he did not have his men actually fighting, they were training. Years later one of his soldiers recalled Lee's "restless activity and untiring perseverance; his indomitable will which surmounted all obstacles; his strict discipline; his thoughtful care of his command; his reckless disregard of personal danger, and the cool judgment he displayed."[22] And Lee established something of a psychological superiority over the Union sailors. Once when gunboats took potshots at the Confederate picket quarters, Lee rushed two rifled cannon down to the shore and fired a half dozen shells at the already retreating enemy. The sailors had begun to scramble out of range at the first sight of Lee galloping toward the scene.[23]

Training and action left its mark upon the aristocratic Legionnaires. Dust and sweat changed their sharp new uniforms into real fighting men's costumes. They sent most of their Negro servants home and abandoned their trunks and valises for lighter loads in more conventional campaign packs. Occasional maladies, like dysentery and typhoid fever, prostrated a large part of the command, killing many, but the rest grew "hard and hairy, brisk at drill and practical at outpost duty."[24]

After the middle of November, the weather became severely cold, and the Legion broke camp at Maple Valley, moving down into winter quarters in a finely wooded area near the junction of the Potomac and Occaquan Rivers on "old Telegraph Road" between Alexandria and Fredericksburg. The troops stayed there until 8 March 1862, but never completely stopped activity. They went on patrols, guarded the country, and built redoubts and breastworks.

The men thought their tasks hard, but they also enjoyed themselves. The commissary kept them supplied with plentiful rations, and the country nearby was stocked well with poultry and dairy products. Hampton frequently entertained his officers with dinner at his quarters.[25]

Lee enjoyed some other moments of leisure too. His friend William D. Pender camped nearby, and the two visited frequently. Lee served as one of the witnesses at Pender's public conversion to Christianity and his baptism—rather odd duty for Lee, who later claimed he had had no serious religious thought in his life until nearly a year thereafter. But Lee obviously was a sober and moral person; for Pender, profoundly religious and virtuous, spent the rest of his short life attempting to make a romantic match between Lee and Pamela, Pender's beloved sister-in-law. Pender wrote his wife that Lee was "the salt of the earth," and "a man that any woman could be proud of and happy with." Later he added, "Take my word for it. . . . Lee is the pink of honor, in morals above the ordinary standard at least, in sobriety unquestionable, and in goodness of heart unequaled."[26]

Lee got a leave sometime while the Legion occupied winter quarters, and he went home. The last page in his 1861 diary lists a number of items that various people had asked him to get for them. These included bandages, caps, cherry bark pipes, heavy shoes, pocket knives, saddles and accessories, and a large supply of toothpicks—a curious demand since one could whittle them. Perhaps the camp cooks prepared unusually tough meat. Lee jotted a reminder to get for himself towels, drawers, a knife, an 1862 diary, and two pairs of spurs. He also bought on this trip the new and "bright Confederate uniform" he was seen wearing in the spring campaign.[27]

Back in camp, Lee and Hampton—always active and restless campaigners—one snowy day took a twenty-man detail on a scouting mission into Maryland. The Confederates often could hear drums, bugles, and brass bands in the Union camp, just across the Potomac River. Hampton wanted to know exactly where the Federals were established and how strong they were. The expedition got up to within sight of a picket and noted the location of certain buildings, but they cut their reconnaissance short when they heard a cannonading to their rear.

Lee, still somewhat brash and without extensive combat experience, listened carefully and overreacted. He immediately concluded that the enemy had run a squadron of gunboats to the Potomac and Occaquan junctions and were shelling his encampment. Lee and Hampton rushed back to Colchester to get support for a counterattack and found that the bombardment was not at their campsite, but on the Potomac.[28] It was only one of the routine little potshot engagements like those Lee himself had taken part in earlier. Though he felt some embarrassment for his overly pessimistic estimate of the situation, the whole episode had comic overtones and amounted to little consequence for Lee. But it did show one important thing about Hampton and Lee—they were active campaigners, not content to sit out all of the cold season in comfortable winter quarters.

On 16 November, Hampton's Legion integrated with Gen. James Longstreet's division. Although the official designation of "Legion" remained until July 1862, Hampton really commanded a brigade after late November 1861. Lee remained with Hampton as the brigade artillerist, although at this stage of the war brigades typically had only one battery, not as much as the battalion that Lee had commanded. The army command and staff faltered for awhile, undecided whether to concentrate larger division and corps artillery reserves or to parcel them out to smaller units. In the spring of 1862, Gen. Joseph E. Johnston divided his force into more divisions.[29] Hampton's command, along with Lee's, went into the new division under Gen. William Henry Chase Whiting, a man on whom the Confederacy pinned high hopes because of his acuity— he had set new records at West Point. But his later performances were so dull that they prompted his critics to infer that he must be on either excessive whiskey or narcotics.

In March 1862, General Johnston ordered a withdrawal fifteen miles to the rear, to a line along the Rapidan and Rappahannock rivers. On 7 March, Whiting directed Hampton to begin moving back at dawn the following day, along difficult, muddy roads with inadequate transportation. The Confederates had accumulated far too much baggage and supplies; and if the retirement was to be prompt and secure, many items must be discarded. Hampton entrusted to Lee the distribution of surplus rations to the nearby poor, even if some items went to Union sympathizers. Lee's men also destroyed large amounts of luggage discarded by the troops.[30]

Normally the brigade chief of staff directed an actual withdrawal, leaving the commander free to oversee the entire operation and to move with the first elements to the new location. The organization of the entire division still remained in flux, and there was no appropriately ranking officer available to serve as chief of staff. With Hampton occupied elsewhere, Whiting chose Lee for the task. Two regiments moved out under Lee's capable direction, and he took charge of disposing the surplus stores at Bacon Race Church, the primary supply depot for troops along the Occaquan. In spite of difficulties, Lee managed to gather up about four hundred stands of arms, a quantity of ammunition, as well as medical and quartermaster's stores and sent them to Manassas. He destroyed only a few unrepairable wagons and harness and some loose cartridges, amounting to several boxes. In an operation overly criticized by press and President for abandonment of equipment and supplies, Lee was complimented by Whiting for the "masterly manner" in which his part of the operation had been planned and executed.[31]

The first large-scale operation in Virginia during 1862, the Peninsular Campaign, began in the middle of March. One of the several scattered Confederate forces, under Maj. Gen. John Bankhead Magruder, occupied a line across the peninsula between the York and James Rivers, with headquarters at Yorktown. Johnston received reports that the Federals were landing in force on the tip of the peninsula. Putting off action until early April, he finally began moving with the main body of Confederate troops, including Lee's artillery battalion, still attached to Whiting's Division, to reinforce Magruder, who meanwhile had succeeded in simulating the presence of a very large force. The Confederates held their lines for several weeks, but knew that they probably would lose in a siege, and decided to fall back, up the peninsula, to fight delaying actions along the way, and perhaps bring about a major battle on more advantageous ground. The Confederate withdrawal from the Yorktown line began on 3 May 1862.[32]

Early on 7 May, John B. Hood's brigade encountered a Unionist fleet of transports, protected by gunboats, landing troops between Barhamsville and Eltham's Landing. Whiting estimated the enemy strength at between twelve and sixteen regiments—considerably more than he had. Nevertheless, Hood attacked and made some advance; but by noon his troops bogged down, and the Southerners could not make further progress. Finally the Northerners took cover in and around their gunboats. The Confederates held a tiger by the tail—they faced a superior Federal force, and they either had to destroy it or get quickly away. Both courses of action seemed very difficult.

Hampton's Legion joined in support of Hood's men, and Lee brought his artillery battalion up toward the river bank. Lee hoped to get the rifled guns in position to fire upon the gunboats that had the Confederate infantry bottled up. He found an advantageous spot on a bluff overlooking the river, but the area was so densely wooded that he could not move the guns into position. Yet, Lee was able to help the Confederates disengage and to achieve something of a victory by firing his artillery from where it was. The Confederate gunners held the northern troops at bay and permitted the Southerners to retire in good order. The Confederates lost eight and had thirty-two wounded; but in the advances they captured forty-six prisoners, from whom they gained valuable information about the disposition of Federal forces.[33] The action as a whole momentarily stymied the Union invasion.

It had been the first taste of combat for Hood's Brigade, and he deemed it a "happy introduction."[34] This was the first of several instances early in the war when Hood saw Lee perform creditably and to Hood's benefit. Unquestionably such events were among the factors that motivated Hood in 1864, when he gave Lee a corps command in the Army of Tennessee.

Hampton praised Lee's actions at Eltham's Landing and cited him for displaying the "soldierly conduct for which he is conspicuous." Two days after the fight, Lee received promotion to lieutenant colonel. He remained with his artillery battalion in the Hampton Legion throughout the retreat up the peninsula, but at the end of May, when the Confederates took a defensive stand near Richmond, he joined Whiting's staff. His friend Pender wrote home that Lee was considered to be the best artillerist in the whole army.[35] Finally, on 31 May, Johnston decided to launch an attack of his own.

The Battle, Fair Oaks or Seven Pines, was a vicious but indecisive confrontation. Whiting's Division hit the left flank of a portion of McClellan's army, south of the Chickahominy River, separated from the main Federal force; but the principal attack went farther to the right. In addition to his battalion command, Lee served as a liaison officer between Whiting and the division's two brigades. The artillery battalion did not take part in the fight.[36] The struggle continued all day, but ultimately the Confederates failed to deliver the decisive blow that they had hoped to inflict. Meanwhile Johnston was wounded and had to relinquish his command.

On the next day, 1 June 1862, Gen. Robert E. Lee filled Johnston's place. General Lee immediately began a reorganization, renaming his force the Army of Northern Virginia, uniting it with the troops under Gen. Thomas J. Jackson, the colorful "Stonewall," and dividing it into two segments, a left wing under Jackson and a right wing under John Bankhead Magruder. Still officially "divisions," now called "wings," in reality they were corps.

In the meantime Stephen Lee had twelve guns under his personal direction. This meant that a minimum of 150 men served under him. He commanded them in a two-hour duel between Confederate pieces at Garnett's farm on the Chickahominy and Union artillery across the river at New Bridge on 6 June. Each side lost two or three men and several horses, but otherwise it was an unimportant affair. Two days later, on Sunday, 8 June, Lee's guns fired shot and repelled a Union attempt to force the Confederate lines that surrounded Richmond.[37] Magruder was much impressed by Lee's performance and requested General Lee to transfer S. D. Lee to the right wing. The general acquiesced in a temporary detachment. Magruder immediately made the lieutenant colonel chief of artillery in his wing.[38]

As chief of artillery, Lee exercised some degree of supervision and advisory responsibility over each battery assigned to brigades, and he personally commanded the reserve. In this reserve were twenty-two pieces, but only ten that Lee considered efficient for field service. In the entire wing, the artillerymen numbered forty officers and 815 enlisted men, with forty-four guns. Lee wrote to the army chief of artillery, Brig. Gen. William N. Pendleton, that if all the guns in Magruder's command were well manned, he would consider the number ample; but, he said, they were not all well manned—and they were not all heavy enough.[39] Magruder displayed his high confidence in his new chief of artillery by delegating to him the responsibility to respond to a threatened attack by placing batteries in the field as he thought best and to call upon nearby infantry brigade commanders for whatever support he deemed necessary.[40]

Magruder and Longstreet began a distinct effort at this time to utilize artillery more effectively by doling out less to smaller units and retaining a larger division, corps, and army reserve. Lee participated in the implementation and an evaluation but did not originate the scheme. At the beginning of the Seven Days campaign, which started on 25 June 1862, the artillery attached to brigades entrenched along the infantry lines, and the reserve battalions occupied the immediate rear. The Confederates planned to move additional guns to any threatened point and to mass guns in concerted fire; but these plans went awry, and the southern artillery would be almost totally ineffective in the upcoming Seven Days campaign.[41]

At the outset of this campaign, Magruder's wing and a brigade under Benjamin Huger—an inadequate line officer whose real forte was staff work—constituted a holding force, occupying a five-mile line stretching southward from a point on the Chickahominy just above New Bridge. Lee's artillery operated from these lines through 29 June.[42] General Lee directed Magruder to hold his position from the enemy "at all hazards [and] to make such demonstrations as to discover his operations." So Magruder charged S. D. Lee to use artillery to "feel" the Federal works "frequently and vigorously." The Confederates not only wanted to withstand an attack if the enemy launched one but also to know that the bluecoats had not pulled back. The Northerners occupied entrenched and well-covered positions; the Southerners had to advance toward them over open fields.

Lee engaged in some sharp artillery contests on both 26 and 27 June. He tried to keep losses to a minimum, shifted the position of batteries under perilous fire, and himself remained on the field. But his men had to take more than usual risk and punishment. Even after the war Lee saw nothing wrong with his having to conduct "feeling actions" in the open against a well-protected enemy, though one officer who observed him at the time called him a "damned crazy fool" for doing it. The amazing thing is that Lee's men remained exactly in position, calmly and consistently firing, despite losses, until Lee ordered them back. They accomplished their goal.[43]

Early on 28 June, Lee conducted a reconnaissance in force and discovered Union working parties attempting to repair the Chickahominy crossing at New Bridge. He moved guns up and drove the Federals off. Very soon a return-fire commenced, and a duel continued until the Confederates ran out of ammunition and pulled back.[44] The Unionists disengaged from contact with Magruder on 29 June, and the Confederate wing pursued. Lee got some of his batteries into action at Savage's Station that day, but they did not join in the fights on 30 June.[45] These engagements, and the one at Malvern Hill on 1 July—a Union victory—ended the campaign.

At Malvern Hill, S. D. Lee was not able to make much of a contribution with his artillery. The Federals occupied high ground in skillful defense. A Confederate infantry assault was to have been supported by massed artillery, including Lee's. Gen. James Longstreet, who led the final and costly infantry charge, later complained that he had understood Lee definitely would come up, implying perhaps that he would not have charged had he known of Lee's inability to give him support. As a matter of fact, Lee encountered withering fire from the Federal long-range guns, and he and his men struggled forward in the hot, choking dust. Despite heavy casualties, Lee still pressed on; but he never got the artillery up in force. Those few batteries that did battle were destroyed in detail—one or two at a time.[46]

Lee's superiors recognized his contributions to the Seven Days campaign and rewarded him appropriately. The failure of the artillery to arrive in time at Malvern Hill was not his fault by any means, and he was not blamed. In the preceding weeks, he had performed outstandingly as chief of artillery, displaying both gallantry and skill. R. E. Lee commended his activity, as did Magruder, who also recommended promotion to full colonel, saying that "Lee has I think no superior in service as an artillery officer and has great modesty, enterprise, gallantry, and skill." On 9 July 1862, Lee received the promotion.[47]

For the next six weeks, Lee performed in a new and different assignment. All the field officers of the Fourth Virginia Cavalry regiment had been killed or wounded, and Lee took temporary command—a duty that required him to apply his West Point cavalry training. His men were still green, so he had to spend some time teaching and drilling them—in an area that the men named "Camp Discipline."[48]

The regiment constituted part of the brigade commanded by Brig. Gen. James "Jeb" Stuart, Lee's former classmate. Lee operated with his cavalry regiment over a wide area from between Richmond and Fredericksburg to the enemy lines and against gunboats on the James River.[49] The Confederate infantry feared the extremely large calibre guns which Union gunboats now carried. Stuart decided to hit these vessels by making use of Lee's ability as an artillerist. Stuart had Squires' Washington Artillery—a battery of rifled guns, and Pelham's Blakely battery detached and placed under Lee's control. Lee conducted the guns to Wilcox's Landing, about three miles downriver from the enemy lines. At 2:00 A.M. on the morning of 6 July, the Confederates opened fire on a transport chugging up the river with some of McClellan's supplies. The artillery inflicted some visible damage, but it was too far out of range to prevent the transport from passing. Stuart sent Lee two more rifled pieces, Rogers' battery; and all the guns moved farther down river, to Wayne Oaks, four miles below Charles City Court House. There at 7:00 A.M. on 7 July, they opened fire on another transport. This time their fire had more effect; and after some twenty shots the vessel turned back, throwing part of the cargo overboard to speed its escape.

Other transports tried to pass, and several gunboats aided them with protective fire. Lee kept his guns busy, moved somewhat further downriver, sank one transport, and compelled the crews of both it and another to scramble into small boats and head for the opposite shore. The gunboats came into range of Lee's guns. They suffered severe damage and never were able to retaliate. The annoyed gunboatmen tried firing shell, spherical case, and grape shot. Still Lee's fire continued. In frustration, the Northerners shelled wooded areas and then bombarded nearby civilian dwellings. Finally when night fell, Lee withdrew and went back to camp. He had thwarted delivery of much of McClellan's supplies and had infused fresh morale into the southern troops. The operations were a complete success.[50]

At times Lee's audacity was mingled with vision—for example, in the use of cavalry. "The sword," he later wrote, "has lost much of its effectivness by the improved revolver, with which the cavalryman will make the dashing charge with more confidence." He recognized that cavalry no longer should charge with the sword, but he insisted that it still could charge. Arming cavalry with repeating weapons was sound, although effectively practiced only by such outstanding Civil War cavalrymen as James H. Wilson. And just as did Nathan Bedford Forrest, Lee also glimpsed the slowly-emerging concept of cavalry riding to a battle and then fighting on foot. "A large body of cavalry, as now armed," he wrote, "is a match for almost any emergency, *it is an army in motion*."[51]

The rest of Lee's cavalry duty passed without significant action. The regiment withstood an attack by other cavalry on 24 July 1862, but reports of the affair have been lost. Lee impressed Gen. R. E. Lee with the "gallant and successful" operation, and Stuart added a word of praise. Lee spent the rest of his time with the horse outfit in drilling and picket duty, activities for which he later recalled frequently being complimented by both Lee and Stuart. Meanwhile serving as president of a general court martial, he also devoted some attention to defending himself in a controversy over the responsibility for the artillery failure at Malvern Hill. A critical correspondent, known only as "the Reverend Mr. Allen," lashed at Lee for his actions in that battle. Lee returned in writing, "It is certainly out of place for *you* to criticize the management of an arm of service you know nothing about," and he went on to contend that Allen's alleged facts were incorrect.[52]

Magruder also became involved, for Lee apparently thought that Magruder too had been critical of him. But Magruder wrote Lee that "I have cast no censure upon you nor said anything which could have prompted others to do so."[53] Nevertheless, Magruder requested that Lee come and talk personally with him about the matter, though Lee could not leave his regiment because he was the only field-grade officer it had. Finally, Magruder wrote a sort of apology to Lee, saying, "I am sure I did not say a word to Mr. Allen or any of my Staff or indeed any one else criticising your management of the artillery." He added, "I do not imagine you will think I have done you injustice after you shall have read my report."[54]

Thus Lee displayed a thin-skinned and testy side of his character, which occasionally would be in evidence for the rest of his life.

Always very sensitive to criticism, he would lash out with vehemence, even to a superior officer, if he thought he was the subject of an unjust evaluation. Only his good fortune and demonstrated successes prevented much adverse comment during the war. And apparently he was diplomatic; for in all his vociferous demands to Magruder that the records do him justice, he did not alienate the general.

Meanwhile some important changes occurred in the Army of Northern Virginia. Robert E. Lee promoted James Longstreet to lieutenant general and gave him the wing, now a corps, formerly commanded by Magruder. General Lee did not particularly like "Prince John" Magruder, the hero of the Williamsburg holding action, and had him transferred to the West. Magruder invited S. D. Lee to go along, but Lee refused[55]—and it was one of the wisest decisions he ever made. He would achieve one of his greatest military successes at the Second Battle of Manassas, just weeks away.

4

Two Battles: Glory and Despair

DURING AUGUST 1862, both northern and southern armies in Virginia made organizational changes, formulated new plans for operations against each other, and began maneuvering. Boldly, Robert E. Lee decided that the Army of Northern Virginia would divide, making it vulnerable to annihilation if caught before re-uniting. Jackson's corps with Stuart's cavalary would move rapidly up the Rappahannock Valley between the Blue Ridge and Bull Run Mountains, turn east through Thoroughfare Gap, and get between Maj. Gen. John Pope's forces and Washington, cutting off Federal communications. Longstreet's corps simultaneously would move up from the south and join with Jackson to crush Pope's force in a giant pincer.

First the Confederates completed their significant reorganizations. S. D. Lee assumed command of a newly organized artillery battalion of six batteries—a heavy concentration of guns. Then the Confederate army began executing its plan. Jackson's corps covered fifty-one miles in two days, successfully reaching the enemy's rear in a prototype maneuver of things to come in the military art: "like an armored force or an air-borne drop sweeping in to establish itself . . . until the other part of the team should drive in for the kill." S. D. Lee's artillery battalion moved with Longstreet's corps.[1]

Jackson concentrated north of the Warrenton turnpike, just above Groveton, and waited. Pope's forces approached from Gaines-ville and appeared to be heading for Centreville, where Jackson knew the terrain would allow Pope to assume a nearly impregnable position on high grounds. Jackson ordered an assault, and both sides fought in a bitter and stubborn struggle, each losing heavily, until the Federals finally withdrew toward Manassas about 9 P.M.

That night the head of Longstreet's columns reached Thoroughfare Gap; and during the same night, the Federal forces supposedly guarding the gap decided to move toward Manassas. Longstreet's troops inched toward Jackson, the bulk of them uniting by the afternoon of 29 August, though Lee and his artillery still remained in the mountain passes. Meanwhile, Pope learned of the fight at Groveton and mistakenly decided that Jackson's corps was in retreat. Blindly confident of imminent success, Pope ordered his entire force to concentrate for a decisive assault. Actually Jackson had selected an admirable defensive position behind an unfinished railroad bed. The grades and cuts provided ready-made entrenchments while the ties and rocks afforded cover for the men. Fighting commenced at 7 A.M. and continued off and on throughout the day.

These skirmishes involved only Jackson's corps, although Longstreet's troops rapidly moved to the vicinity and made contact with Jackson's flank late in the afternoon. Night brought a temporary end to the fighting, while the Union forces regrouped into a single mass and the Confederates made some important movements. Jackson's men on the right abandoned the advanced positions they had won, and all returned to the strong defensive line along the unfinished railroad. Longstreet's corps stretched out next to them, at an angle bending to the front so that the Confederate army occupied a four-mile-long line shaped like an open V, facing the enemy to the east. Lee's artillery battalion, with the last of Longstreet's forces, received orders late in the evening to march toward the front.[2]

Lee and his men marched in darkness. They encamped just before dawn on the thirtieth, after a tiresome trek, not knowing precisely where they were in relation to Jackson's corps, only that they were somewhere on the Warrenton Turnpike. At daybreak Lee discovered that his bivouac occupied exactly some of the positions involved in the previous day's battles. Lee's battalion was very close to the Confederate division then on picket duty.[3]

Lee consulted with Maj. Gen. John B. Hood, one of Longstreet's division commanders and closest to Jackson's corps, and then decided to put his battalion on the same spot that had been occupied the day before by the Washington Artillery of New Orleans. In this position, Lee could support Col. Stapleton Crutchfield's artillery battalion near Longstreet's center, and also could fire across Jackson's front. Lee's artillery, adjacent to Hood's brigades, constituted the exact midpoint of the Confederate lines.[4]

In a position that could not have been better, the guns pointed northeast and were nestled along a commanding ridge about a quarter of a mile long. They overlooked a field of fire embracing some two thousand yards—over a mile to the front! Immediately opposite Jackson's lines stretched nothing but an open field, of which Lee's fire could sweep any part. Beyond that, to the east, was farmland with corn fields, orchards, and fences—an inviting expanse for enemy skirmishers—and still farther to the east was timberland, an obvious assembly area for a Union assault force. Gen. R. E. Lee himself inspected Colonel Lee's position and declared, "You are just where I wanted you; stay there."[5] The Confederates were ready; they had completed all their strategic maneuvers. Only one question remained: would Pope be reckless enough to thrust his infantry into the waiting jaws?

The answer soon came. Saturday, 30 August dawned clear and bright. Remembering Lee's unhampered field of fire, one battalion member recalled that "we had a grand view of the plains of Manassas, reaching as far as Centreville."[6] The first Federal infantry became visible at 7 A.M., some two thousand yards away. Lee's guns opened fire, forcing the enemy, even at that distance, to move back. The Federals returned the volley with long-range guns.

During the morning the act was repeated many times. At every appearance of Union infantry, Lee's artillery harassed and drove them back. They answered with fire from their own big guns, but did no damage to Lee's emplacements. Lee himself, setting the example and raising morale among his troops, helped with some of the firing. Once he sighted a gun for 3,500 yards, aimed at a Federal caisson, and killed two of the wheel horses with his second shot.[7] Meanwhile, the Federals continued preparations for a massive charge.

Throughout the morning Lee's artillery engaged only a far-distant enemy, some of the other nearby Confederates almost growing complacent. One regimental commander actually sat under the

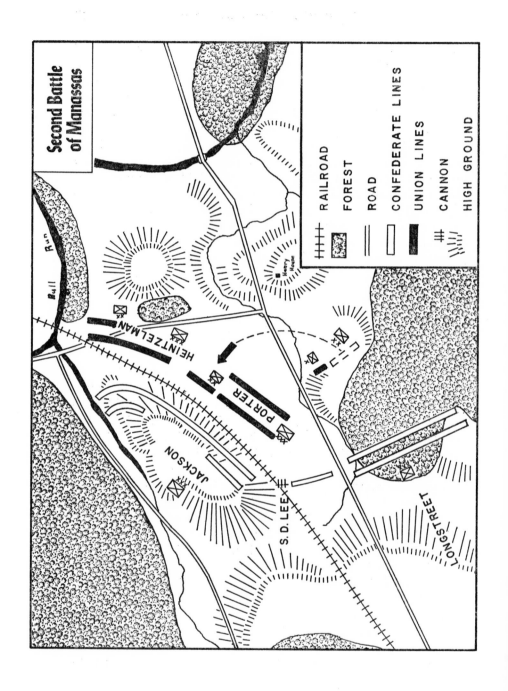

Second Battle of Manassas

RAILROAD
FOREST
ROAD
CONFEDERATE LINES
UNION LINES
CANNON
HIGH GROUND

Bull Run

Henry House

HEINTZELMAN

PORTER

JACKSON

S. D. LEE

LONGSTREET

shade of a persimmon tree, eating his breakfast of dry crackers and boiled bacon, watching Lee direct fire at a line of troops too far away to recognize as soldiers until sunlight glinting off their bayonets betrayed them.[8] Around noon the Federals tested the position with an advance, driving in the few Confederate skirmishers. The artillery drove them back, and then suddenly all firing ceased. An ominous silence prevailed.

During the day a huge concentration of Federals massed behind the timber opposite Lee's position. Finally, at about 3 P.M., the Unionists advanced in heavy force against Jackson's left, "glittering lines of battle in magnificent array," one Southerner recalled. Suddenly came a crash of musketry. Regiment after regiment of bluecoated soldiers moved toward Jackson's lines. The Confederates fought back furiously, some quickly running out of ammunition. One, two, three charges were thrown back. At intervals, Southerners scrambled out and stripped the dead and wounded of cartridge boxes. The Federals were so close that some confederates resorted to throwing rocks into the faces of the advancing foe.[9]

Jackson sent a desperate message to General Lee, requesting reinforcements. Lee immediately ordered Longstreet to send a division; but by the time Longstreet received the order, huge masses of Federal troops were crossing the field of fire of S. D. Lee's guns. It was about 4 P.M. One of S. D. Lee's men rushed up to him, gesticulating wildly, shouting, "Here they come, Captain! Here they come!" S. D. Lee, "cool and self-possessed," as always, one of his officers wrote, ordered every howitzer turned toward the threatened points in Jackson's front. Lee had "planted artillery so thick . . . that cannoneers almost elbowed each other."[10]

"The heavens rocked with the roar of the Confederate batteries," wrote one soldier, and "Such a blaze of artillery as I never heard," another recalled. For thirty full minutes, regiment after regiment— thousands of Federal troops—charged into the open. Lee's guns belched an incessant fire. Twice, Federal reserve forces moved out to assist faltering assault columns. Suffering tremendously from Lee's fire, some Northerners charged toward his guns. Three regiments slashed desperately forward. All finally were repulsed, some of their dead falling within two hundred yards of Lee's guns.[11]

Capitalizing on Lee's successful fire, Longstreet quickly sent the rest of his artillery to the position. So thirty guns joined in the final destruction of the Federal assault, sweeping the last blue waves from the field. Lee had the short-range guns moved to within five hundred yards of their targets, but they finally had to quit firing because the thick smoke created a blinding curtain over the battle-field. This smoke also hampered any chance of Federal counterfire. Only two Union batteries even fired on Lee, and these overshot their mark. Finally the Confederate army counterattacked. The Army of Northern Virginia at last delivered the kind of heavy blow against the northern troops that R. E. Lee had tried and failed to achieve all through the Seven Days Campaign.[12]

S. D. Lee's performance had been magnificent. His men never ceased their fire, though two of the batteries were in action for the first time. The enormous expenditures of each gun—certainly not less than one hundred fifty rounds apiece—ranked this as one of the greatest muzzle-loading artillery conflicts of history. It also made Lee something of a hero. His name was on the lips of every soldier in the army. Some even said, with obvious extravagance, that "never, in the history of war, had one man commanded so much artillery, with so much skill and effect as he did."[13]

Apparently, however, Lee did not receive as much credit and adulation from his superiors as he did from other admirers. In later years many persons cited Second Manassas as one of Lee's two or three outstanding Civil War accomplishments. Even R. E. Lee supposedly said to him, the first time they met after the battle, "Young man, come here! I want to thank you for what you did yesterday. You did good work." But the general gave Lee no special personal credit in his official report. He mentioned only that Lee occupied the same position as Walton's Washington Artillery the day before and that under Lee's "well directed and destructive fire, the support-ing lines were broken and fell back in confusion."[14] That was all: no high praise; and no promotion.

Longstreet exhibited an even cooler attitude. In his official re-port, he blandly stated that "Colonel S. D. Lee, with his reserve artillery placed in the position occupied the day previous by Colonel Walton, engaged the enemy in a very severe artillery com-bat. The result was, as on the day previous, a success." Then years later, in 1878, Longstreet and Lee fought a bitter and lengthy literary debate. The argument revolved around a misunderstanding between the two over what the other said: Lee thought Longstreet implied that Lee's artillery deserved no credit for the Confederate success; Longstreet believed that Lee claimed responsibility for having selected the position. Actually in 1878 Longstreet did attach considerably less than singular importance to Lee's contribution and he altered his interpretation only slightly in Lee's favor by the time he published his memoirs in 1896.[15]

Perhaps, just perhaps, R. E. Lee and Longstreet gave S. D. Lee the exact amount of credit he did deserve. He may merely have been a lucky man in the right place at the right time with the right things. He himself wrote many times later that he always had felt his services in the next battle, Sharpsburg, just two and one-half weeks after Second Manassas, were more significant than those at Second Manassas.[16] From one purely military point of view, it appears that he was right. Yet Second Manassas was a great Confederate victory. Whether mainly through luck or through skill, Lee had been the man of the moment. Many more such moments, and the outcome of the war might have been different.

Now, with the Army of Northern Virginia enjoying the flush of victory, the Confederates invaded the North. Though short of vital supplies, including ammunition, some even without shoes, high morale made them feel invincible. The campaign was important. Before moving into Maryland, Gen. R. E. Lee implemented a new scheme of artillery organization within his army. Basing decisions upon S. D. Lee's effectiveness in massed position at Second Manassas, the Confederates centralized all the guns into battalion-size units: one artillery battalion attached to each infantry division, and a reserve retained for both corps and for the army (though the plan was not rigidly adhered to). Lee's battalion and the Washington Artillery of New Orleans constituted Longstreet's corps reserve.[17] S. D. Lee moved his men and guns into Maryland with the most advanced infantry columns. By the afternoon of 7 September, the mass of the Confederate army reached Frederick.

Boldly General Lee decided to divide his army into four parts. One would go immediately to Hagerstown (S. D. Lee with this force), and each of the other three parts would maneuver so as to converge on Harper's Ferry from three directions—north, east, and west. The move began with a march through Frederick on Wednesday, 10 September. The townspeople's reactions indicated that most Marylanders were uncooperative. "The citizens crowded the streets and windows to see the troops pass," one soldier wrote. "Ladies were demonstrative, and waved their handkerchiefs; but the men looked coolly on as though afraid to express their feelings either way." The soldier then continued with a delightful little tale: "On a small gallery stood a buxom young lady. . . . On her breast she had pinned a small flag, the 'stars and stripes. . . .' Some soldier sang out, 'Look, h'yar, Miss, better take that flag down; we're awful fond of charging breastworks!' This was carried down the line amid shouts of laughter. The little lady laughed herself, but stood by her colors."[18]

Perhaps the contrast between Lee's ragged Confederates and the well-equipped, well-fed Federals that the Marylanders were accustomed to seeing influenced their decision. Just two days after the Southerners evacuated Frederick, elements of the Union army entered the town. Washington officials had hastily thrown this army together. Initially the force lacked cohesiveness, and many of the men woefully needed training. In desperation President Abraham Lincoln had turned to the discredited but masterful organizer, Maj. Gen. George B. McClellan. In four days he had remarkably shaped the ranks, now swollen to nearly 90,000 strong, into a formidable fighting machine and had gotten it on the march.[19]

Could the Confederates accomplish their tasks before McClellan's superior numbers crushed them? On 12 September, S. D. Lee, with the column under James Longstreet, finally reached Hagerstown. Things momentarily looked better. Here even the Marylanders seemed inclined toward southern support. "People here are more demonstrative; and we have much polite attention shown us," one soldier wrote. "Many young girls approached us as we marched through the streets, and presented us with beautiful flowers." But time was short. If McClellan got between Hagerstown and the graycoats trying to take Harper's Ferry, the Army of Northern Virginia might be destroyed. One day, two days went by. On the night of 13 September, Gen. R. E. Lee ordered several forces southeastward toward the critical mountain passes.

All day on 14 September the Confederates desperately fought delaying actions against the superior Federal numbers punching through the gaps. Early that day, S. D. Lee's artillery began to support Daniel Harvey Hill's hard-pressed infantry division. Lee's artillery and some of Longstreet's infantry joined Hill's troops in bitter fighting around Turner's Gap. The struggle lasted late into the night, but finally the Federals enveloped both Confederate flanks, and the Southerners withdrew. At other locations, too, the Unionists achieved even easier successes. The bluecoats secured clear passages into the Valley.[20] Then late on 14 September came word from Stonewall Jackson: Harper's Ferry was about to fall.

Again there seemed to be hope. If Jackson could take the place by early the next morning, the main parts of the Army of Northern Virginia could meet each other at Sharpsburg, Maryland. There a low ridge extended north and south of town—providing good defensive position. The Confederates might do battle with Mc-Clellan's army and win, making the campaign a great success after all. Longstreet's divisions began a night-long march toward Sharpsburg. S. D. Lee's artillery battalion moved out at midnight and crossed Antietam Creek at 8:00 A.M. on 15 September.[21]

Lee placed all but one of his batteries in a north-south line facing Antietam Creek, just west of a road roughly parallel to it. Nothing happened during the morning. At 1:00 P.M. the first Federal infantry appeared across the stream. Lee's guns belched, and the bluecoats scrambled back to safety. Soon the Unionists reappeared, this time with several long-range guns. Lee's artillery again scattered the northern infantry, but now the Southerners received galling punishment from the supporting enemy guns. More duels occurred, though at long distance. The fire killed no one, but it wounded several men and disabled some horses. At least Lee managed to keep the Federal infantry constantly shifting positions all day.[22]

Luckily for the Confederates, McClellan did not force a battle on the fifteenth. Eighteen thousand Southerners stretched thinly along a three-mile line. By noon some 75,000 Federals faced this gray army within striking distance. But McClellan procrastinated, and time slipped away. By nightfall the Southerners knew they would accept battle roughly along the lines they then occupied, so they began shifting units and bolstering for defense. S. D. Lee moved his battalion slightly farther west, just behind the crest of the ridge, to a spot immediately southeast of a Dunkard Church.[23] At

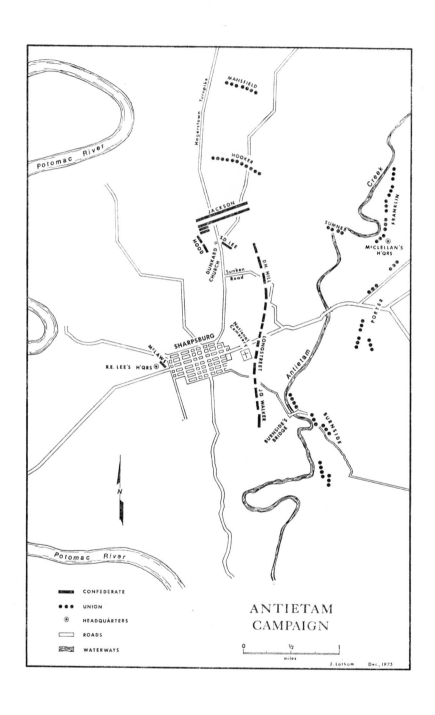

MANSFIELD

Hagerstown Turnpike

Potomac River

Creek

HOOKER

FRANKLIN

JACKSON

SUMNER

S.D. LEE

HOOD

McCLELLAN'S H'QRS

DUNKARD CHURCH

Sunken Road

D.H. HILL

PORTER

SHARPSBURG

National Cemetery

Antietam

McLAWS

LONGSTREET

R.E. LEE'S H'QRS

J.G. WALKER

BURNSIDE

BURNSIDE'S BRIDGE

N

Potomac River

CONFEDERATE
UNION
HEADQUÁRTERS
ROADS
WATERWAYS

ANTIETAM
CAMPAIGN

0   ½   1
miles

J. Latham   Dec., 1975

this point he was very close to the extreme left of the Confederate line, now loosely held, since Jackson's men would be placed there as they arrived.

During Tuesday, 16 September, Jackson's men trickled in. From early morning the Confederates watched Federals massing toward the left. Long lines of blue crossed Antietam Creek, marched north-westward, and took positions opposite the Confederate front and left flank. Busy crews of bluecoated axemen cleared hilltops of timber to emplace deadly twenty-pound Parrott guns. Still the Federals tried no offensive thrusts until near sundown.[24]

Two Union brigades from Maj. Gen. Joseph Hooker's corps slashed into the Confederate left, opposite the North Woods. A spirited combat ensued, lasting until dark. Areas of ground changed hands several times. The artillery on both sides entered the fray. Not all of Jackson's men had arrived. The Federals almost broke through. S. D. Lee rushed two howitzers toward Maj. Gen. John B. Hood's faltering lines and arrived just in time. The enemy advance halted, Jackson's units slipped into place on Hood's left, and night finally brought an end to the firing.[25]

Lee performed very creditably. Longstreet declared that Lee "took a distinguished part" in the fighting on the sixteenth. But that day actually was only a prelude—a calm before the storm of battle that marked 17 September 1862 as the bloodiest single day in the entire war. In Lee's words, "Sharpsburg was artillery hell." In this battle, one of his subordinates wrote later, Lee was "destined to win our soldier-love."[26] Previously Lee's men had come to respect him, admire him, follow him. Now, because of his great bravery and efforts, he won from them an even deeper adulation.

The battle began at 3:00 A.M., in a drizzling rain that fell during the night. Flames of fire slashed into the darkness. Skirmishers from each side, unseen by their enemies, began moving toward each other. Fierce encounters between small groups continued until dawn. The morning broke grey and misty, but the skies cleared early. Harsh sunshine brought a muggy morning and a hot, sweltering afternoon.

The day's fighting amounted to five separate Federal assaults from right to left (or north to south.) Each major onrush occurred at a different time, four in the morning and one in the afternoon. The Confederates repulsed them all—or ultimately stymied them by successful counter assaults. Lee's battalion participated in the first three and in the last.

During the morning Lee's guns fired with tremendous effect. His battalion occupied one-third of a mile, between Hood's Texas Brigade and another under Daniel H. Hill, the erstwhile mathematician and "southern viewpoint" textbook author. Lee's men stood atop a ridge, with a commanding view on all sides of the valley below, but they could not see any assaulting enemy troops until these were very close, because the woodlands and cornfields afforded unusual concealment.

The first hammer blow hit the Confederate lines from the north, directly against the left flank, at 6:00 A.M., and continued for more than two hours. Meanwhile the second assault commenced in support of the first, this one from the northeast. Initially Lee turned his guns to the left and had them fire over the heads of the adjacent Confederate infantry. This fire had some effect, but onward still came the powerful Federal forces. Then as the second assault developed, more nearly from his left front, Lee had to turn again toward the right. Firing in this direction, Lee could more easily damage the enemy because he did not have to worry about friendly infantry in between, but his men now had less cover. Firing from more exposed positions, they suffered heavy losses. (Several knolls had afforded a measure of protection from the enemy in the first assault, from the North Woods.) In the bitter and hard-fought struggles, everyone was involved, and "colonels and generals fell like privates."[27] Both sides sustained many casualties.

The battlelines became fluid—troops moved forward, back, and forward again. As the morning passed, the Confederates first halted a Federal advance, then counterattacked only to be thrown back. Then the Federals launched a third assault, commencing about 9:00 A.M. and drove the Southerners rearward a quarter of a mile, where desperate fighting again restored a line. Thus between 7:00 and 9:00 A.M., the battleground was east of the Hagerstown Pike; then for the rest of the morning, the southern lines bent and fell back. Lee's men participated in the significant fighting in the wooded, hilly area west of the pike.

Much of the struggle occurred at close quarters, so all units suffered extremely heavy losses, even the artillery. One battery finally ran out of ammunition and had to withdraw. Two other batteries lost so many horses and men, and sustained so much equipment damage, that Lee had to order them to the rear to refit. They were in such bad shape that they could move the pieces only by leaving portions of the caissons behind. One battery even lost a gun on the field. All four horses and six men that served the piece were disabled. Lee tried several times to retake it, but enemy troops swarmed around and stopped the attempts.[28]

Lee did his best in the thickest of it all, "fighting magnificently." He personally supervised some of the firing, including that by the farthest advanced and most exposed guns. Once, when the Confederate infantry moved forward, Lee accompanied two howitzers into the cornfields with two hundred infantrymen who together checked and held at bay an enemy force many times larger.[29]

After the Federals launched their 9:00 A.M. assault and began forcing the Confederates to give ground, Maj. Gen. Hood ordered Lee to take a message personally to Gen. R. E. Lee. The young colonel found the general about halfway between Sharpsburg and the Dunkard Church and delivered the urgent message: without reinforcements the Confederate left soon would crumble. General Lee replied calmly, "Don't be excited about it, Colonel; go tell General Hood to hold his ground, reinforcements are now rapidly approaching between Sharpsburg and the ford." Colonel Lee replied, "General, your presence will do good, but nothing but infantry can save the day on the left." Later recalling the incident, Lee continued, "I started to return, and had not gone over one hundred yards, when he called me, and pointed to McLaw's division, then in sight, and approaching at a double quick."[30]

Returning to his battered battalion, Lee mustered the operable guns along a ridge between the Dunkard Church and Sharpsburg, west of the pike. He again commenced an effective fire by shooting over the heads of D. H. Hill's infantry. Then finally as the Federals made their deepest plunge into the Confederate lines, Lee contributed significantly to the last repulse. Actually Confederate reinforcements blocked the advance, and the Federals then suffered severely because southern troops fired upon them from three sides. But Maj. Gen. John G. Walker, a Confederate division commander, credited Lee's artillery blasts with finally breaking Sedgwick's troops and forcing them to flee "in great disorder back to the cover of the 'East Wood,' beyond the Hagerstown Road."[31]

Lee's battalion had done all that it could; its energy and resources now were exhausted. At about 10:00 A.M. he moved the command a mile southward to rest, refit, and replenish ammunition. McLaw's division provided ample additional strength on the Confederate left, and thereafter the lines in that sector remained static. By 10:30 A.M. the fourth Federal charge slammed into the Confederate positions farther south. But Lee's men did not return to the fighting until mid-afternoon.[32]

As the day wore on the Union forces continued to launch attacks, gradually shifting their primary efforts from the Confederate left, to center, to right. The significant fighting during the hot, sultry afternoon began at 1:00 P.M. and continued for many hours.

S. D. Lee gathered the available remnants of his battalion and, beginning at 3:00 P.M., joined in the fighting that checked Maj. Gen. Ambrose Burnside, who was trying desperately to force a crossing of Antietam Creek. Twelve of Lee's twenty-six pieces were all that he could refit after the wreck suffered in the morning. One of the reemployed batteries, under Capt. William W. Parker, known as the "boy's battery" because the personnel were all so young, had fought well during the morning, though now they seemed too tired and battered to fight again. Lee gathered Parker's tired gunners around him and shouted: "You are boys, but you have this day been where men only dare to go. Some of your company have been killed; many have been wounded. But recollect that it is a soldier's fate to die. Now, every man of you who is willing to return to the field, step two paces to the front!" One of the men later wrote that "As Lee spoke these words he seemed a very god of war, and his eyes flashed command, not entreaty."[33]

Enough courageous boys stepped forward to man a section, and Lee proceeded with these and the rest of his available force toward the front. Again Lee's men engaged in several hours of bitter and desperate fighting and significantly aided the Confederate effort. Lee separated the guns into three groups and sent them in support of the hardest pressed infantry. One brigadier general credited Lee with rendering "material aid."[34]

The boys from Parker's Battery were too weak to roll their guns forward after each discharge. Under standard artillery practice the gunners stood clear when they fired, let the guns roll back under the recoil force, and then rolled them forward to the original position. After each shot, the guns recoiled, and the boys reloaded and fired again from the continually regressing position. Nevertheless, the boys kept firing, as did all of Lee's men, until dark. And though they fell back, they doubtless contributed to saving the Army of Northern Virginia from a rout. Years after the war Lee generously exaggerated that Parker's Battery "had made him a general."[35]

During the night of the seventeenth, Gen. R. E. Lee met in council of war with all his generals. S. D. Lee was present, and years later wrote an account of the proceedings. Many subsequent historians based their accounts of that meeting upon Lee's recollection. Apparently Lee embellished the story as years passed, making it "better" and more dramatic by quoting the various generals and having them express great pessimism and beliefs that the army should recross the Potomac that same night. "If I read their faces aright," Lee said, "there was not one but considered that General Lee was taking a fearful risk."[36]

S. D. Lee probably recalled the war council as he did because he misunderstood R. E. Lee's immediate intentions. Because S. D. Lee accompanied Stonewall Jackson on a reconnaissance the next day, and was asked for his opinion about the possibility of an offensive operation, he concluded that R. E. Lee seriously considered moving the next morning to hit McClellan's army. Actually R. E. Lee had concluded that an offensive was out of the question, but was confident that the Confederates could and would defend their positions if McClellan again attacked.[37]

Apparently the Confederate leaders looked upon the possibility of an attack by McClellan the next day as highly probable. But as the hours slipped by on 18 September and the attack did not materialize, the Confederate commanders began toying with a previously proposed plan to turn McClellan's right flank.[38] S. D. Lee accompanied Jackson on a careful reconnaissance and observed overwhelming strength and heavy preparations by the enemy at that point. Thus the Confederates concluded that nothing further could be gained in Maryland, and they crossed the Potomac that night into Virginia.

Again, years after the campaign, Lee vividly recalled the reconnaissance, and he published distorted accounts of the exact words he claimed were exchanged between himself, Jackson, and R. E. Lee. S. D. Lee gave the story greater significance than it deserved—implying that Jackson already believed offensive operations were impossible, but concealed this from him in order to get his completely frank opinion. R. E. Lee supposedly disagreed with Jackson and other generals who advised retreat, but would trust the word of "an artillerist in whom he had confidence."[39] At this late date S. D. Lee felt frustrated that his fame was not more widely recognized, and so enhanced his alleged status in R. E. Lee's eyes.

Actually, S. D. Lee did not need to place extra importance on his actions at Antietam; in reality they were quite laudable. Longstreet credited him with being "in active combat . . . from the first shot made before daylight." Brig. Gen. Richard B. Garnett praised Lee's "bravery and intrepidity," which "should add fresh fame to the high reputation he has already won." Infantry Col. Eppa Hunton wrote in his report that, "I cannot close . . . without mentioning the gallant conduct of our artillery, which fought near us [including] . . . Colonel Lee's." Scholars have been equally enthusiastic: "Sharpsburg was a day of glory for the Confederate Artillery. . . . Without Colonel Lee's guns to hold the enemy at bay," it is likely that D. H. Hill would have been "swept from the field," and at Sharpsburg, "the most shining figure was Colonel Stephen D. Lee."[40]

This was high praise indeed for an artilleryman in such a costly battle. The Army of Northern Virginia lost slightly more than nineteen percent of its personnel on 17 September. Lee's battalion suffered ten killed and seventy-five wounded, casualties of almost twenty-nine percent—an unusually large loss for artillery. His normally eighty-man-strong batteries now mustered an average of only sixty-four. Lee, later reminiscing with a friend, declared that Sharpsburg was the greatest battle he had been in during the entire war, and the acquaintance recalled that as Lee related the tale, "though it was a piece of enchanting eloquence . . . Stephen D. Lee was the saddest man I ever saw." Little wonder that Lee told E. Porter Alexander to "Pray that you may never see another Sharpsburg."[41]

Nevertheless Lee and his men had good reason to be proud. They fought long, hard, and well. In less than three weeks the Army of Northern Virginia enjoyed the glory of victory at Second Manassas

and suffered despair, frustration, and bloody stalemate at Sharpsburg. Lee deserves much credit for his part. His actions markedly
affected the outcome of both battles. These engagements proved to
be his last great adventures with the Army of Northern Virginia.
His exemplary performance "put a wreath around his stars"—he
became a general officer—and he soon transferred west to face a
new foe.

5

Outdoing the Prophet

FIVE DAYS AFTER the terrific struggle at Sharpsburg, still on the march back into the Shennandoah Valley, Lee observed his twenty-ninth birthday. The Army of Northern Virginia finally went into camp along Opequan Creek, a southerly tributary of the Potomac River. There the army found food and safety, while stragglers who had dropped behind after the Second Manassas campaign, and others later returning from Maryland, trickled in. Harvest time arrived, and living became easier for the Confederates. Lee spent some of his time leisurely gathering fruit in nearby orchards and dining occasionally with his friend Pender. The latter wrote to his wife, "You have no idea of our luxurious living. We even have a milk cow and what my dear wife has not, coffee and sugar."[1]

Even greater rewards than good food soon came to Lee. President Jefferson Davis telegraphed R. E. Lee, asking for the name of an accomplished artillerist to be made a brigadier general and sent west to help with the defense of Vicksburg, Mississippi. The general unhesitatingly named S. D. Lee, and on 6 November the newly named brigadier journeyed to Richmond for promotion ceremonies and briefings on his new assignment. He did not arrive at the capital until the next day, but his rank dated from the sixth.[2]

The inevitable question arises: was S. D. Lee, "kicked upstairs?" Frequently when R. E. Lee desired to be rid of a particular officer, he suggested to Confederate officials that the man could be more useful to the cause if stationed elsewhere. In this case he desired to make a place in his artillery for the man who became S. D. Lee's successor, E. Porter Alexander. R. E. Lee regretted losing such a fine artillerist as S. D. Lee, but he "never experienced trouble replacing artillery officers," since "that service drew educated men . . . with natural leadership and . . . intelligence." He wrote to President Davis saying, "I feel that I am much weakened by the loss" of S. D. Lee; and although Davis replied, "if you require Lee, he will be sent back to you," R. E. Lee did not exercise the option.[3]

Less than a year later, R. E. Lee needed a new division commander and wrote to Davis, "I think it probable that some meritorious officers . . . on duty in Gen. Johnston's Department may be without a command. If Gen. Stephen D. Lee is in this situation I would recommend that he be ordered to this army to take charge of Wilcox's brigade in case of the latter's promotion."[4] Therefore R. E. Lee obviously thought well of S. D., but the return did not take place. As a matter of fact, just two days after R. E. Lee penned his request, S. D. himself was promoted to major general. In any event, S. D. Lee permanently had ended his service with the Army of Northern Virginia. On 10 November 1862, with wide and varied military experience behind him, he proceeded to a new adventure, in Mississippi, and there soon met his first test as a general.

By the closing months of 1862 the war in the west was going badly for the South. The bloody battle of Shiloh in April had taken a frightful toll. The Federals had pushed down the Mississippi River to Memphis, which they occupied, and up from the Gulf to take New Orleans. Many irate citizens who lived in the western part of the Confederacy believed that President Davis and other high officials had neglected the area in favor of Virginia—channeling the best troops, guns, and supplies to the forces protecting Richmond. The accusation, at least considering intent, was not correct; but in a sincere effort to achieve greater Confederate strength in the West, Davis requested that an accomplished artillery officer be transferred from R. E. Lee's army to take direct charge of defending Vicksburg, strategically the most significant city on the Mississippi River still in the hands of gray forces. After S. D. Lee was selected for the assignment, Davis spoke at Jackson, Mississippi, affirming his faith in the new brigadier, saying "I am happy to state, after an attentive examination, that I have not been mistaken in the General of my choice. . . . It is but faint praise to say he has no superior." Davis also said: "I selected a General who, in my views, was capable of defending my State and discharging the duties of this important service. . . . He was sent to Virginia at the beginning of the war, with a little battery of three guns. With these he fought the Yankee gunboats, drove them off, and stripped them of their terrors. He was promoted for distinguished services on various fields. He was finally made a Colonel of cavalry, and I have reason to believe that, at the last great conflict on the field of Manassas, he served to turn the tide of battle and consummate the victory. On succeeding fields he has won equal distinction. Though yet young he has fought more battles than many officers who have lived to an advanced age and died in their beds. I have therefore sent Gen. Stephen D. Lee to take charge of the defenses of Vicksburg."[5]

Lee's transfer did constitute a considerable bolstering of Confederate command resources in Mississippi. In the preceding months, often under fire, he had on occasions carried standards and personally rallied faltering troops. He consistently had demonstrated that he was brave, soundly competent, energetic, and resourceful. Most important, he was rugged, hardworking, and popular with troops. One newspaper observer wrote that "Lee never seemed to suffer, yet he shared the hardships of his command in every way. . . . He carried neither tent nor camp equipage—only such baggage as he could tie behind his saddle."[6] On campaigns Lee shared the fighting men's frugal meals and meagre shelter. Unluckily, however, he had the misfortune of serving for more than seven months in Mississippi under officers less competent than he.

In addition to some poorly selected personnel, the southern command system in the west suffered from instability, complexity and cumbersomeness. "Department" boundaries and responsibilities varied. In late 1862 the mediocre if not incompetent Lieut. Gen. John C. Pemberton had departmental charge of Mississippi and East Louisiana, with headquarters at Jackson, Mississippi. A bit of Confederate windowdressing, Pemberton was one of the few northern-born generals who cast his lot with the South, and then rose in rank more by accident than by good performance. Earlier in charge of the Department of South Carolina, Georgia, and Florida, he was transferred both because no further serious threat seemed imminent in that area and because he had grown unpopular there. Then he got promoted, not for ability but for the sake of command unity. Clearly, Davis intended that Lee be primarily responsible for Vicksburg, but Pemberton sent his special assistant, Maj. Gen. Martin Luther Smith, an engineer officer who had directed the unsuccessful defense of New Orleans, to Vicksburg to oversee the engineering emplacements. As a major general Smith ranked Lee, but he exercised only a vague supervisory control. He could issue orders to Lee in Pemberton's name, but generally Lee enjoyed a free hand. In the battles of late December 1862, and early January 1863, Smith stayed inside the city and supervised the interior defenses, while Lee operated in the field.

Arriving at Vicksburg by rail in mid-November, Lee immediately examined the town and weighed the possibilities for its defense. In a letter to his friend and successor in Virginia, Col. E. Porter Alexander, Lee said: "Mississippi is one of the strangest places I have ever seen—nothing but ravines and bluffs—it is difficult to find sufficient level ground in this vicinity even to encamp the troops." Nevertheless the available men and fortifications pleased Lee, and he concluded, "the only difficulty is . . . supply . . . ; the Yankees can never really *take* Vicksburg—there is scarcely a place . . . where they could advance with company front of seventy-five yards . . . and our batteries are strong."[7]

Lee also noted both charm and strength in another asset: the Vicksburg citizenry. "The people are a polished, hospitable set and seem bent on making a last stand," he wrote. The people in turn liked Lee and put him up in "one of the finest houses in town." One newspaper writer proclaimed on 17 December that "Lee . . . is winning golden opinions from all who have seen anything of him since his arrival. He appears to be emphatically 'the right man in the right place' . . . ; he is an officer of industry and ability—a man who devotes his whole time and energies to the cause and to the health and comfort of his command. We are pleased with his plain, free and easy manner." While making such impressions, Lee also found time to socialize, and wrote Porter Alexander that, "there are lots of pretty girls here. I am afraid they will be the *death of me.*"[8]

The city of Vicksburg is situated on the Mississippi River near the southwestern end of a long series of hills running inland from the water almost at a right angle. The Yazoo River touches the

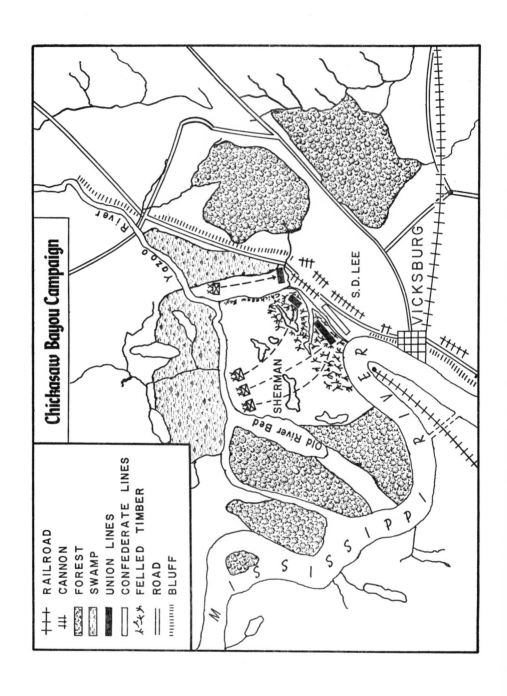

Chickasaw Bayou Campaign

Yazoo River

S. D. LEE

VICKSBURG

Chickasaw Bay

SHERMAN

Old River Bed

MISSISSIPPI RIVER

Legend:
- RAILROAD
- CANNON
- FOREST
- SWAMP
- UNION LINES
- CONFEDERATE LINES
- FELLED TIMBER
- ROAD
- BLUFF

foot of these hills at Haynes's Bluff and runs along the northeastern side to Snyder's Mill where it arches away from the hills and empties into the Mississippi about six miles north of Vicksburg. During the Civil War most of the ground in the area enclosed by the bluffs and the two rivers was low and marshy, cut by lakes and bayous, and was then heavily wooded with dense undergrowth, except for the clearings for a few small plantations.

A county road from Vicksburg to Yazoo City, called the Valley Road, ran along the foot of the bluffs, a feature of much importance in the Confederate defensive plans. Northwestwardly from the bluffs was swamp and a series of semiconnected lakes, once a bed of the Yazoo. This stretch of water could be forded only at three or four dry crossings. Chickasaw Bayou ran through the bluffs, touched and joined the lakes, but continued northward and emptied into the Yazoo.

Circumstances dictated that any Federal attack from down the Mississippi River would have to come across the swampy ground to the north of Vicksburg, but the Confederates failed to perceive this in advance. The Southerners established heavy batteries above the city on the Mississippi and for some months prevented Federal vessels from operating on the strip of river between there and Port Hudson, Louisiana. Thus they held a connecting link between the main part of the Confederacy and its trans-Mississippi territory. Relying upon river batteries and entrenchments surrounding the city in an arc from the bluffs to the Mississippi River, the Confederates also had an outpost at Snyder's Mill with three regiments of men and strong fortifications. A raft blocking the Yazoo proved sufficient to stop all Federal attempts to get up that river.

Earlier in the fall of 1862 Gen. Ulysses S. Grant had assumed command of all the Union forces in Northern Mississippi and at once began efforts to capture Vicksburg, making plans for a three-pronged attack. He suggested that Maj. Gen. Nathaniel P. Banks, in command of northern forces in Louisiana and not subject to Grant's orders, lead a force up the Mississippi River. Meanwhile Grant's subordinate, Maj. Gen. William T. Sherman, would move down the river from Memphis, and Grant himself would bring troops southward through Central Mississippi toward Grenada, then turn west in a coordinated attack upon Vicksburg.

As things turned out, Banks did not leave Baton Rouge, and other Confederate troops thwarted Grant with brilliant cavalry raids upon both Federal communications and supply depots. Grant retired to Memphis, but did not notify Sherman, who continued moving toward Vicksburg. Sherman was by no means being sent to certain defeat. His effective strength amounted to over 30,000 troops. Lee had only a "reorganized brigade" of about 2,700 men. About 2,400 other Confederate soldiers were on duty in and around Vicksburg.[9]

By 4 December, Lee had his brigade reorganized and ready for action. The command consisted of two light artillery batteries with eight guns and four infantry regiments. On Sunday, 21 December, Lee's troops, along with the entire Vicksburg garrison, stood in review before President Davis and Gen. Joseph E. Johnston,[10] the department commander whose headquarters were in Tennessee. Then, three days later, on Christmas Eve, the Southerners enjoyed a last gay moment before battle—many Vicksburg citizens and Confederate officers attended a grand ball, unaware that even as they danced Sherman's transports and gunboats neared the city.

The Southerners had telegraph outposts along the river—on the Louisiana side, where they were safer from northern forces operating out of Memphis. A telegrapher spotted Sherman's boats just below Lake Providence, Louisiana, and wired the news to Philip H. Fall at Desoto, Louisiana, just across the river from Vicksburg. The weather was tempestuous; high waves churned in the river, and it was a dark, cloudy, cold, and drizzly night. Under these adverse conditions Fall crossed to Vicksburg in a rowboat, scrambled up the muddy bank, and rushed to the ballroom. Lee was dancing with a local belle as Fall, covered with mud, delivered his message to General Smith. The older general turned very pale and in a loud voice exclaimed, "This ball is at an end; the enemy are coming down the river!" Lee courteously bowed to his partner and left, immediately beginning preparations to fight.[11]

Drummer's "long roll" aroused the Confederate troops at 3:00 A.M. on Christmas morning. Lee rushed with his brigade to the imminent battleground lying between the Mississippi and Yazoo rivers and the bluffs. The men immediately began digging entrenchments along the line of bluffs, using at first the only tools available

—their bayonets. Across the ground over which the Federals would have to charge were only five possible routes: at the race track two miles from the city; at Indian Mound, two miles farther inland; on the road parallel to Chickasaw Bayou; at Colonel Blake's plantation; and finally, at a wide area near Snyder's Mill. An abatis of fallen timber made an almost impassable obstacle at the race course, and fortifications were very strong in the entire area around Snyder's. Lee correctly surmised that an attack had the greatest chance of success if it came over one of the other three approaches. Realizing that the Valley Road would allow him to shift troops rapidly if necessary, Lee located his forces in two concentrations toward the center and left of the line: one regiment and two guns at Indian Mound, four regiments and an artillery battery at Chickasaw Bayou, and a regiment between these two places.[12]

Lee continued improvements of his positions for nearly three days—until they were attacked. He ordered a large force of Negroes out from Vicksburg and set them to work felling trees across the lake at the two dry crossings opposite Indian Mound and at the intersection of the lake and Chickasaw Bayou.[13] Lee also scattered advanced units up near the Yazoo River both to hinder the unloading of the enemy troops from their boats and to give ample warning of Sherman's approach.

Pemberton had been informed several days previously of the large fleet of gunboats and transports coming down the river, and he had immediately begun moving extra defensive forces toward Vicksburg. He had various units scattered nearby—at Port Gibson, Natchez, Grand Gulf, Jackson, and Grenada. Ultimately the Confederates concentrated 12,000 troops for the defense, but they arrived over a period of days—until 30 December. When the most decisive action of the campaign occurred, on 29 December, the Federals still outnumbered the Confederates by more than three to one.[14]

Sherman's forces landed at Johnston's and Lake's plantations early on 26 December and spent about twenty-four hours debarking. Confederate pickets had fired on the Federals the previous day, and they now continued the harassment. Lee reinforced these advanced positions with slightly more than a regiment of infantry and a section of artillery. General firing continued all day, both sides sustaining slight casualties. As the Federals moved into open ground, Confederate artillery sent them scrambling back into nearby woods. Finally the Northerners moved up some guns and returned the artillery fire until dark.[15]

Newly promoted Maj. Gen. Dabney Maury arrived that night with four hundred men and joined Lee on the battlefield. Cultured, competent, and gifted with a literary flair, Maury had risen rapidly from his first important position as colonel and chief of staff and had shown gallantry at Pea Ridge, Iuka, and Corinth; but he knew little of the Vicksburg situation. "The night was black as a wolf's mouth," Maury recalled, and "a cold rain was falling." Even though he outranked Lee, Maury generously deferred to Lee, saying "I am here with only four hundred men, but the whole division will be here soon after daylight. Please dispose of my force where and how you think best." With commendable candor Maury admitted, "I don't know anything about conditions here. I don't know where your line lies, I don't know where the enemy is; in fact, I don't know where I am." Obviously it was best that Maury entrusted Lee with the new troops' placement, but remarkably he even assured Lee, "You shall have all the glory, and I will be responsible if anything goes wrong."[16] So Lee's brigade gradually received reinforcements; it became a "provisional division," and Lee remained in command.

General skirmishing commenced on 27 December. Heavy clouds remained in the sky, and the intermittent cold drizzle continued. The artillery pieces on both sides fired all through the day. The Federals pushed along the entire line, driving most of the advanced Confederates rearward, but no major assaults occurred. Lee mused that "they evidently had excellent guides, attacking us at every point where it was possible. . . ."[17]

Attacks on all these points came again the next day. The sky had cleared; but frost settled on the open grass, and ice formed on the lakes and the bayou. The 28th Louisiana Infantry Regiment and a company of light artillery held an advanced position at Chickasaw Bayou. They exchanged fire with the Unionists for six hours, from about daylight to noon, and then fell back under pressure. The Federals cheered and stormed forward, confident of success. But another of Lee's regiments, the 26th Louisiana, still had to be reckoned with. They too were highly confident troops, occupying a slightly advanced line near the edge of the woods in which Sherman's men were pursuing the other nearly vanquished Louisianans. Lee watched the Federals as "a volley from the Twenty-sixth Louisiana . . . , near the edge of the lake and in temporary rifle pits, brought them to their usual prudence, and allowed the gallant Twenty-eighth to move in safety."[18]

As the northern advance bogged down, the Federals brought up more and more artillery, which soon joined with the sharpshooters in pounding away at the thin Confederate line. The Southerners suffered their heaviest losses of the entire campaign here, considering the small numbers engaged, because part of their position bent along the Chickasaw Bayou and left the men exposed to an enfilade fire. At the 26th Louisiana Regimental Command Post, Lt. Henry B. Lee—S. D.'s cousin and one of his aides—had part of a finger shot off by an enemy bullet. Retreat would expose the Confederates to an even more punishing fire, so they remained in place until Lee ordered the trenches vacated at 2:00 A.M.[19]

Lee felt certain that Sherman's main attack would come at Chickasaw Bayou. The area contained the widest stretch of cleared land, and for two days the Federals had moved more troops to the vicinity. Furthermore, Lee wrote, "it was the only place where much boldness was displayed." Therefore Lee audaciously decided to allow initial Federal progress at the Bayou and planned a big kill in the open field beyond. He removed all obstacles at the Bayou, had the men quietly vacate the advanced positions long after midnight, and placed a considerable number of troops near the foot of the bluffs on the forward slope so their fire might have more of a sweeping effect. These troops hastily dug new pits with their bayonets. Meanwhile, Lee received two additional regiments, which he used to bolster his rear lines.[20] He probably had a total of just under 6,000 men.

Sherman also did some thinking and maneuvering during the night of 28 December, but he made less fortunate decisions than Lee. After a personal reconnaissance of the entire front, Sherman became convinced that Indian Mound and Chickasaw Bayou offered the only two possible points for a successful assault. "I determined to make a show of attack along the whole front, but to break across . . . at the two points named," he wrote. He snorted to a subordinate that it would eventually cost at least 5,000 men to take Vicksburg, "and we may as well lose them here as anywhere else."[21] Everyone and everything possible would be thrown into a grand Federal charge on the next day.

On 29 December came the decisive action in the campaign. Heavy, lead-colored clouds covered the sky. Icy winds slashed through the fields. Many blue-clad troops gazed apprehensively at the water marks ten feet above their heads on some of the trees. Meanwhile the Confederate guns belched incessantly. "The deep toned thunder of the artillery was almost drowned in the ominous roar of musketry," wrote one soldier, "while enveloping the whole, hung thick folds of smoke."[22]

Lee directed the troops personally, often exposed dangerously. Capt. Paul Hamilton, Lee's adjutant, was killed while standing by his chieftain, but Lee remained steel-nerved and tenacious. Once Lee stood between two trees and studied the front through field glasses when suddenly a cannon ball crashed into one of the trees, just a foot or two from his head. Coolly, he removed his glasses and merely looked at the tree for a moment then went on with his task. Later another cannon ball cut his horse from under him, but he escaped unhurt. One of the men wrote admiringly that "his presence was very inspiring to us all." Another said, "I have seen a good many brave men, but none surpassed Gen. S. D. Lee in cool bravery."[23]

The Confederates had no trouble stopping the Federal assaults at all points except at Chickasaw Bayou. The Unionists made five attempts to storm the lines at Indian Mound, but natural obstacles and effective fire thwarted them all. At Chickasaw Bayou the blue-clad troops worked during the night trying to bridge the lake with pontoons, but dawn revealed that they were working at the wrong water—only a slough running parallel to the bayou. The Federal infantry stormed forward at daylight and cautiously examined the recently vacated Confederate positions—apparently not understanding why they had been abandoned. Meanwhile, the Federal engineers again tried throwing their pontoon bridge across the lake, but Lee had eight artillery pieces arranged to crossfire over the lake, and a few well-directed shots stopped the bridging operations. Nevertheless, Lee immediately shored up his line behind the point of the attempted bridge by moving two infantry regiments. Then, since no enemy appeared at Snyder's Mill, he ordered one regiment there to join his main forces.

Nothing further happened until about 10:00 A.M. when the Federals opened up a furious cannonade. This tremendous barrage continued for an hour then ceased as suddenly as it had begun. The hills echoed mockingly. Then in the new silence that followed began the bloodiest part of the campaign, which might well be called "Sherman's folly." Some 4,000 men from the Union division commanded by Brig. Gen. George W. Morgan moved up in a concerted assault. They bunched up, able to cross the lake at only two points. The terrain provided a "funnel-effect," and by the time the Federals could begin dispersing they were in the killing zone. They fanned out while charging upslope across an open field, heading toward a concave Confederate battleline.

Artillery fire alone stopped the first charge. "This terrific fire," Lee said, "literally swept these troops off the ground and those not killed or wounded fell to the ground with them." Morgan rallied his remaining men and charged again, slashing more to the left. "A passage was forced," he recalled, "over the abatis and through the mucky bayou and tangled marsh to dry ground. All formations were broken; the assaulting forces were jammed together, and, with a yell of desperate determination, they rushed to the assault and were mowed down. . . ." Again Lee made maximum use of artillery in conjunction with infantry; Morgan remembered "a storm of shells, grape and canister, and minie-balls which swept our front like a hurricane of fire."[24] At the head of his largest and most important command up to that time, Lee was doing very well.

Lee ordered his infantry to hold fire until the enemy was within one hundred yards. At no point did any Federals get closer than fifty yards to the Confederate lines. Finally the Northerners sought cover behind logs, debris, and even the bodies of their fallen comrades. Observing this action, the 26th Louisiana and part of the 17th Mississippi Regiments, showing a readiness for combat that Lee had instilled, spontaneously stormed forward while their enemy still lay face down. The Federals were so stunned that twenty-one officers and over three hundred enlisted men were captured as well as four stands of colors and five hundred rifles. The remainder of Morgan's troops fled in mass confusion, leaving their dead and wounded behind.[25]

The only other significant assault hit the Indian Mound. There the Union's 6th Missouri succeeded in getting across a narrow sandbar, but then found the bank too steep to climb. Lee's men nearby, the 31st Louisiana Infantry with two artillery pieces, kept the Federals huddled against the bank and penned in this muddy spot until nightfall. Then under the cover of rain and darkness, they withdrew one company at a time.

Rain and sleet brought more cold during the night. A few Southerners built fires, which burned only feebly. One group that had shown great skill and aggressiveness received a special visit. Up came General Lee, all alone, with a water bucket of whiskey. "Gentlemen, I have come especially to congratulate you," he said, "and also to bring something along to warm you."[26]

Before nightfall Lee had sent litter bearers to bring in the Federal wounded, but they were mistakenly fired upon. After dark some eighty Union wounded were picked up and taken to Confederate hospitals. This kindness probably gave rise to the charge made later that the Southerners plundered the dead and wounded of their clothing and equipment. Of course, the charge was unfounded, and Morgan himself admitted as much in his account of the battle.[27]

Sherman considered several plans during the next few days but did little except to have his men entrench. On 31 December, a truce was arranged for the burial of Union dead, but apparently Sherman expected a counterassault later. Rain continued to fall, and he feared that his positions might flood. Furthermore, he wrote, "from our camps we could hear the whistles of the trains arriving in Vicksburg, could see battalions of men marching up toward Haynes's Bluff, and taking post at all points in our front. I was more than convinced that heavy reinforcements were coming to Vicksburg." So, he continued, "I became convinced that the [better] part of wisdom was to withdraw."[28]

The optimum time for a Confederate counterassault would have been early on 30 December. The southern generals, however, felt that they still had insufficient troops for such an undertaking that day and in fact expected Sherman to advance. Lee later wrote that, "It was not credited that an American army of that size would after so feeble an effort return to their boats." The day after Sherman's grand assault, Maury assumed command, and Lee thus lost authority to order a Confederate attack. Like Lee, Maury anticipated another attack, rather than perceiving an opportunity for a counterattack. Lee was allowed to keep his "provisional division" for a time, and he became a temporary major general—signing his official report with that rank—but he would continue in the next few months to have only "temporary" grades and assignments. This situation prompted the men of the corps he later commanded to nickname him "Old Temporary."[29]

The Confederates continued making ready for Sherman's expected attacks. On 1 January 1863, scouts reported the Federals concentrating to assault Snyder's Mill. Lee moved there that night with four additional regiments but learned a few hours before daylight that the bluecoats were reembarking. He rushed back to Maury at Chickasaw Bayou and requested permission to pursue the enemy to the river. Taking four regiments up near the river bank, he discovered two Federal regiments drawn up in line of battle on the bank under cover of the gunboats. Lee advanced his men as skirmishers, some getting to within one hundred yards of the boats. The troops engaged in blistering fire, but the Federals opened up with boat howitzers. Lee could do nothing more. His men remained in place, harassing the troops boarding the boats, but unable to move any closer. The next day, 3 January, Sherman's expeditionary force steamed down the Yazoo to the Mississippi and headed back to Memphis. Sherman was in such a hurry that he left all his entrenching tools behind.[30]

Southerners long remembered Chickasaw Bayou, where they justly credited Lee with giving "old Sherman a good drubbing." One southern newspaper article extravagantly proclaimed in 1908 that the Chickasaw Bayou battles "deserve as historic a place in history as that of Thermopylae." A Confederate veteran contended that "of all the genuine, clean-cut victories, save, perhaps that of 2nd Bull Run, Chickasaw Bayou is in the lead."[31]

Lee received considerable praise and honors for his actions. Maury wrote that, "throughout the operations . . . I have relied . . . upon his admirable military judgement. He is one of the most energetic, prompt, and efficient soldiers it has ever been my good fortune to serve with, and I hope the distinguished services he has rendered . . . may be acknowledged by his advancement in rank and command." Pemberton wrote that "to Brigadier-General Lee, . . . great praise is due for his energy, courage, and ability. . . ."

Lee received authorization to designate a suitable officer from his staff to carry the captured standards to Richmond. The Confederate government in turn authorized all the regiments in the battles to inscribe "Vicksburg" on their flags. When Lee made his first appearance before his troops after the battles, they shouted, "Three cheers for General Lee, the hero of Chickasaw Bayou." Perhaps the most touching tribute Lee received was a beautiful black stallion that one of his regiments purchased for $1,700 and presented to him as a token of their admiration.[32]

Even some of the enemy—though not Sherman—admitted Lee's triumph. One, identified in a newspaper account only as "Colonel Allen of Ohio," said in a speech that "Stephen D. Lee was the most active, pugnacious, and efficient of any of the gallant fighters on the Confederate side." Brig. Gen. John Milton Thayer, a brigade commander in Morgan's division, said that Chickasaw Bayou was "a repetition of Balaklava, although mine was infantry and Earl Cardigan's force was cavalry."[33]

Although Lee effectively utilized combined arms, his artillery at Chickasaw Bayou did make that battle similar to the famous and costly charge of the "Light Brigade." Unquestionably the handling of artillery was one of Lee's keenest skills as a soldier. Jefferson Davis had judged correctly in moving an accomplished artilleryman to the west. Lee's victory had contributed incalculably to the Confederate war effort.[34] If he had not been at Chickasaw Bayou, or if he had lost, Vicksburg would have fallen in December 1862, depriving the Confederacy of its trans-Mississippi territory six months earlier.

The Confederates should have counterattacked, but on 30 December, Lee lost responsibility for the decision. After 1 January Lee believed that "reinforcements had arrived in sufficient numbers to enable Gen. Pemberton to take the aggressive had he so desired."[35] Nevertheless, Lee remained quite discreet and almost always defended the actions of those above him, although actually he believed that historians early would notice *his* greatness.

Lee certainly had performed creditably during the Chickasaw Bayou Campaign. He displayed sound military ability, boldness, and a willingness to meet his enemy. Placing defensive troops at the foot of Walnut Hills, removing the obstacles at Chickasaw Bayou, and utilizing the funnel-effect to make a big kill showed a remarkable exercise in generalship. He made logical decisions when faced with a rapidly changing situation, and he acted quickly whenever speed was required. Personally on the scene, he took charge of the action and influenced its outcome by directing the battle as it progressed. He had outdone the "prophet of modern warfare."

With his courage, daring, and example, Lee set a standard for brigadier generals. He displayed *coup d'oeil*, that quintessential quality of generalship, the ability to assess at a glance the terrain, the enemy and friendly dispositions. Making hasty, but accurate and adequate estimates of situations, he took sound and decisive steps to insure resourceful executions and positive results. The engagement at Chickasaw Bayou bore a striking resemblance to the Battle of Fredericksburg, 13 December 1862. S. D. Lee, on only a smaller scale, duplicated one of Robert E. Lee's most noted tactical achievements. Little wonder, then, that the influential Virginia newspaper editor, E. A. Pollard, wrote that S. D. Lee "had one of the best founded reputations of the war,"[36] and high hopes now rested upon him in the further defense of Vicksburg.

6

Conflict, Ratholes, and Defeat

WITH SHERMAN GONE from the scene and no aggressive action to contend with, "Old Temporary" Lee and his men settled into the environs of Vicksburg, where they manned defensive trenches for the first two and one-half months of 1863. Their guns performed efficiently throughout the winter, and only an occasional insignificant Federal vessel got past. Commanding a "provisional division" and continuing to receive official compliments, Lee began to think that he soon would be promoted to the rank of major general, but this honor did not come to him until much later.[1]

Lee continued to enjoy popularity with his men. He sometimes shared their labors, and he pleased them by always delivering orders in person. "No neatly-dressed aids-de-camp with their foppish airs and tones of authority" carried his instructions, recalled one admiring subordinate, who continued: "We distinctly remember the appearance of General Lee. . . . A huge rough overcoat enveloped his form, . . . pants thrust carelessly into his high, military boot-tops, while his fine, manly features lighted up with smiles beneath his slouched hat. . . ." Lee encouraged occasional "hilarity and mischief" because he liked to see his troops full of life. "His actions and manner, so pleasant and affable, soon won for him the deep admiration and heartfelt esteem of the whole regiment." Lee's men also observed and appreciated a practicality in his ways, and they believed that he never asked anything of them that he would be unwilling to perform himself.[2]

On one occasion, a young sergeant in the 17th Louisiana Infantry Regiment desired a furlough and sought Lee's approval. The general said sternly, "We cannot spare any of our good soldiers," and he added that in order to increase their readiness for enemy attacks, "they should be drilling every day."

"But that does not apply to me," argued the sergeant, "for I am well drilled."

"I shall try you," said Lee. "Take position! . . . About face! . . . Forward march!"

Just about the time he finished marching back to his place in the defensive lines, the sergeant realized that he was not going to get the leave; but doubtless his fellow soldiers appreciated the humor and had another good story to tell about their popular commanding general.[3]

Lee was correct to insist upon constant readiness, because Sherman's Chickasaw Bayou defeat had not lessened Grant's determination to take Vicksburg. The persevering Union commander tried various approaches, by constructing new canals and by utilizing the Federal navy to move troops along rivers and bayous in the vicinity. The first four of these episodes, Grant's Canal project, the Duckport Canal project, the Lake Providence Expedition, and the Yazoo Pass Expedition, all failed because of natural barriers and successful Confederate counteroperations. Lee played no direct role in these actions, as he remained with his "provisional division" in and around Vicksburg.

The Confederates had effective forces to the east but not on the western bank of the Mississippi River. Grant needed to secure a foothold on the high ground either above or below the city. To deter him, the Confederates defended a river front extending two hundred miles to both north and south. Even though Pemberton did not have sufficient troops to garrison such a line, he could move forces to any threatened point if he received adequate and timely intelligence concerning Grant's movements. Pemberton had far too little cavalry, however, and no navy. Lee later mused in conversation with Pemberton that "the want of cavalry" was at the root of all the southern difficulties in defending Vicksburg.[4]

In spite of the failures of the Union Navy in the operations of the next few months, Lee appreciated the enormous advantage which naval power conferred upon the Union, saying some years later, "Although it is a matter of speculation, it seems as if the navy and its work during the four years . . . was as decisive in results as were the mighty Union armies which were in the field."[5] Of course he was referring to the navy on the western waters.

Lee volunteered to lead a force against the next and most extraordinary of Grant's attempts to reach Vicksburg—the Steele's Bayou Expedition, called the Deer Creek Expedition by the Confederates. The Union fleet tried to approach the city through two hundred miles of narrow, twisting bayous—Steele's, Black, Deer Creek, Rolling Fork, and the Sunflower River, into the Yazoo just above Snyder's Mill. Lee received an order to attack if possible on Black Bayou, to create obstructions closing Deer Creek to navigation, and also to try getting behind the Federals, penning their fleet within the labyrinth of small waterways.[6]

The Federal admiral himself, David D. Porter, commanded the flotilla that on 16 March 1863 ran into Steele's Bayou. Natural hazards hampered the way, making the route just barely wide enough for passage of the gunboats. Porter's apprehensive subordinates expressed fears that the fleet super-structures would sustain great damage in the perilous, closely overhung waterways, but the admiral boldly replied, "All I need is an engine, guns, and a hull to float them."[7]

Nevertheless the Federals had to contend with Lee as well as with the natural obstacles. On 22 March, Lee made final preparations for launching his counteroffensive and issued orders that three days' rations be cooked and packed. He eventually united three regiments for the operation, the 3rd, 22nd, and 28th Louisiana Infantries. The troops moved up the Yazoo River, some in the steamer *Peytona* and some in the side-wheel mail packet *Dew Drop*. Farther upriver, the men transferred into a fleet of flatboats, skiffs, canoes, and "every conceivable small floating craft." Often they had to stop and cut trees which snarled the passage with intertwined branches.[8]

On 24 March the Confederates arrived at Wilson's, six miles from the mouth of Deer Creek, and there commenced building earthworks and obstructions in the waterway. The weather was unseasonably cold, and the area was sporadically flooded and uniformly muddy—a "cheerless waste of waters," one soldier recalled. Several Negroes lived in cabins nearby, and each had a dugout canoe tied to a door post—supposed by some of the southern soldiers to be precautions against rising water.[9]

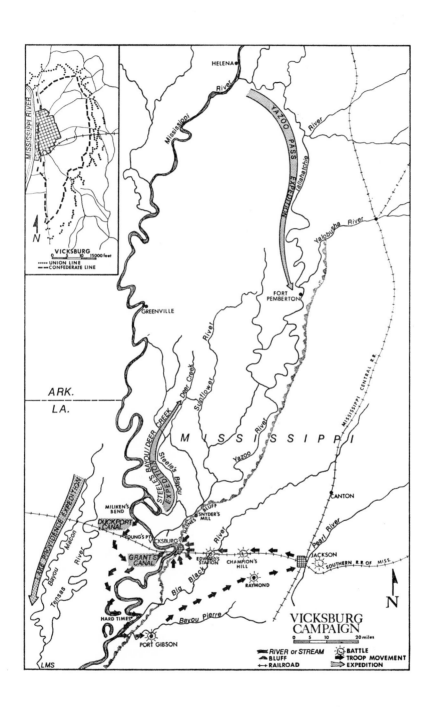

HELENA

Mississippi River

YAZOO PASS EXPEDITION

Tallahatchie River

Yalobusha River

GREENVILLE

FORT PEMBERTON

Sunflower River

Deer Creek

ARK.
LA.

Coldwater River

MISSISSIPPI CENTRAL R.R.

M I S S I S S I P P I

Yazoo River

CANTON

STEELE'S BAYOU/DEER CREEK EXPEDITION

Steele's Bayou

HAINES BLUFF
SNYDER'S MILL

MILIKEN'S BEND

DUCKPORT CANAL

LAKE PROVIDENCE EXPEDITION

Bayou Macon

Tensas River

YOUNG'S PT.
VICKSBURG

GRANT'S CANAL

Yazoo River

EDWARD'S STATION
CHAMPION'S HILL

RAYMOND

JACKSON

Pearl River

SOUTHERN R.R OF MISS.

Big Black River

HARD TIMES

Bayou Pierre

PORT GIBSON

LMS

N

VICKSBURG CAMPAIGN

0   5   10   20 miles

RIVER or STREAM
BLUFF
RAILROAD
BATTLE
TROOP MOVEMENT
EXPEDITION

VICKSBURG

0   5   10   15000 feet

...... UNION LINE
—— CONFEDERATE LINE

MISSISSIPPI RIVER

N

After Lee's men worked on the obstructions for two days, northern forward observers noted that Lee had emplaced enough impedi-
ments to warrant canceling the expedition, so Porter began backing
his transports rearward, as the narrow way would not allow them
to turn around. At 2 A.M. on 27 March Lee heard of this move. He
considered moving his force up for an attack but did not because
the few boats he had were inadequate and no all-land route existed.
So Lee sent seventy-five men to try felling trees in the Federals'
rear. The Southerners waded through water three and one-half
feet deep, and only a few of them got into Porter's rear. Sherman,
who had been moving with infantry behind the Union fleet, led
his men on an eerie night march and with superior numbers drove
Lee's troops off. Sherman's troops also had marched in this hip-
deep water, through a dense jungle-like area, using candles thrust
into their rifle muzzles as the only light.[10]

Lee remained in position at Wilson's for several days to make
sure that the Federals continued their withdrawal. Then, leaving
an outpost on Deer Creek, he moved the remainder of his men
back to Haynes's Bluff and himself returned to Vicksburg, arriving
on 29 March. His operation at least had accomplished its primary
objective, thwarting the Federal offensive. Lee had saved Vicksburg
a second time. His skill, energy, and initiative continued to pay
dividends. Again he received official commendations, from both
Maj. Gen. Dabney H. Maury and Maj. Gen. Carter L. Stevenson,
the latter a division commander in Pemberton's army and one of
the few southern generals officially declared a traitor by the United
States War Department because of his delay in forwarding his
resignation. Dispelling any insinuation that perhaps Lee should
have done more, Stevenson exonerated him, saying that "not even
the energy of General Lee . . . could overcome the difficulties in
his way. . . . Had it been possible he would have done it."[11]

Lee's "provisional division" gradually reduced in strength to a
"reinforced brigade," and the Confederates spent the rest of March
and the first few days of April 1863 waiting calmly in their defensive positions. But Grant did not leave them in peace very long.
The flood waters already had begun to recede, and more dry land
appeared. Grant could now move men and equipment overland on
the Louisiana side of the river. If a substantial part of the fleet
could run below Vicksburg's batteries, the Federals could cross the

river in force between Vicksburg and Port Hudson and then attack overland. As an aid to his planned operations, Grant formulated several diversionary actions.

The first of these diversions was to move a division under Maj. Gen. Frederick Steele by water from Young's Point, Louisiana, to Greenville, Mississippi. Steele moved in the first week of April. He went overland to Deer Creek and then south along the west bank of the stream. The maneuver was not only a possible threat to Vicksburg; but, more important, Steele was in the area that served as a primary source of commissary supplies for the Confederates at Vicksburg.[12]

On 7 April 1863, Lee moved out with a reinforced brigade to repel Steele and hopefully engage and defeat the Federals. Lee proceeded up Deer Creek to a position twenty miles above the junction of that stream with Rolling Fork. At 8:00 P.M. Lee's cavalry scouts reported that Steele was falling back, leaving a path of destruction as he went. Lee ordered two infantry regiments to pursue, planning to give battle in the morning.

But Steele chose not to fight, and Lee had too few cavalry to catch him. Steele went all the way back to a camp seven miles from Greenville, burning thousands of bushels of corn and carrying off large numbers of livestock. Lee loaded the salvageable corn and stray cattle on the Confederate vessel *Golden Age* and sent a message requesting reinforcements. On 12 April Steele's men boarded their boats and steamed away. Lee advised his superiors to send a larger force of cavalry to the area for any future operations, though "it should be borne in mind," he warned, "that corn will now be scarce."[13]

Returning to Vicksburg on 15 April, Lee reported on Steele's destructive acts. Meanwhile Grant had marched the bulk of the Union forces overland from Milliken's Bend to a point in Louisiana, south of Vicksburg; then on the night of 16 April Porter ran a part of his fleet past the Vicksburg batteries. Shortly before midnight, pickets in skiffs warned the Confederates of the fleet's approach, but the shock effect of the move, so soon after the Confederate high command had turned all of its attention to the Deer Creek area, undoubtedly affected the Southerners. Porter ran twelve boats past, though all were hit and one sank. It was a significant

Federal success. Now Grant could march men southward on the Louisiana side of the river and use the boats to get them across into Mississippi below Vicksburg. Lee still had some supervisory responsibility regarding the artillery batteries, but he did not participate in the 16 April operations. He took a very active part, however, when another large portion of the Union fleet ran past Vicksburg a week later.

Meanwhile Grant launched two more diversions. Between 17 April and 2 May, Col. Benjamin H. Grierson led one thousand cavalrymen on a raid from Memphis to Baton Rouge. At the same time, Sherman's corps made an elaborate feint from the north of Vicksburg, landing at Haynes's Bluff. Pemberton never realized what Grant really was up to and continued to expect an attack from above the city.[14] On the night of 22 April, five Federal transports, a gunboat, and twelve barges ran past the batteries. The Confederates sounded an alarm at 11:30 P.M. and opened fire upon each vessel as it came into view. Shots hit all the transports, and one southern officer reported that "the escape of any seemed miraculous, considering the number of large projectiles sent crushing through them." One vessel ran into the Louisiana shore, and its crew abandoned it, while another sank.[15]

Lee reported that the "firing was generally good" but that it had been lessened in effectiveness because the guns produced huge clouds of smoke that settled over the water and hampered the gunners' vision. Some vessels used these clouds as screens and slipped past unobstructed. Lee wrote in an analysis of the Vicksburg campaign that these two passings, one on 16 April and the other on 22 April, demonstrated that the Vicksburg batteries alone never had been an adequate defense. He correctly claimed that the Southerners sorely missed naval strength and cavalry forces.[16] Grant had accomplished two major feats—he had troops on the west side of the river below Vicksburg, and he had naval vessels to move him across and to stock him well with supplies. On 29 April Grant unsuccessfully tried to cross some of his forces at Grand Gulf; but when the defending batteries proved too strong, he moved south to a point opposite Bruinsburg and crossed the next day.

On 1 May, one of Grant's corps, under Brig. Gen. John A. McClernand, attacked the southern forces holding Port Gibson.

The attacking Northerners numbered about 23,000 men, while the defending Confederates had only 8,000. The rough terrain prevented McClernand from committing the mass of his forces at any one time. Battle raged all day in a series of furious engagements, the Confederates slowly falling back. They withdrew under cover of darkness, each side having suffered about 800 casualties.

One of the Confederate casualties resulted in Lee changing commands. At Port Gibson the Confederates lost a brigade commander, Brig. Gen. Edward D. Tracy. The men of Lee's reinforced brigade by this time manned specific and critical defensive positions in and around Vicksburg, and the Confederate commanders wished to leave these soldiers where they were; but Tracy's brigade needed a new commander—one capable of leading it in active campaigning. Since Lee seemed obviously the best man available for the job, he assumed a new command, composed of the 20th, 23rd, 30th, 31st, and 46th Alabama regiments, a brigade in Maj. Gen. Carter L. Stevenson's division.

Finally Pemberton assembled an army of 17,500 men organized into divisions under Stevenson, John S. Bowen, and William W. Loring, to maneuver in the field against Grant. Other Confederate forces remained in Vicksburg, and some were located in Jackson, Mississippi, under the nominal direction of department commander Gen. Joseph E. Johnston, who still remained at his headquarters in Tennessee. But Pemberton did not launch a united counter-offensive—as Johnston somewhat unclearly urged.[17]

The Union general quickly united his own men and cut loose on a bold, audacious inland move. He pushed rapidly toward Jackson, planning to defeat the southern troops there before they either evacuated or moved to reinforce Pemberton. The Confederates got only a brigade into Grant's line of advance. The Federals clashed with this relatively small resisting force at Raymond on 12 May, pushed past, and reached Jackson two days later. General Johnston had arrived two days earlier, assuming personal command; and as the Federals approached he decided to withdraw, to save as many troops and supplies as possible. He staged a holding action with part of his forces and sent word to Pemberton to meet him at Canton, Mississippi, where the Confederates would unite.

Grant intercepted a copy of this order and immediately moved out of Jackson toward the west. By this time Pemberton's army was only a few miles outside of Edward's Station, between Jackson and Vicksburg. Pemberton wavered indecisively. He had received conflicting instructions from higher authorities. President Davis had telegraphed that he should definitely hold the city; General Johnston wanted him to ignore Grant and move to Canton. Pemberton finally decided to obey Johnston's orders, but too late. The armies clashed in the Battle of Champion's Hill, also called Baker's Creek, on Saturday, 16 May 1863.

Champion's Hill, a little more than four miles to the east of Edward's Station, is a crescent shaped ridge, about seventy-five feet in elevation, near where the Champion plantation home was located. Three roads led eastward from Edward's Station, and eventually all went to Raymond. Each of Pemberton's three divisions covered one of these roads.[18] The Confederate line stretched out about three miles. Stevenson's division occupied the left. One brigade remained in Edward's Station with the supply trains, while the three others, with Waul's Texas Legion and some cavalry, numbered about 5,000 effectives. Lee's brigade occupied the extreme left flank of the army's line, facing east and holding a three-fourths mile front beginning at the intersection of the three roads, a mile from Champion's House. Every brigade had skirmishers out for about one mile.

Skirmish fire began at daylight, grew very hot by 7:00 A.M., and continued to increase. Lee realized the strategic importance of the crossroads and emplaced a battery of six guns there. He also anticipated that the Northerners might do exactly what they eventually *did* in the battle—attack from the north and northeast in an attempt to roll up the Confederate left flank. He sent out a reconnaissance patrol and received word by around 9:00 A.M. that a strong Union column was approaching from the northeast.[19]

The blue forces that hit the Confederate left outnumbered the defenders by two to one. Lee's sound action in suspecting a flanking attack and sending a patrol which gave him advance warning was of crucial importance. Under fire, Lee moved his brigade to the left and turned it to block the Union threat. He sent word to the brigade commander on his right, explaining what he was doing and requesting support to close the gap thus opened.

As the Northerners continued their massive build-up, firing toward Lee's new front, General Stevenson gradually moved his entire division line in a counterclockwise direction. The Confederate line of battle thus formed somewhat in the shape of the number 7. Pemberton expected the main attack along the vertical, but it actually came from the horizontal above. In the bitter fighting, Lee had to maneuver various units from time to time in order to prevent his left from being hit. Stevenson asked for reinforcements from the Confederate right, which Pemberton did not send until after midday. On several occasions Lee rallied his various hard-pressed regiments, grabbing their battle flags and leading the men in person. Three horses were shot from under him, several balls tore through his clothing, and he was slightly wounded in the shoulder.[20] His arm later turned black from the elbow upward—he obviously suffered severe pain—but he did not have to be relieved of duty.

As the Federals moved farther and farther to the west, attempting to turn Stevenson's left flank, Pemberton finally shifted Bowen's division to the north. The Confederate battle line then stretched essentially west to east rather than, as it had previously, from north to south. The added weight of defending troops forced Grant to move more of his own men to the reinforced area.

Meanwhile Lee's beleaguered lines were being forced back in some spots. Certain areas of the battleground changed hands several times as the day wore on. Finally the Federals took Champion's Hill, and most of Stevenson's brigade had to retire and form a new battle line west of the crossroads.

Just about the time that Lee's brigade was breaking again, Bowen's division moved in from the south. One of the reinforcing troops recalled that, "After going in a run for I suppose a half mile, we turned to the fight and took position in a sweet potato patch just in the rear of General S. D. Lee's brigade who was being forced back. . . . General Lee, making a terrible appeal to his men to rally—for God's sake to rally and drive the enemy back." The man was impressed with Lee's commanding form: "I could see him and hear his voice above the din of battle." He also saw the disorganized condition of Lee's lines and doubted that any rally at all was possible, but the brigade did re-form, "as if by magic," he thought, a "magnificent scene."[21]

Two more Federal divisions joined the other attacking Unionists at about 3:30 P.M. By the weight of numbers, they routed Bowen's

division. Confederate division commander Loring moved his men
into a holding action while the rest of the defeated Southerners retreated. With an attack coming from his front, a menace of gradually extending attacks from the left, and finally a gap to his right
vacated by retreating Confederates, Lee had to withdraw his own
brigade.

Lee regrouped his men; and, having been cut off from Stevenson,
his division commander, he reported to General Loring, the nearest
senior officer. Loring's division and two other brigades, Lee's one of
them, held off the Federals while the main Confederate forces
crossed Baker's Creek. Lee then conducted his brigade across, but
Loring's division could not cross. The Union troops secured all the
crossings, and Loring had to march around his enemy, finally to
make contact and unite with General Johnston, thus being saved
from Pemberton's folly when the latter fell back into Vicksburg.

The battle of Champion's Hill was the bloodiest action of the
series of conflicts near Vicksburg. Lee's brigade had withstood much
of the heaviest firing. It was badly battered, many were killed, and
almost a whole regiment had been captured. Pemberton had lost
nearly four thousand men, while Grant sustained casualties of
twenty-five hundred.[22]

Lee's personal contributions were notable. His sound military
knowledge, his alertness, and his initiative had helped save the
Confederates from worse disaster. His actions on the field did much
to spur the men to greater effort. Without Lee, Pemberton's army
might have been shattered. As usual, Lee received warm compliments and congratulations from his superiors.[23] But the Confederates had succeeded only in staving off a defeat. Champion's Hill
constituted a significant victory for Grant. The South was a wide
step closer to losing Vicksburg.

The citizenry at Vicksburg soon heard of the great conflict at
Champion's Hill. One of Lee's dearest acquaintances, Emma Balfour, a married resident of Vicksburg, heard that he had been
killed, no doubt because he was cut off from the rest of Stevenson's
division. She wrote in her diary: "General Lee's brigade four times
met the shock of battle—going where we were most hotly pressed.
. . . General Lee repeatedly rallied his men—appealed to them by
all their love of home and country to rally, threatened to shoot the

first who ran, but all to no purpose. . . . Lieut. Underhill . . . wept as he related all this, said he never saw such daring, such generalship, but alas it was all of no avail. He said he was not ashamed of his tears, for God never made a purer, braver or nobler man! I too wept. . . ." Later on the same day, 17 May, she received more cheering news, and wrote, "General Lee is alive and unhurt. See how God shields the brave!"[24]

At the moment Mrs. Balfour wrote, Lee was busy helping the Confederates salvage men and material, moving back toward Vicksburg. Not knowing that Loring's division could not rejoin his force, Pemberton ordered that a stand be made near a bend in the Big Black River—about six miles west of Edward's Station. He hoped to keep the bridges open long enough for Loring to come up and cross. The Confederates occupied a line about a mile long, touching the curving river at both ends.

Before dawn, on 17 May, the Union army began pushing toward Vicksburg again and immediately came into contact with the defending Confederates. The Federals at once launched an attack and quickly discovered a vulnerable point. On the extreme Confederate left the earthworks had been washed away by a recent overflow of the river. The Northerners easily moved up to this point and threatened to roll up the flank. Afraid of getting cut off from any escape, the Southerners broke, heading in disorder for the bridges.

Lee's brigade received orders to cover the retreat across the river. He stationed men along the banks, and they provided protection for the demoralized, retreating army. Lee's troops remained in position, performing creditably, until relieved by Baldwin's brigade, the last of Pemberton's force to cross. Lee crossed the river with the bulk of his brigade, but one of his regimental commanders misunderstood the order and remained. The 23rd Alabama "gallantly engaged the enemy during the entire day," Lee reported, "leaving its position about midnight and joining the brigade at Vicksburg."[25]

In the retreat, Lee had a close call. He and his adjutant, Capt. William Elliott, considered emplacing troops at one of the bridges where a part of Pemberton's forces planned to cross. Lee received word that the Confederates still controlled the road leading to this bridge, and he rode with Elliott to reconnoiter. As they approached, they saw troops nearby. Supposing them to be Confederates, the two officers galloped ahead. Actually the troops were Northerners. In fact, a Federal company with six pieces of artillery in support had secured the bridge then deployed in a nearby woods. They saw Lee approaching and decided to ambush him. Two Federal soldiers donned gray shirts and rode out as decoys. Lee and his adjutant rode up to within six paces of the two enemy soldiers and within seventy-five yards of the larger body hiding in the woods. "Who are you?" Lee called out, and the Federals replied with the same question. "I am General Lee," he answered.

"All right General, come on." Apparently Lee suspected the trap and began to take action at the same time that the Federals drew pistols and demanded his surrender.

"No you don't," Lee cried, as the two Confederates put spurs to their horses, wheeled around, and thundered away. The Federals discharged their pistols, the infantry in the woods opened fire, and the artillery belched out several charges. But Lee and his companion kept riding. Miraculously they were unscathed.[26]

After the Confederates crossed the Big Black, they burned the bridges, halting Grant's pursuit. The Unionists began repairs, while parts of the Confederate army trickled into Vicksburg all day on 17 May. Stevenson's division, including Lee's brigade, got there in the afternoon. All able-bodied Confederates assumed defensive positions either in the trenches that surrounded the city or in the river battery emplacements. The lines ran along a ridge which essentially surrounded Vicksburg, varying from one mile to one and one-half miles in distance from the city, and touching the Mississippi both above and below the city. The high ground was dotted with a system of angular fortifications including one square fort, a redoubt. Rifle pits connected all these installations. Along the entire eight-mile line, Pemberton had something over 19,000 fighting men to face Grant. Stevenson's division manned the right third of the Confederate line. Lee's brigade occupied the left portion of this sector, extending from a cut made for the Vicksburg and Jackson railroad, a vulnerable spot, south to include the square fort. He had 1,268 effectives.[27]

Meanwhile Grant's troops threw a pontoon bridge across the Big Black, crossed on the morning of 18 May, and on the same day surrounded Vicksburg. The Federals numbered 71,000 men in all, but a large portion of them had to remain detached and watch for

Johnston's force. For an actual assault on Vicksburg, Grant could utilize a maximum of about 35,000 men. These Federals spread out in a concentric arc on the outside of the defending Confederate lines. Grant could either wait for Confederate supplies to run out or try to storm and break through the lines.

Since the bluecoats wished to avoid a long siege if possible, on 19 May Sherman's corps launched an assault from the north. The attack was bloodily but rather easily repulsed. The Federals lost a thousand men in this operation, which accomplished no more than to ascertain that the defense lines were very strong indeed. Confederate casualties were slight.

Grant's other two assaulting corps were not yet in good position for attack but did advance several hundred yards closer to the siege line. A small but determined charge hit the part of Lee's line through which the railroad cut passed. Mrs. Balfour could view the scene from her gallery. "It was terrific!" she wrote in her diary; "I was up in my room sewing and praying in my heart, oh so earnestly for our cause, when Nancy [her Negro servant] rushed up actually pale, exclaiming, 'Oh Mistress, the Yankees are pouring over the hill and our men are running.' " But Lee's men rallied and repelled the attackers. The Federals renewed their charge and were repulsed three times.[28]

"General Lee's praise is in every one's mouth," Mrs. Balfour noted. Lee was very much a hero with much of the Vicksburg citizenry. They remembered his victory at Chickasaw Bayou, and they heard reports of his laudable performance at Champion's Hill. Even though the big assault of 19 May did not come at his sector, the populace thought that surely if Sherman attacked, Lee must have been chiefly responsible for the repulse. In fact, some Federals actually thought that Lee was Pemberton's second-in-command. Even many of the soldiers thought of Lee as one of their special leaders. One spoke of him in a letter that when the later student of the war "looks at the page that tells of those who struck so nobly and so well in freedom's holy cause, his eye will rest upon the name of none that will shine with a brighter, purer, steadier luster than that of Brigadier General Stephen D. Lee, Vicksburg's noblest, best, and most skillful commander."[29]

During the night of 19 May, after the Federals made their first charge, the Confederates set fire to some houses in front of their lines, to remove obstruction from the fields of fire. The former residents of these dwellings, as well as many others who lived inside the city, moved into the numerous caves in the area. Lee advised his friend, Mrs. Balfour, to secure one too because "there will be no safety elsewhere." He called these shelters "ratholes"; and when he told this name to Mrs. Balfour, she replied that "it seemed to me that we were all caught in a rat hole."[30]

For the next two days, both armies worked to strengthen their lines. Lee wrote that "all the knolls in front of my line were at once seized by the enemy, and batteries erected thereon for their artillery, their sharpshooters in the meantime keeping up a continuous and annoying fire." The Federals maintained a heavy harassment both day and night, from all along the lines and from boats on the river. Lee estimated that between fifteen and thirty artillery pieces stood directly in his front. While Grant opened up supply lines, the Union fleet all but completely sealed off Vicksburg. Meanwhile the Confederates added to various fortifications along their line, built traverses to protect against enfilade fire, and made covered approaches from the camps in the rear.[31]

Still Grant wished to try another assault. He feared that a prolonged siege would cost perhaps as many men as an all-out attack, and he wished to secure Vicksburg quickly, then perhaps move with the mass of his forces against Johnston's army. So he issued orders for a general onslaught along the whole Confederate line. Noting the momentary success near the railroad cut on 19 May, the Federals prepared a heavy concentration to hit that portion of the line guarded by Lee's brigade.

The Confederates knew that Grant intended to try another assault. As Lee wrote, Federal "preparations did not partake of the slow methods of a siege program, but rather of the hasty preparation for immediate battle. The troops everywhere were being pushed up as near as possible to the Confederate lines, and were being massed under shelter in the deep vales in full view. . . . Nervous tension of all within Confederate limits, was kept to the highest pitch."[32]

Admiral Porter bombarded the city from gunboats all night on 21–22 May. Early on 22 May, the Northerners on the entire front cannonaded for over two hours. Lee recalled it as "continuous and unceasing; the artillery fire being accompanied by the ringing, steady cracking of the sharpshooters' rifles. We then knew that the assault was to occur."[33] The Confederates had prepared the defense well. Grape and canister artillery rounds had been arranged near the guns. Every trench had a supply of extra rifle ammunition. A Federal staff officer remembered how the lines had looked to Grant's men: "A long line of high, rugged, irregular bluffs, clearly cut against the sky, crowned with cannon which peered ominously from embrasures to the right and left as far as the eye could see. Lines of heavy rifle-pits, surmounted with head logs, ran along the bluffs, connecting fort with fort. . . . The approaches to this position were frightful. . . ."[34]

"About half past 10 o'clock A.M., as if by magic," Lee recalled, "every gun and rifle stopped firing along Gen. Grant's exterior line. . . . The silence was almost appalling." And, he said, "Suddenly there seemed to spring almost from the bowels of the earth, dense masses of Federal troops, in numerous columns of attack, and with loud cheers and huzzahs, they rushed forward, at a run. . . . Their advance over the rough ground which compelled them to open out was a grand and awful sight. . . ." Another account of the scene indicates that, "For a space of three and a half miles a swarm of blue appeared . . . the rough hills and valleys changing color with the regular movement of the advancing Federals. They continued with the determination of a machine gone wild."[35]

The Confederate troops withheld their fire at first. Then at a signal they all rose in the trenches and began blasting. Reserves fired while others reloaded. Volley after volley poured into the attacking waves. Artillery sent forth double-shotted charges of grape and canister. Very quickly the general assault crumbled. As Lee put it, "no troops in the world could stand such a fire."[36] Federal soldiers made only one lodgment in the Confederate line, at the railroad cut in Lee's sector. Lee had recognized the point's vulnerability and had established the main line of works some eighty to one hundred yards to the rear of a salient fort guarding the cut with forty soldiers. Four regiments stormed the little fort. The Federal engineers had built forty scaling ladders, fifteen to twenty feet in length, and the attackers carried them forward. Though suffering heavy losses, the Federals got several groups into the fort by sheer weight of numbers. Their corps commander, John A. McClernand, sent Grant word of the momentary success. So the Northerners continued the general assault and sent reinforcements to exploit the breakthrough.

This decision proved very costly for the Federals because there really was no breakthrough. Lee's lines behind the fort held firm. The twenty to thirty blue-clad soldiers in the fort managed to hold it only for a time. They annihilated one assaulting party which attempted to retake it, but Lee immediately requested another party, made up of volunteers, to storm the fort. Two companies from Waul's Legion, Lee's reserve, agreed to try. Lt. Col. Edmund W. Pettus, who had been in command of the fort before the Confederates evacuated it, asked for permission to lead the attack. Three privates from the 30th Alabama Regiment also joined Waul's group.

They charged with bayonets, fiercely and with stunning rapidity. Only three men in the assault party sustained wounds; none was killed. Fifty Northerners had crowded into the fort by this time, and all that survived the assault were captured—including a lieutenant colonel and a set of colors. Remembering that the first assault party had been wiped out completely, Lee praised Pettus' accomplishment, saying "a more daring feat has not been performed during the war."[37]

Meanwhile McClernand mistakenly believed that success was within his grasp and renewed the attack. Grant ordered his other corps commanders to commit their reserves and create diversions in McClernand's favor. The result was a considerable loss of over 3,000 Federal troops, with no breaches of the Confederate defenses. Southern losses were much less, though no exact number can be ascertained. Pemberton's army suffered 2,872 casualties—killed, wounded, or missing—during the period from 19 May through 13 June 1863.[38]

Grant's army settled down to hold the lines and inflict attrition, the unsuccessful assaults of 19 and 22 May having convinced him of its necessity. The Northerners conducted this operation very methodically and efficiently, and the Confederates did not receive outside help. The inevitable surrender came after forty-seven days of besiegement.

Supply was an important factor to both sides. Grant continued to receive replenishments of food and ammunition; Pemberton had to rely almost entirely upon what was already inside the city. The Confederates had captured a number of arms from the Federals in the two large assaults—Lee's brigade reported gathering a large amount of ammunition and some "beautiful Enfields" abandoned by the enemy in front of the lines. Southerners outside Vicksburg managed to smuggle in several million percussion caps by floating them on logs through the Federal fleet. Aside from such exceptions, the defenders had to make do with what they had. There was plenty of food, but Pemberton rationed it, keeping enough in reserve to feed his army if he tried a breakout later. The populace had to settle for many undesirable types of subsistence, for example, mule meat and an occasional rat.

Grant's army did try twice more to break the Confederate lines by force, once on 27 May with naval support and once in late June with underground mines. The defenders sank the attacking gunboat and destroyed the other approach by countermines and by creating a second line of defense works behind the craters that did open. Otherwise the Federals simply waited. At the same time the bluecoats kept up a constant harassing fire. "Everything, even the size of a man's hand, was shot at," Lee remembered, and "there was not a quiet hour day or night, when any one could sleep without being disturbed by piercing shot or shrieking shell or sharpshooting."

Pemberton ordered ammunition to be rationed while all but forbidding the artillery to fire except to repel assaults and restricting the infantry from firing except for one man every ten paces. "This was soon discovered by the Federals," Lee said, "and it made them bolder." He complained that ammunition was being rationed too much and later asserted that "the approaches could have been delayed by a free use of ammunition."[39]

Both sides suffered from exposure to the elements. It rained frequently, and the days were hot. Damp fogs and heavy dews added to the misery. Both armies lacked sufficient pure water for drinking, and many soldiers contracted diseases. Pemberton's troops did not have enough water for washing, and the bodies of many men became infested with vermin. But in spite of all their privations, the troops remained cheerful. The Confederates worked to make their trenches more comfortable and wider, with traverses to prevent the artillery from being enfiladed. They put up headlogs and sand bags for protection and tied blankets up overhead to get some shade from the oppressive sun. They often shouted greetings to their enemies, even occasionally exchanging joking remarks. The talking got easier as the siege proceeded, when the Union lines got close to the Confederate works—only thirty feet at several points from Lee's front by the end of the siege.

Lee did not share the fraternal spirit that many of his men had with the enemy, although he was compassionate. For example, the Federal soldiers killed or wounded in the 22 May assault lay where they fell until nearly dark on 25 May. Lee called it "one of the most striking incidents of the horrors of war." Finally he arranged a truce so that the sick could be cared for and the dead buried. A northern general engaged Lee in conversation and invited him over for a drink. Lee coldly declined. At one point the bluecoat asked how much longer the truce was to continue, and Lee snapped that it made no difference, since its purpose had been fulfilled in their front; as far as he was concerned, hostilities could commence at once. The Federal officer apologized for any offense and observed that Lee's lines seemed very strong. "Yes sir," Lee snarled, "I think I can hold them . . . ," and the conversation ended.[40]

Lee spent most of his time with his troops, infusing them with deep loyalty and devotion. He acted toward them in such a way as to win a high degree of cooperation and willingness. More than forty years later, a veteran corporal remembered Lee's treatment and professed a belief that Lee's characteristics compared favorably with those of the illustrious Robert E. Lee. And one veteran, who had been a young lieutenant and aide-de-camp to General Stevenson, recalled that during the siege Lee seemed "as gallant a soldier as ever wore a sword," and later told of Lee weeping over the death of a troublesome little talkative private—"a perfect chatterbox." He said, "I saw hot, burning tears trickling down his bronzed cheek."[41]

Although Lee shared many of the men's privations, he found comfort with Mrs. Balfour. She had him and his staff in to lunch on several occasions, and every day she sent buttermilk out to them. Some evenings he took tea at her house. Mrs. Balfour possessed admirable literary talent, and no doubt she charmed Lee with her conversation. She teased him, asking him not to allow Grant to shoot so near that her flower pots might break; but another entry in her diary reveals what a sensitive, cultured person she was—and also describes the scene during that early summer siege of 1863: "In the midst of all this carnage and commotion, it is touching to see how every work of God, save man, gives praise to Him. The birds are singing as merrily as if all were well, rearing their little ones, teaching them to fly and fulfilling their part of nature's program as quietly and happily as if the fearful work of man slaying his brother man was not in progress. . . . The flowers are in perfection, the air heavy with perfume . . . and the garden bright and gay with all the summer flowers. . . . Nature is all fair and lovely—all save the spirit of man seems divine."[42]

By early July Pemberton had both despaired of receiving any help from Johnston and decided that without aid the Confederates could do nothing effective against Grant. Hence Pemberton began to consider surrender. He called his general officers together in council on the night of 2 July and offered them two choices: either capitulate or make a desperate attempt to fight their way out.

The six-week siege had taken a hard toll of Confederate strength. Wounds, sickness, hunger, and exposure had debilitated more than 10,000 of the defenders. Nearly all the generals considered their commands too weak or enfeebled to withstand the hardship of an evacuation attempt. Lee urged a fight. He had written to Stevenson the day before that: "I consider my brigade in tolerable condition; and though they are weak from forty-five days' confinement, . . . I consider them equal to undergoing the fatigue which would be incident to our evacuation . . . taking in view its importance and the interest of the Confederacy." But even Lee admitted in his official report, written several weeks later, that his men "physically . . . were much weakened by their arduous duties and poor rations, and at the time of the surrender I did not consider more than one-half of my men able to undergo the fatigues of the field."[43]

So, in the Confederate officers' conference on 2 July, Lee's arguments seemed very unconvincing. The question in most of the generals' minds was simply to "surrender or not, and if so when?" Brig. Gen. Francis A. Shoup took it upon himself to draft a set of surrender proposals—asking for considerably better terms than Grant might conceivably offer. All of Pemberton's subordinate generals signed Shoup's proposal except Lee. Pemberton chided Shoup and the others, saying that he knew Grant never would agree to such requests. Furthermore, Pemberton urged that the decision be made soon, or else Grant was likely to assault them and inflict fearful casualties.[44]

From the junior officers upward, all voted affirmatively except

Brig. Gen. William E. Baldwin and Lee. Baldwin declared, "I object to a surrender of the troops, and am in favor of holding the position, or attempting to do so, as long as possible." Lee said, "I do not think it is time to surrender this garrison and post yet. Nor do I think it is practicable to cut our way out. When it is time to surrender, the terms proposed by Grant are as good as we can expect."

Actually Lee was being both realistic and practical. "I still have hopes of Johnston relieving the garrison," he insisted. And Lee was not alone in urging the greatest reason for holding out a little longer: to avoid surrender on 4 July, Independence Day. But Pemberton persuasively argued that the Confederates could get better terms then "than on any other day of the year."[45] That may have been so, but the propaganda value and effect on morale were tremendous: coming on that day the event elated Northerners and crushed Southerners. The impact of Vicksburg's fall would have been lessened by the passage of only another twenty-four hours.

Steadfast to the end, Lee submitted a note through channels protesting the surrender decision. Pemberton ignored it and sent word that he would like a meeting with Grant. Lee had done all that he could, and that ended it; he never bickered with his associates even when he disagreed with them. Lee never became disrespectful or contemptuous of Pemberton as did many other Southerners. "I have always felt great injustice was done General Pemberton," Lee wrote years later. "While he may not have been a militant and successful soldier, . . . the odds against him were too great."[46] So they were. On 4 July 1863, Vicksburg fell, and every Confederate soldier there, 29,500 men, became prisoners of war—including Lee.

The Confederates captured at Vicksburg received paroles and moved into camp at Demopolis, Alabama, under the charge of their own provost marshals. In this instance, the northern army did not wish to be bothered with administering and supplying a prison camp. The southern soldiers signed promises to refrain from fighting until exchanged and from serving the Confederacy in any military, police, or constabulary force, or as guards at prisons, depots, or stores. Lee signed the agreement on 5 July 1863, but he did not have to wait very long for an exchange.[47]

7

"... The Most Enterprising of All in Their Army"

EARLY IN THE war most prisoners received releases and exchanges, but later the North—with its larger population—tightened the procedure. Nevertheless both sides continued to engage in numerous trades to free specifically desired persons. Sometimes a large number of privates might be exchanged for a general officer. A Confederate agent declared Lee exchanged on 13 July, and three days later Secretary of War James A. Seddon wrote that Lee could return to duty.

On 17 July Pemberton recommended to President Davis that Lee be promoted to major general and assigned to command the cavalry in Mississippi. "In my opinion," Pemberton wrote, "nothing will so effectually check Grant as this appointment." On 3 August—seven weeks prior to his thirtieth birthday—Lee became a major general. His orders required him to report for duty to Gen. Joseph E. Johnston, department commander.[1]

Johnston and the Mississippi citizenry expressed pleasure over Lee's appointment. Johnston termed Lee a "gallant" and "spirited soldier," and Lee enjoyed considerable popularity. One newspaper article proclaimed that Lee had "inspired universal confidence in the people, and contributed greatly to drive away despondency. Always cheerful, always hopeful and confident, his presence . . . is hailed with joy."[2]

But Lee's assumption of command on 18 August brought something less than joy to Grant and Sherman. Neither of them had heard of Lee's exchange, and both revealed concern. Grant immediately ordered that a flag of truce be sent through the southern lines to learn more facts about the exchange. "I do not think Gen-

eral Lee would act in bad faith, but I would like to know . . . ,"
Grant wrote. Sherman made other inquiries and showed even
greater concern, saying: "He was one of the Vicksburg generals, and
the most enterprising of all in their army."[3]

A rather lengthy correspondence over the legitimacy of Lee's exchange ensued and opened the way for other serious problems also
to be discussed across the battle lines. Sherman contacted Confederate Brig. Gen. William H. "Red" Jackson about Lee. Jackson
promised to deliver Sherman's letter to Lee and also reported learning that some of Jackson's own scouts had fired upon some of Sherman's troops while the poor victims were bathing. "I gave orders
that this practice must be discontinued at once," Jackson declared,
"also all similar ones at variance with the usages of civilized warfare."[4] So the war still retained a touch of chivalry—and cleanliness.

The controversy over Lee's exchange soon ended too, but not before another series of heated letters. Union General in Chief,
Henry W. Halleck, wrote Grant on 9 September that "Neither General S. D. Lee nor any other officer or man paroled by you has been
exchanged." For one more week the Federals continued to consider
Lee a parole violator, but finally on 17 September the incident
closed. Sherman, notified by Richmond authorities, at last became
convinced that Lee had acted in good faith.[5]

The cavalry units under Lee initially were scattered widely,
poorly organized, and rather inefficient. The principal scene of the
war in the west had shifted to Tennessee. One can only guess the
Mississippi cavalry's strength in the late summer and fall of 1863,
but from Lee's letters and from organizational charts, it appears to
have been approximately 5,000. Lee observed that "this command
is generally not in good condition"; especially "the partisan and
State troops are not reliable, being in poor discipline and over one-
half the number on the rolls being at their homes." As newspaperman E. A. Pollard analyzed, "It was a disheartening command
where the utmost bravery could secure but little glory." Lee was a
vigorous administrator, who looked after training, morale, and
equipment, first and always a professional soldier. This trait, however, sometimes proved rather a liability than an asset when dealing
with irregulars or state troops. Often prima donna, always tem-
peramental, they required delicate handling and careful persuasion.
Even here Lee showed above average capability. As Frederick

Thiele, a recent student of Civil War cavalry, observed, Lee's efforts bore fruit, but too late to "save the state."[6]

If Lee could not save the state, he did at least keep it in the war. Johnston, with departmental headquarters at Meridian, Mississippi, was charged with general defense of a wide area, Mississippi, East Louisiana, and later Alabama. Clearly one of the South's best strategic field commanders, nevertheless he did not possess the degree of insight and independence appropriate for the role that President Davis had thrust him into. Lacking sufficient guidelines, he played by ear and defended equally the entire geographic area under his purview. Lee, also not equal to much thinking that far transcended his general instructions, and not the kind of soldier who would do other than his commander advised anyway, responded accordingly.

Lee initially chose Canton, Mississippi, as the cavalry base. The Southerners had something less than one-third the number of troops to oppose the Federals, operating principally out of Memphis, Tennessee, and Vicksburg, Mississippi, attempting to make further thrusts and slashing divisions into Confederate territory. Lee wrote to Mississippi Gov. John J. Pettus recommending promotions for the men he considered the better commanders. He also opened communications with the commanders of the district of Western Louisiana and the Department of Louisiana and Texas, to promote coordination of efforts and cooperation where possible. Lee then dispatched details to round up all deserters from his command, and he stiffened discipline and tightened policies—especially regarding furloughs. As usual, Lee's methods rapidly had an effect. On 17 September 1863, Sherman wrote to Halleck that, "this class of men must all be killed or employed by us before we can hope for peace. . . . I have two brigades of these fellows to my front, . . . Stephen D. Lee in command of the whole. . . . Am inclined to think when the resources of their country are exhausted we must employ them. They are the best cavalry in the world. . . ."[7]

Sherman took command of the Federal operations in Mississippi, while Grant journeyed into Tennessee to help William S. Rosecrans against Braxton Bragg's army, the principal Confederate force in the west. With many southern troops sent from Mississippi into Tennessee as reinforcements, Sherman meanwhile attempted to wear down resistance by ravaging towns, cutting Mississippi into pieces, and destroying the crops. Initially he tried small raids. Two groups left on 16 August, one from Yazoo City, another from Grand Junction, Mississippi. Some of Lee's cavalry units opposed these movements but failed to halt the Federals until they united at Grenada, Mississippi, and burned about one-fourth of the town and most of the railroad rolling stock located there. Then more of Lee's troops concentrated, and the Northerners withdrew toward Memphis. On 28 August another raid slashed out from Vernon, Mississippi, but Lee's men met this one and drove it back.[8] For all the rest of 1863 the Federals confined their operations to Tennessee and extreme Northern Mississippi.

Above all else, Lee wished to be an active, fighting general. He told his men that they should "seek and never to avoid an opportunity of striking a blow against the enemy. . . ." Lee himself devised a scheme to try a surprise attack, hitting one of the strong points on the Memphis and Charleston Railroad, then being used by the Federals. Johnston approved of the plan, and Lee began readying his men. They gathered supplies, at several points and in secret, with the hope of deception. Lee picked 2,500 cavalrymen and six pieces of artillery for the expedition.[9]

Lee's plans changed slightly as a result of a telegram that Bragg sent to Johnston on 29 September, asking for immediate assistance. Johnston agreed to send Lee's cavalry through North Alabama into Middle Tennessee, hoping to cut an important and vulnerable rail artery—a long single-track, with a series of wooden trestles, bridges, and a tunnel. Perhaps if all the cavalry under both Johnston and Bragg had operated in concert, this line could have been destroyed.

Not only did Johnston and Bragg elect not to unite their entire cavalry forces, but they and their subordinates also failed to cooperate with much effectiveness. Lee and Johnston expected that Bragg would order the cavalry from the Army of Tennessee under Maj. Gen. Joseph Wheeler, the famous "Fightin' Joe," and later even were led by Bragg to expect it. But nothing of the sort occurred, apparently because Bragg gave his subordinates too much discretionary authority and too little positive direction.

Lee arrived near Tuscumbia, Alabama on 9 October 1863, examined the fords in the Tennessee River, and found stragglers from Wheeler's cavalry. Wheeler had taken his corps on a long sweep into Middle Tennessee, penetrating almost to Nashville, but then recrossed the Tennessee River and suffered a severe defeat while fighting Federal cavalry on 7 October at the Battle of Farmington. His command nearly wrecked, Wheeler believed that from six to eight thousand Federal troopers were pursuing him and was thus disinterested in joining Lee for any more fighting.

Lee at once decided that he could not cross the Tennessee River alone and wrote to Bragg indicating willingness to cross either with Wheeler or with other reinforcements. The stakes were high here with Rosecrans' army bottled up—a devastating stab at its supply lines could have brought decisive results. But Lee had not only to worry about the forces believed to be following Wheeler but also about Sherman's whole corps, which then labored at rebuilding the Memphis and Charleston Railroad while moving eastward across Northern Alabama to join Rosecrans' army. Already Lee's hopes for a surprise attack seemed demolished. Yet he stayed in camp near Wheeler for more than a week, urging Wheeler to cooperate. They exchanged frequent correspondence: "I will cross the river at any moment with you," Lee promised, or even "with such a part of your force as will enable me to cope with the enemy. . . . I think it is a favorable moment to cross . . . , but we should act in concert." Wheeler continued firm in his stand. "I think I ought to wait until I can hear from General Bragg," he insisted. On the nineteenth, Bragg authorized Wheeler to take his command to Guntersville, Alabama, some ninety miles southeastward, ending any contact with Lee.[10]

Meanwhile the advance of Sherman's corps forced Lee into an engagement. On 20 October Lee moved westward and clashed with some of Sherman's units about fourteen miles from Tuscumbia. The Southerners drove the enemy's advance troops rearward to Cherokee Station and there encountered a large force of bluecoated infantry. On the next morning this infantry attempted to push on toward Tuscumbia, and Lee hit it with his full weight. A brisk fight lasted for one hour, but superior Federal numbers caused Lee to fall back several miles. During the next four and one-half days, Lee skillfully used artillery and selected numerous favorable defensive positions, further delaying the Northerner's inevitable, but slow, entrance into Tuscumbia.

At Tuscumbia, on the twenty-seventh, Lee fought one more severe skirmish and then withdrew to a new position eight miles eastward. Then suddenly, on the next day, Sherman began moving in the opposite direction. Lee's command followed closely. Again, at Cherokee Station, Sherman concentrated and repulsed a small Confederate assault. The opponents disengaged, and Sherman's command crossed the Tennessee River, abandoning its efforts at railroad rebuilding. Grant needed the men quickly for his concentration before Missionary Ridge.

Bragg desired that Lee remain as long as possible in North Alabama, but Lee felt that Sherman's disengagement left little further use for his cavalry there. Furthermore the Southerners' supplies began to run short. So Lee returned to Mississippi. Bragg wrote that Lee's delaying actions against Sherman, and the successful prevention of Sherman's completing his work on the railroad, had been "of great value to us." Lee had done, Bragg said, "noble service in North Alabama."[11]

Lee soon received his most important and valuable reinforcement: Brig. Gen. Nathan Bedford Forrest, a natural military genius and great cavalry leader, transferred to Johnston's department. Forrest had suffered abrasive relations with his previous superiors, notably Bragg; and on 29 October, President Davis acquiesced in the transfer. Johnston felt that Lee and Forrest should have separate areas of responsibility, but Davis emphatically stated that, although Forrest might operate in North Mississippi, enabling Lee to be drawn further south, Lee should remain senior officer over all cavalry in the department.[12]

On 16 November 1863, Forrest reached Okolona, Mississippi, Lee's headquarters, amidst speculations that the command arrangement could not work. Many observers felt that Forrest—older, unorthodox, and not a West Pointer, would be unable to function under a man like Lee. Their backgrounds could not have been more different. Lee's culture and more genteel upbringing contrasted starkly with Forrest's roughhewn façade. During Lee's financially lean youthful years, Forrest had grown wealthy as a slave trader. While Lee had studied French, Forrest was famous for butchering English, even inaccurately reputed to be illiterate. But Lee handled the situation beautifully.

He wrote to Forrest, "Whether you are under my command or not, we shall not disagree, and you shall have all the assistance and support I can render you." Lee acknowledged Forrest's ability, and remarked flatteringly that, "I would feel proud either in commanding or co-operating with so gallant an officer as yourself and one who has such an established reputation in the cavalry service to which I have been recently assigned." And Lee enclosed a general order to his staff officers to fill Forrest's requisitions as often as practicable.[13]

Lee and Forrest, although very different types who employed different methods, functioned well together, as a disagreement over discipline illustrates. Lee once encountered two members of Forrest's command whom Forrest had sentenced to be shot. One was thirty or thirty-five years of age, the other in his teens. "The boy must not be shot," Lee declared and insisted that he receive a pardon. Lee later said that he would have liked to pardon the older man too but was afraid that action might insult Forrest and completely demean the latter's disciplinary techniques.[14]

Aside from Forrest's outstanding ability to get the most out of his men, he made great contributions as a recruiter. He reported to Lee with a "brigade" of only 271 men. Lee raised Forrest's force to about 450 and approved of Forrest's proposal to go into Western Tennessee, perhaps for the entire winter, on a troop-raising expedition. In order to help Forrest get into Western Tennessee—long since under Federal control—Lee escorted him as far as Saulsbury then turned westward, appearing to threaten a raid on Memphis. Forrest passed unnoticed into Tennessee, while Lee destroyed a long stretch of the Memphis and Charleston Railroad and burned a wooden trestle bridge at Saulsbury. Then Lee made a quick march to Moscow, Tennessee, inflicted sharp losses upon the surprised Union garrison, and withdrew into Mississippi.

Although by the middle of December Forrest wrote that his venture "was succeeding beyond my most sanguine expectations," the Federals prepared a force of nearly 15,000 men to go after him. Warned by scouts in time, Forrest started south two days before Christmas. He had raised about 3,000 men, bringing Lee's cavalry in Mississippi close to 10,000 at year's end.[15]

Lee wrestled with numerous problems in late 1863 and early 1864. Lack of supplies constituted the most vexing one. "My command . . . are clad but scantily in summer clothing," he wrote on 4 November 1863, "poorly shod, and without blankets." One of his subordinates wrote, "for God and country's sake, . . . send me skillets, ovens, pots, or anything that will bake bread or fry meat. . . . I cannot fight any more until I get something to cook in."[16]

Somehow Lee managed. Besides supplies, he also needed better organization and efficiency. He continued reshuffling command arrangements and searching for the right man to do each job. He wrote to friends, like Louis T. Wigfall at Richmond, trying to expedite assignment of higher commissions for the men who impressed him. He evaluated others, sometimes deciding that they were too highly placed. One, Brig. Gen. George B. Cosby, whose principal accomplishment was his service as chief Confederate negotiator in the February 1862 surrender of Fort Donelson, did not measure up at all. Lee gave him every opportunity, then wrote Cosby that "It is my belief that there are but few officers or men in your command who have confidence in your judgment and ability on the field, and there is an aversion on their part to go into battle under you." Lee suggested that Cosby request a transfer, since "I have yet to find the first officer who is willing to remain with or serve under you." Several weeks later, Cosby departed.[17]

Sometimes Lee also had to contend with troops that were too zealous. Some of them tended to disregard the rights of the populace. Mississippi citizens considered the cavalry's presence of little use when the troopers destroyed property or created domestic disturbances. One complaint, concerning a few of Lee's men who forced people living near their camps to give them food and who occasionally stole possessions, reached the attention of the secretary of war. Lee conducted an investigation to identify the guilty parties, and the case dragged out over many months; but nothing positive could be established. Lee wrote defensively that "I regret to state that there are many irregularities in my command, as in all others." This did not, however, satisfy the secretary of war, who wrote that "the fact is notorious that the cavalry in Mississippi generally have been lawless and rapacious in their dealings with the property of citizens." The secretary ordered that careful attention be paid to preventing such depredations.[18]

Unquestionably some citizens brought troubles with the troops upon themselves. Many Southerners continually engaged in illegal trade with the enemy. Johnston informed Lee that the secretary of war directed soldiers to confiscate wagons and teams employed in such trade. Yet some civil authorities, especially in North Mississippi, issued writs to recover items seized by Lee's troops. Johnston authorized Lee to ignore the writs, but the problem remained a troublesome one because numerous persons believed that they did have permission to trade cotton for absolute essentials such as salt. Lee tried to be consistent, eliminating all trade, but he never knew when his decisions might be overruled. Even the Mississippi governor, Charles Clark, sometimes intervened in behalf of the citizens.[19]

Another problem for Lee arose because so many private individuals sought and received authorization to raise volunteer cavalry units. At first glance these outfits looked like assets, but in actuality many of the organizations never got past the planning stage; and everyone who had volunteered for such duty remained exempt from the draft. Furthermore, even when a new unit did complete muster, it took a very long time to become efficient, especially as cavalry. "I consider it much better," Lee insisted, "to equip tried troops as cavalry in place of forming new cavalry organizations." As it was, the new cavalry merely hindered the building up of other branches in the service, and it appropriated an unjustified share of the gradually more scarce cavalry horses.[20]

Good horses not only were scarce; they also were appallingly expensive. Lee had lost two horses earlier in 1863, both his own property, and worth a total of $780. Confederate law provided for reimbursement in such cases, so Lee filed a claim to purchase new mounts. It is a sad commentary on Confederate administration that the claim remained unpaid for over a year and required that Lee and numerous others engage in time-consuming red tape: evidence and affidavit gathering, correspondence, and even personal inquiries made by officers.[21]

Lee also had to give attention to numerous other details. He worked to secure a military court for each cavalry division, since punishment for offenses might be delayed for months. He finally got the courts, but not until April 1864. Meanwhile Lee became involved in pressing charges against derelict soldiers; in administrative decisions concerning prisoner exchanges; in providing supplies for the inmates of the Mississippi Lunatic Asylum; and, in addition to all this, even some minor combat operations. Johnston wrote approvingly of Lee's performance and added that "with another such officer in the West our cavalry would be far more efficient."[22]

In December 1863, shortly before Christmas, with Bragg discredited Johnston left Mississippi to assume command of the Army of Tennessee, and Lt. Gen. Leonidas Polk, the erstwhile Episcopal bishop, also a West Pointer, took over the department. Polk established his headquarters at Meridian, Mississippi and determined to divide the cavalry command between Lee and Forrest, each operating in his own specific region. Polk drew an east-west line through Prentiss, Mississippi, and gave Forrest responsibility north of the line, Lee responsibility to the south.[23] Forrest meanwhile was promoted to major general. This arrangement of divided cavalry did not last long, but before it changed again Lee's forces clashed with Sherman's.

In January 1864, Sherman organized at Memphis a force of nearly 26,000 men, mostly infantry with some artillery and cavalry support, to slash into Mississippi. In addition, Brig. Gen. William Sooy Smith took charge of 7,000 Union cavalry, planning to move southward from Tennessee and join Sherman at Meridian, Mississippi. "The rebels still maintained a considerable force of infantry and cavalry in the state of Mississippi," Sherman said, "threatening the river. . . ." He hoped to check this action, thereby freeing for use in the Atlanta campaign a large group of Federal troops then manning garrisons. Further, Sherman said, "a chief part of the enterprise was to destroy the rebel cavalry commanded by General Forrest, who were a constant threat to our railway communications in Middle Tennessee." Lee later snorted that "it is necessary for General Sherman to explain the object, for otherwise it might not be discovered by the military student." Lee viewed Sherman as inept. "He is very much overrated in my opinion," Lee allowed, and "if he ever displayed any generalship—I never saw it." Indeed Lee even viewed Sherman as something of a war criminal.

Sherman conducted this campaign utilizing his later famous destructive techniques, leaving burned buildings and desolation to his rear. Lee named this the "Sherman Torch" and never ceased, for the rest of his life, contending that Sherman had been wantonly vindictive. "Was this the civilized warfare of the nineteenth century?" Lee asked. Over three-fourths of what Sherman destroyed was private property, Lee asserted, and he genuinely believed that history would condemn Sherman.[24]

On 4 February Polk received word that Sherman's command had

moved from Memphis to Vicksburg and then turned toward Jackson. Polk began a series of troop movements, decisions and counterdecisions, designed to stave off the invasion and to establish priorities for defense within the Department—a vexing task. The complex Confederate departmental system, and the inadequate broad guidelines Davis provided, produced a system that expected too much of the area commanders. Polk did not know Sherman's intentions, so he wished Lee to "Detain the enemy as long as possible from getting into Jackson," and he rapidly shifted some of the Mobile garrison northward to help. Lee initially had only 2,500 men in Sherman's front; and in the first encounter, on the same day—the fourth—Sherman's 25,000 men, advancing along several roads, easily pushed Lee backward toward Jackson.[25]

At Jackson Lee received one thousand men as reinforcements, bringing his total strength to 3,500, but even this proved far too little to stop Sherman. On the morning of 6 February, the Federals occupied Jackson. Lee moved eastward, watching the Pearl River, still not knowing which way Sherman intended to head. Sherman crossed on 7 February, and Lee hit him again, scattering the blue-coated foraging parties. But Sherman then tightened up into a single heavy column; and, as Lee said, "it was impossible to damage the enemy much as he marched in perfect order. . . ."[26]

Polk still believed that Sherman meant to take the important city of Mobile, so Polk ordered Lee to cover the Mobile and Ohio Railroad south of Meridian in order that the Mobile garrison might be increased rapidly. Lee realized by 11 February, however, that Sherman obviously intended to take Meridian, and Lee moved to make one last attempt to prevent that. In the afternoon of 12 February, Lee's men dashed against the Federals at Decatur, Mississippi. The Confederates disabled twenty Union wagons, by killing all the mules, but could not take the wagons away. Five minutes after the charge, the Federals advanced in line, and Lee had to withdraw. At daylight on 13 February, the Union advance continued. Meridian fell the next day.

Polk moved into Alabama and established a new headquarters at Demopolis. Meanwhile, on 11 February, he heard from Forrest about William Sooy Smith's advance from the north with 10,000 men and 31 artillery pieces. Polk invested Lee with command of "all the cavalry west of Alabama" in Polk's department, a total of

12,500, and ordered Lee and Forrest to make a concerted resistance. On the morning of 18 February, Lee started toward Starkville and arrived at dawn four days later, "having moved as rapidly," Lee said, "as the jaded condition of the horses would permit." Smith had commenced to retreat twenty-four hours previously and went safely back into Tennessee. Not really as incompetent an officer as he seemed here, Smith, actually only slightly outnumbered, had been duped into thinking that Forrest had many thousands more troops than was the case and that Lee's juncture would mean certain annihilation.

Bitterly disappointed, Lee had hoped to win a decisive engagement with Smith, even was momentarily irritated with Forrest, though it quickly passed. Rapid new developments left little time for further reflection. Sherman spent a week in Meridian, burning much of the town and tearing up the railroads ten or twelve miles in every direction; but without Smith's cavalry, Sherman elected to return to Vicksburg. Lee rushed a part of his command to harass the Federals, at Sharon, where the Confederates captured twenty wagons and killed or captured two hundred bluecoats, but that was all that could be done. Sherman recrossed the Big Black River on 4 March, ending the Meridian expedition.

The campaign was a mixed victory for both sides. Sherman achieved much of his objective, but by no means all. He had swooped through Mississippi and destroyed key towns, although many acres of crops still grew unmolested. Lee and Forrest accomplished quite a bit in that they finally warded off forces with superior numbers—though Sherman had done a tremendous amount of damage. Polk issued congratulations to his cavalry, their having ridden between six and eight hundred miles in five weeks and having done much. The achievement, Polk declared, "marks an era in this war, full of honor to our arms." To his thanks he added the "thanks of his countrymen to Generals Lee and Forrest and the gallant spirits who follow them."[27]

The next two months, March and April 1864, were months of relative inactivity in Mississippi. Lee and Forrest traveled to Demopolis, Alabama, mostly by railroad handcar, to confer with General Polk. There they decided that Forrest should go into Tennessee for more recruits and horses. His famous capture of Fort Pillow,

Tennessee, and the controversial alleged massacre of the largely black garrison, took place on 12 April. Lee, not directly involved, later played an important role in attempting to vindicate Forrest and ascertain the truth of the episode.

Lee meanwhile remained in Mississippi, reorganizing and attending to the procuring of replacement horses, recruiting more men, rounding up deserters, questioning suspected spies, stopping robbery and pillage, enforcing the tax-in-kind laws, and continuing his efforts to curb illegal trade with the enemy. Within weeks he greatly improved his situation. New men and new horses were rare by 1864, but the indomitable Lee tirelessly and ingeniously searched them out. Using persuasion, and sometimes a forceful personality, he ferreted out resources and commenced effective utilization. As an organizer, a master of logistics and training, and a disciplinarian, he showed no fault. More than a courageous man of operational competence, he could instill high standards in camp.[28]

Considerably heavier responsibilities soon fell upon Lee. He asked Polk to relieve him from command over Forrest's cavalry, believing Forrest competent to act alone and that his own geographical area of jurisdiction had grown too large. No evidence indicates that any friction between Lee and Forrest prompted this decision. Lee insisted that he preferred an active command in the field for himself and that he was attempting to prevent becoming an administrative desk soldier. The War Department, however, disagreed with Lee's objections and even named him to command all of the cavalry in Polk's department, recognizing his significant administrative ability as the source of higher morale.

On 13 April Lee assumed the new command, moving his headquarters to Columbus, Mississippi. In that town he met the young girl whom he would marry less than ten months later, but he had little time for courting now. On 4 May 1864, Polk received orders to take the department's infantry forces to join Johnston in North Alabama. Davis directed that Lee be put in charge of the department, Polk sending needful instructions from time to time.[29] As things turned out, Polk never returned, and Lee became full-fledged department commander, another step upward.

8

"Soldiers Must Do as They Are Ordered"

ON 5 MAY 1864, Lee began acting in temporary command of Polk's department, and on 9 May took over in his own right. Polk remained with Lee at Demopolis, Alabama, between those dates. Lee expressed apprehension over the planned arrangement, saying that he preferred a field assignment and that he expected difficulties if left in charge of the department because Maj. Gen. Dabney Maury, in command at Mobile, outranked him. Polk preferred to keep Lee near him anyway and telegraphed President Davis suggesting that Maury be given the department and that Lee accompany Polk to Georgia. "To be deprived of General Lee's services in the campaign before us," Polk reasoned, "would be a serious loss to the service," but Davis replied that Maury's command, the Department of the Gulf, remained separate and Lee's presence in Central Mississippi seemed necessary.[1]

These developments show clearly both how much Polk had been impressed with Lee's capability as a combat commander and how important Davis considered the departmental system. This administrative structure, functioning either as Davis insisted or otherwise as he forced by default, provided for a general defense of the Confederacy's total area. It provided for strategic response at any threatened spot, it served as something of a morale sustainer for the populace, and it provided some beneficial propagandistic effect by adding to the appearance of stability and cohesiveness. Nevertheless it drained a lot of able officers from field commands, and its allocation of resources woefully lacked coordination. Davis entrusted some very good officers, like Lee, with departments but then failed to provide them with adequate guidelines and supervision, simply hoping for too much from them.

Lee realized that parts of his department needed special protection: the grain producing prairies of Northeastern Mississippi—the "breadbasket" of the Confederacy; and the industrial region in South-Central Alabama, especially the machinery and shops at Selma and Montgomery, Alabama, and the railroads—vital arteries of transportation and supply. He also had to pay attention to Mobile, as Davis expected him to help Maury if that place were threatened seriously. In addition, Davis also expected Lee, as he did all department commanders, to aid other departments when practicable.

Here lay the fatal flaw in the departmental system. With inadequate coordination no individual commander, not even the great Robert E. Lee, was able to make enlightened and maximally beneficial decisions concerning the relative needs of his and other departments. Davis passed the buck to them, except in rare instances as after Fort Donelson and before Chickamauga; and instead of issuing orders, he mildly suggested that troops should be sent on long-range missions if they could be spared from their immediate duties.

In the late spring and summer of 1864, the Confederate Army of Tennessee needed Lee's aid in disrupting the lines of communications of the Union army under Sherman. Davis hoped for Lee's help but did not ask very urgently, especially since troops had been taken from Lee's department with Polk's departure. And Lee had important logistical and political considerations, to say nothing of actual military threats. The Federals were effectively applying Grant's strategy of pinning down all Confederate reserves to prevent further concentration. To achieve such a concentration, the South would have to give up something. Davis failed to face this necessity. Under such conditions, each departmental commander naturally almost always looked first to the needs of his particular area of responsibility. Lee, perhaps more than most, distinguished himself by coming as close as he did to sending aid to another department.

While Lee personally preferred active campaigning to administrative command, he quickly and accurately sized up his job—then did it. He had the mind of an extraordinarily competent and selfless soldier, displayed clearly in the letter he wrote to Dabney Maury shortly after taking up his new duties: "I asked to be relieved from the command and that you be assigned, which was declined. . . . I thought of you and your rights. . . . I would much prefer having a command in active service, but soldiers must do as they are ordered."[2] How true, and yet how rare it was to find such a man as Lee among the Confederate generals. Always willing to engage in unglamorous activities, he never failed to exceed the standards set by the lesser men with whom his government and its military abounded.

His task required a most careful and skillful manipulation of available resources. On paper he supposedly had 35,676 men; but with huge numbers absent and others debilitated, he actually had only 15,758 effectives. The cavalry constituted a particular problem because many of the men had either no horses or inadequate supplies. Lee ordered that the dismounted men be organized into garrison units for temporary duty at Selma, where at least they could serve as a safety factor.

Joseph E. Johnston applied great pressure on Lee, urging that troops be sent to aid his army; and at first Lee seemed very receptive to the idea. In late April Lee made several requests for the necessary authorization from Polk and from Gen. Samuel Cooper at Richmond. On 16 May Lee ordered Forrest to concentrate 3,500 men at Corinth in preparation for moving into Middle Tennessee. But although on 17 May Cooper gave permission for the movement, that same day Lee also learned from scouts of a new Federal expedition from Memphis. Immediately cancelling Forrest's planned departure, Lee prepared to protect his department.

When the expected northern offensive did not commence immediately, Lee again considered aiding Johnston. Forrest personally wanted to go into Middle Tennessee, though he disagreed with Lee over the number of troops required for an effective campaign. Finally on 31 May Lee dispatched Forrest, but on 3 June had to call him back. Federal Brig. Gen. Samuel D. Sturgis had moved from Memphis with 3,300 cavalry, 5,000 infantry, and 22 guns to "smash things" in North Mississippi.[3] The Federal strategy was working.

On the night of 9 June 1864, Lee and Forrest met in council at Booneville, Mississippi, where allegedly they "planned the battle of Brice's Cross Roads."[4] Actually they did not lay a tactical *plan* for the battle, especially not for the smashing victory that ensued. They discussed the situation and deemed their available forces probably insufficient to stop Sturgis, so they decided that Lee would attempt gathering reinforcements while Forrest faced Sturgis to harass and delay him. On the next day Forrest met and decisively defeated Sturgis. Outnumbered two to one, Forrest's men inflicted more than 600 casualties and captured more than 1,600 Federal troops and 16 of the artillery pieces as well as the entire supply train. The bluecoats certainly had not intended for their pindown strategy to be so costly! Astounding vigor and good luck made the victory Forrest's alone.[5]

The Brice's Cross Roads victory reflected great credit upon Lee, as well as Forrest, being a major achievement within the department. Lee's promotion to lieutenant general came thirteen days later, although the battle was merely the catalyst since the President had for some time been considering promoting Lee. But until 14 June the possibility existed that, as originally planned, Polk might return to command the department. On that date Polk received a mortal wound. So Davis named Lee to the lieutenant generalcy, exactly three months before Lee's thirty-first birthday, thus making Lee the youngest man on either side to have that rank.[6] It was a special testament to Lee's capability, to be chosen over Dabney Maury, an older, experienced, and successful general.

The southern populace and press certainly approved of Lee's promotion. Many newspapers contained favorable comments about him. The Memphis *Daily Clarion* published a laudatory biographical sketch: "He has won distinction on every field, and when the faithful chronicler of the times closes his book, the part played by Stephen D. Lee will be found among the brightest annals of our struggle."[7] Another reporter wrote a remarkably insightful analysis: "The rare military merits of Gen. Lee have always been better known to the army than to the people at large, but unlike some of our leaders, confidence in his capacity, and reliance upon his judgment are not confined altogether to the authorities at Richmond.

"Whenever Gen. Lee has been in command he has impressed the soldiery under him and the people about him, with a belief that he was fully equal to any emergency. . . .

"Perhaps Gen. Lee may not heretofore have flashed quite as

resplendent a sword as some others . . . but his has ever been as brave and true as any other. . . . He has generally had to contend against heavy forces with inadequate numbers to oppose them . . . yet, in spite of all obstacles, his services have been conspicuous to all. Lee has, we believe few, if any enemies. He has never had any bickerings or feuds with the officers with whom he has to deal. . . .

"He is quick and brave—he has never yet failed to exalt himself to the exigencies of the occasion. . . ."[8]

The Battle of Brice's Cross Roads precipitated a fresh controversy over the Confederacy's attitude toward black troops and a renewed attention to the Fort Pillow "massacre" of 12 April. Shortly after the action at Fort Pillow, Forrest wrote to Lee that "so much has been said by the Northern press in regard to the engagement," he was sending a civilian judge to obtain statements from the Federal survivors. This and subsequent investigations revealed that all the Negro troops stationed in Memphis had taken an oath to avenge Fort Pillow and that they would show Forrest's troops no quarter. Thus at Brice's Cross Roads, where the Federals had two colored regiments, the blacks fought furiously; and, even when beaten, many refused to surrender because they expected to be slaughtered after capture.

On 17 June 1864, Maj. Gen. Cadwallader C. Washburn, the Union officer commanding the District of West Tennessee, wrote to Lee about Brice's Cross Roads. "I felt considerable solicitude for the fate of the two colored regiments . . . ," Washburn stated, "until I was informed that the Confederate forces were commanded by you. When I learned that, I became satisfied that no atrocities would be committed." But subsequent information caused Washburn to change his mind, and it then seemed to him "that the massacre of Fort Pillow had been reproduced at the late affair at Brice's Cross-Roads." He closed with a request that Lee give him a specific statement of the treatment that black troops could expect. "If it is contemplated by the Confederate Government to murder all colored troops that may by the chance of war fall into their hands, as was the case at Fort Pillow," he wrote, "it is but fair that it should be freely and frankly avowed."

Lee's temper flared, and both he and Forrest penned letters to Washburn on the matter. Forrest wrote that "I regard captured

After graduating from the United States Military Academy at West Point, Lee was commissioned a second lieutenant and served in the United States Army from 1854–1861. (Library of Congress)

Statue of Stephen D. Lee in the Vicksburg National Military Park. Lee was active in the organization of the park and served as its chairman. (Library of Congress)

Commissioned captain in the South Carolina Army in 1861, Lee later became a captain in the Confederate States Army and rose through every rank to lieutenant general at the age of thirty. (Library of Congress)

Stephen D. Lee and his wife Regina Lilly Harrison. The photographs were taken in 1865 at the time of their wedding. (Family possessions of John Glessner Lee)

Portrait of Stephen D. Lee in the Battle Abbey in Richmond, Virginia. (Virginia Historical Society)

In this collage painting "Lee and His Generals" by George B. Matthews, Stephen D. Lee is shown ninth from the left. (National Archives)

During the last thirty years of his life Lee became an active and productive historian, politician, educator, and champion of women's rights. The above photograph shows Lee as he appeared in the 1880s and the photograph on the opposite page shows Lee in the 1890s. (Southern Historical Collection, University of North Carolina; S. D. Lee Museum, Columbus, MS)

The Stephen D. Lee home in Columbus, Mississippi. Now a museum, the house was built in 1847 by Thomas C. Blewett, grandfather of Lee's wife, Regina Harrison. (Mississippi Department of Archives and History)

Stephen D. Lee, who died in 1908, outlived most of his Civil War contemporaries. After the Civil War he worked to build a New South as fervently as he had fought for the Old South. He is shown above as he appeared in the 1900s. (Stephen D. Lee Chapter, United Daughters of the Confederacy, Columbus, MS)

negroes as I do other captured property and not as captured soldiers, but . . . it is not the policy nor the interest of the South to
destroy the negro—on the contrary, to preserve and protect him.
. . ." Lee approved of these remarks and added that "the case
under consideration is almost an extreme one. You had a servile
race, armed against their masters and in a country which had been
desolated by almost unprecedented outrages." He reiterated the
southern position on Fort Pillow: that the garrison never surrendered, the colors never struck, the fort's commander issued all the
liquor rations he had before the fight, and the Negro troops displayed especial fanaticism; and in spite of all this over two hundred
prisoners—both some black and some white—finally were taken
and still remained in southern hands.

Then Lee concluded with a specific denial that a massacre took
place at Brice's Cross Roads. "As regards the battle," he said, "I do
not think many of them were killed. They are yet wandering over
the country, attempting to return to their masters." (What Lee
meant by the last phrase is not completely clear.) "With reference
to the status of those [blacks] captured," he continued, "I will state
that, unless otherwise ordered by my Government, they will not
be regarded as prisoners of war, but will be retained and humanely
treated. . . ." And he closed with perhaps his most eloquent wartime statement: "It is my intention, and that also of my subordinate officers, to conduct this war upon civilized principles, provided
you permit us to do so. . . . We are engaged in a struggle for the
protection of our homes and firesides, for the maintenance of our
national existence and liberty. We have counted the cost and are
prepared to go to any extremes, and although it is far from our
wish to fight under the black flag, still if you drive us to it we will
accept the issue."

Of course neither side had any intention of adopting an official
policy of no quarter; and Washburn's answer, followed by Lee's
forwarding copies of all the correspondence between himself, Forrest, and Washburn upward through Confederate command channels, ended Lee's involvement in this largely propagandistic controversy. The letters eventually reached Jefferson Davis, and he
approved of the way the matter had been handled.[9] Lee meanwhile
had turned to other less monumental but very demanding and
troublesome problems.

As department commander Lee had to see that sick and wounded soldiers received care and treatment. Sometimes, as was the case after Brice's Cross Roads, he asked civilian communities for help. He telegraphed the people of Columbus, Mississippi, for example, asking for "eatables and delicacies" to feed four hundred men. Lee also took pains to avoid moving the severely wounded men, sending medical and bodily sustenance to them instead. He gave considerable attention to seeing that surgeons were assigned to as many different units as possible.[10]

Numerous other matters also required Lee's attention. He finally gave personal sanction to some cotton trading with the enemy in order to secure vital supplies, an action that raised more problems. For example, the Unionists desired guarantees of safety for boats when sent for such cotton, guarantees which a lower-echelon Confederate commander refused to give without specific authorization from Lee. Furthermore, many of the southern soldiers who were required to help with the transactions had themselves been deprived of their cotton by the Confederate government, and it was not easy to make them understand the necessity for this trade.[11]

Lee also had transportation difficulties and could not move many of the supplies collected. Some bacon remained in warehouses for months awaiting distribution. The president of the Mississippi Central Railroad wrote Lee that it was "almost impossible to keep this road in safe running order for want of shovels, axes, and some framing tools" and that recent heavy rains had covered "the track with sand in some places to the depth of two feet."[12]

Furthermore, many of Lee's men had as much as six months' pay due them. He wrote Gen. Samuel Cooper at Richmond that "the want of money, both by the officers and men, is great, and interferes with the proper performance of duty." Lee's request for a remedy reached James A. Seddon, the secretary of war, but Seddon wrote, "I have sent up so many similar applications and indorsements that it is useless to press them further on the Secretary of the Treasury."[13] There simply was nothing that Lee or anyone else could do; his men had to go still longer without pay.

Yet, defense of his departmental area remained by far the greatest problem Lee faced. Numerous reports indicated that the Federals planned further raids and even full-scale attacks. Sherman, now in command of the Union army fighting toward Atlanta, determined to keep Forrest busy and occupy Lee's attention so as to prevent the Confederates from shifting any more troops into Georgia or hitting Sherman's supply lines. In late June 1864, Maj. Gen. Andrew Jackson Smith moved out of Memphis with 14,000 blue-clad men of all arms—infantry, cavalry, and artillery—and on 5 July turned southward from La Grange, Tennessee. To oppose this thrust Lee could assemble only 7,500 men, almost all from Forrest's command. The cordon dispersion strategy required Lee to keep his remaining forces at other important points. Furthermore, indications were that the Federals soon intended to attack Mobile, and Lee felt constrained to deal rapidly with Smith then reinforce Maury, who continually called for help.

Lee made several attempts to increase his force before meeting Smith. First he asked President Davis to see that the Mississippi state reserve forces be called into active service. Davis responded both with a note to the adjutant general to "let it be promptly done" and with a letter to Mississippi Gov. Charles Clark urging cooperation. Then Lee tried to get help from forces in Louisiana. None of these efforts was successful. By the time troops were specifically ordered from Louisiana to Lee's department, Lee already had fought the Federals, and the militia proved to be of limited value because many of them balked at being utilized for anything other than local defense (e.g. within their own counties).

Lee's situation continued to grow more complex. Forrest wrote reporting his force insufficient to meet Smith's command and furthermore that Forrest was suffering with boils. "If the enemy should move out," Forrest declared, "I desire you to take command of the forces." Meanwhile, another small enemy expedition moved into Mississippi from the west and advanced toward Jackson. Lee dispatched troops to block this threat. Then the Confederate authorities at Richmond decided that Lee should assume direct responsibility for Mobile, Lee now outranking its commander, Maj. Gen. Dabney Maury, and there being an official attempt at departmental consolidation.[14]

Meanwhile, from the north, Smith moved into Mississippi in close formation, as Lee said, "exceedingly cautious and careful." Except for a small skirmish above Ripley on 7 July, the Federals proceeded unopposed through New Albany to a position just north of Pontotoc, arriving on 10 July. There Smith stretched his forces

out into a line of battle one mile long, cavalry carefully guarding
the flanks and rear against surprise. On 11 July the Federals pushed
back the slight Confederate resistance and occupied Pontotoc and
a nine-mile stretch of road southward toward Okolona. Lee hoped
to rush up with reinforcements and fight Smith there, but on 12
July Smith only sent out reconnaissance parties on various roads,
all of which the Confederates checked and drove in.

Abruptly on 13 July, much to Lee's surprise, Smith abandoned
efforts to move farther southward and marched toward Tupelo,
eighteen miles due east of Pontotoc. Lee could get no force in front
of Smith, so Forrest hit the rear while Lee, directing two brigades,
marched hard with troops moving along parallel roads and attacked
the flank. But none of these efforts achieved any success, and Smith
moved on to Harrisburg, a ghost town which had been deserted
when the railroad was built through Tupelo a few miles eastward.
Smith had his men bivouac in a semicircular line of battle, and
during the night they strengthened their defenses with fence rails,
logs, timbers from houses in the village torn down for the purpose,
cotton bales at one point, and anything else that they could find.[15]

Lee and Forrest decided to attack the Federal line on the next
morning. Whether Forrest actually agreed or, as his biographer says,
"merely acquiesced in what he could not help," is a matter of considerable controversy. Lee wrote in 1901 that he and Forrest "were
in perfect accord as to delivering battle," but in the same account
Lee also admitted that Forrest had "considered the Confederate
troops inadequate to defeat Smith."[16] Whatever the case, the decision was sound strategically. Lee still gave first consideration to his
duty as department head: he needed to halt Smith's destructive
march. Lee had the ablity to make hard decisions. Instead of wilting
as had Pemberton earlier, he chose to give battle against heavy odds.
For his biggest moment as an independent commander, Lee formulated a rather complex plan. Three Confederate brigades, Hinchie P.
Mabry's, Tyree H. Bell's and Crossland's Kentuckians, would assault the Union right and center, while Phillip D. Roddey's division
swung around to hit the enemy's left. Chalmers' division would remain in reserve and form a second line for the entire front. Capt.
John W. Morton, Forrest's chief of artillery, suggested that all
twenty of the Confederate artillery pieces be concentrated on the
left center, but Lee—so unlike himself—ordered the guns doled

out, one battery to support the Kentucky brigade, another with Bell's brigade, and a third to accompany Roddey.[17]

Success required an exceptional degree of coordination, at which Lee failed. First, almost all the southern troops were cavalrymen, unfamiliar with complicated infantry maneuvers. The open terrain required a wide, general advance, but for that the curved enemy line necessitated that every Confederate unit move at a slightly different speed. The venture called for extremely careful planning and very tight discipline. Yet, according to Lee's 1901 account, at the last minute before commencing, Lee offered Forrest a choice of wing to command, a decision that should have been made and understood by all many hours before.

The original plan called for a signal gun to be fired, Lee recalled, "on the Pontotoc road between Bell and Crossland as the order for a general and simultaneous advance." But just before the troops began to move, Lee and Forrest still remained together on the Confederate left. The two generals compared their watches and agreed upon a time for the attack to start. Forrest then rode away at full speed to Roddey's right, nearly a mile away. At the proper time, Lee ordered the left wing forward—"at the signal agreed on," he wrote. Years later most of Forrest's subordinate officers contended that the signal gun did not fire, but at least some of the troops thought it had. Actually the evidence implies that Lee and Forrest abandoned the signal gun idea when they synchronized their watches and picked a specific time for the attack.[18]

In the heat and dust of that blistering morning, 14 July 1864, some men moved sluggishly while others charged with unrestrained ardor—and all semblance of coordination crumbled. Crossland's Kentucky Brigade rushed unsupported into the concerted Federal fire not only from the front but also from both flanks. Lee then got his other brigades moving forward, one after another in piecemeal fashion. Then he tried to get some of Chalmers' reserve troops into the action, but Chalmers received conflicting orders from Forrest to move toward the right and elected to obey Forrest, his immediate superior.

Forrest meanwhile failed to engage his wing at all. He stated in his report that he rode to the far right of the Confederate line, conferred with Roddey, and "after giving him the necessary orders in person I dashed across the field at a gallop for the purpose of select-

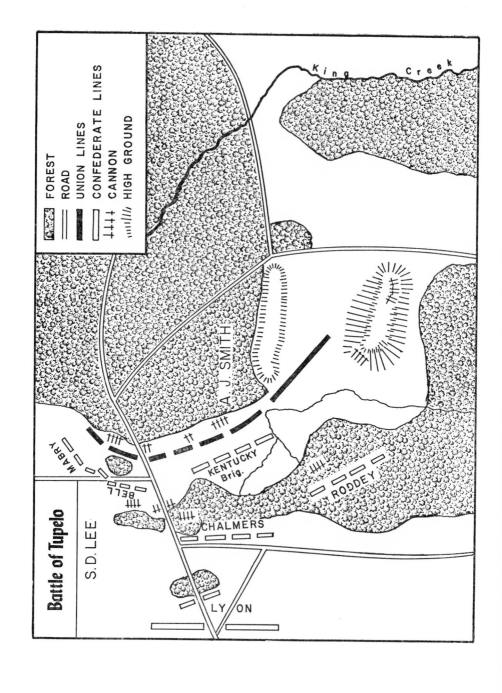

Battle of Tupelo

FOREST
ROAD
UNION LINES
CONFEDERATE LINES
CANNON
HIGH GROUND

King Creek

A. J. SMITH

MABRY

S. D. LEE

BELL

KENTUCKY Brig.

RODDEY

CHALMERS

LYON

ing a position in which to place his troops, but on reaching the front I found the Kentucky brigade had been rashly precipitated forward. . . . I seized their colors, and after a short appeal ordered them to form a new line. . . ." So, "wishing to save my troops from the unprofitable slaughter I knew would follow," he chose not to push Roddey forward.[19] Thus, although perhaps through misunderstanding rather than insubordination, Forrest disobeyed Lee. The Kentuckians were in Lee's sector of the battle. At the very time that Forrest was meddling with their premature charge, Lee expected him to be leading Roddey's flanking movement.

The battle itself brought mixed results. Lee's men charged back and forth for nearly three hours and finally retired into defensive lines, but—except for pushing one brigade slightly forward—the Federals made no countermovements. During the night the Northerners burned what remained of Harrisburg, unwittingly providing the Confederate artillerymen with good targets. The Southerners also tried a small night attack, precipitating what General Chalmers called "the heaviest fire of small-arms which was heard during the engagement," but the attack accomplished little.[20]

In the end, Lee achieved his strategic victory by default; Smith chose not to press on, and instead the Federals retreated all the way back to Memphis. Lee reported the battle as "a drawn fight," though Smith wasted no time in establishing his title as the man who had "whipped Forrest." Some Confederate officials, most importantly Braxton Bragg, hailed Lee's accomplishment as a "very important victory," but southern public opinion by and large was reserved: Lee and Forrest had won no victory, though Smith had retreated badly whipped. Considering only casualties, the Southerners suffered quite a defeat. Lee lost 210 killed and 1,116 wounded—more than forty percent of the approximately 3,000 actually engaged—a tremendous loss. In comparison, the Federals with nearly twice the numbers engaged, lost only 77 killed and somewhat over 55 wounded.[21]

The battle satisfied neither side, but the Confederates really had more reason to be pleased. As one student correctly observed, if George G. Meade on the day after the Battle of Gettysburg had withdrawn his forces in the direction of Baltimore or Philadelphia, leaving Robert E. Lee in possession of the field, history would have recorded the South as victorious there—in like manner then, the fight near Tupelo was a Confederate victory.[22]

Certainly Lee had been let down; things had not gone as he directed. What if they had? Partisans of Forrest tend to claim that southern losses would have been needlessly higher. But one of the Unionist soldiers later wrote perceptively that "had Forrest carried out his part of the plan of battle, we would have had more to contend against, with probably more loss, while it is doubtful if the Confederates would have suffered any more."[23] It is possible that with more cooperation and coordination Lee might have achieved a greater success; but against the odds he faced, and with the mission as he perceived it, he did quite well.

Lee submitted no detailed report of the battle because he realized Forrest's value and desired to give him the benefit of the doubt. This was the only engagement on which Lee wrote no official report. Thirty-seven years later Lee indicated that he had not written the report because of the call that transferred him to the Army of Tennessee less than two weeks after the battle. But in 1878 he wrote a friend that he knew a report would have resulted in an investigation. The blame probably would have been laid on Forrest, and this, Lee said, "could have paralyzed him and his command."[24] Lee chose the wise and magnanimous action that helped the Confederacy the most; not the one that vindicated himself or brought punishment on Forrest merely for the sake of the record.

Lee had little time to reflect on Tupelo; circumstances at last propelled him into the kind of assignment he most desired—action with troops in the field—this time as corps commander. Since early May 1864, a Federal army (now under Maj. Gen. William T. Sherman) had been campaigning in Georgia against the Confederate Army of Tennessee under Gen. Joseph E. Johnston. As the summer wore on Johnston gradually fell back before superior numbers, and the Federals got closer and closer to Atlanta. President Davis, disgruntled with Johnston's cautious defensive policy, and amidst complex circumstances fearing for the safety of Atlanta, decided to name a new army commander. He gave the position to one of Johnston's subordinates, Lt. Gen. John B. Hood, who assumed command on 16 July 1864. Lee then gained command of Hood's old corps.

Hood was less than two years older than Lee; and in previous combat injuries, he had lost one leg and had one arm badly mangled. Yet, Davis considered Hood "practically the only possible 'successor,'" to Johnston,[25] because by the time Davis acted he felt the replacement should be someone already with the army. Davis had considered Robert E. Lee, William J. Hardee, Braxton Bragg, Alexander P. Stewart, James Longstreet, Ambrose P. Hill, Wade Hampton, Pat Cleburne, and Benjamin F. Cheatham—apparently, however, not S. D. Lee. Though farfetched to suggest that the junior lieutenant general in the Confederacy might have been thought ready for such a position, Lee was at least as good as several of those considered.

As a corps commander, Lee outperformed his peers but showed some weakness in independent operations. Potentially, with seasoning, he could have been an excellent corps commander, but he needed experience and growth. Intrinsically he had the prerequisites to be a great division commander, and ironically this was one of the few assignments that he never sampled. As things turned out, he became Hood's best subordinate—and he did well in crucial instances. He had been a better man than was needed for most of his previous jobs, yet he rose haphazardly and finally rose too rapidly. During the next five months, Lee showed, however, that he could serve creditably even in a task for which he had insufficient tactical experience. "It did not take us long to realize that he was a man of unusual ability," his new adjutant general wrote, "and we rejoiced in the good fortune that had sent us so able a commander."[26]

9

Trying Times with the Army of Tennessee

HOOD KNEW QUITE a lot about Lee, since they had been together for three years at West Point; then early in the war they saw each other in the Army of Northern Virginia. On 19 July 1864, Hood wrote the war department requesting a new corps commander and suggested three names, one of which was Lee's. President Davis gave the matter his personal attention and took only one day to decide upon Lee.[1]

Between the time he assumed command on 17 July and when Lee arrived on 25 July, Hood had engaged his army in two devastating battles, bitter, hard-fought, and indecisive engagements. The Federals did not get Atlanta, but they inflicted severe losses upon the Confederates, and Lee found the army in a state of low morale and ineffectiveness. Hood believed, and convinced Lee after initial briefings, the cause was in large part the army's experiences with entrenchments.

Analyzing the army's campaigns just before and after Lee arrived, Hood later recalled Lee as saying, "I consider it a great misfortune to any army to have to resort to entrenchments; its *morale* is necessarily impaired from their constant use." Lee felt it indispensable to have bold and unafraid soldiers, since "troops once sheltered from fire behind works, never feel comfortable unless in them." Further, "An army, accustomed to entrenchments, has its efficiency impaired as a whole," also affecting offensive operations against "even temporary breastworks." And, "When orders were given to attack and there was a probability of encountering works, they re-

126

garded it as reckless in the extreme . . . and therefore did not generally move to the attack with that spirit which nearly always ensures success."[2] Of course Hood twisted Lee's meaning slightly, for his own vindication.

Lee had extensive experience with entrenchments and doubtless knew how formidable they were. Yet he also knew that high morale was essential. Having been briefed by Hood, and remaining scrupulously aloof from the gossipy attacks that the other generals in the army made upon Hood's lack of touch with the new tactical necessities imposed by increased firepower, Lee initially accepted Hood's thesis. Under these circumstances, it is much to Lee's credit that he also could improve spirit. The troops received him "most favorably," thought Braxton Bragg—President Davis' chief military advisor— and Lee's adjutant recalled "the skill he showed in handling the troops, his personal courage, and many other admirable traits of character, which soon endeared him to the men of the corps."[3]

Certainly not least among the reasons for the army's lowered morale was the severe lack of strength in all units. Lee had only 11,900 effective troops, organized into four artillery battalions and three infantry divisions, one under the aggressive and efficient Maj. Gen. Henry D. Clayton, one under Maj. Gen. Carter L. Stevenson —in whose division Lee had served before Vicksburg fell—and one temporarily under the dangerously inexperienced Brig. Gen. John C. Brown. Another 4,653 men were present but not fit for duty, and a staggering 21,334 were absent. Both of the other corps in the army, under Lt. Gen. William J. Hardee and Lt. Gen. Alexander P. Stewart, also had more men absent than present; Hood had fewer than 40,000 effective infantry.[4]

The corps generals all were competent, and all had demonstrated unblemished gallantry and considerable intelligence. Hardee had authored a standard textbook, *Rifle and Light Infantry Tactics*, and Stewart had held a university professorship. The troops pinned nicknames on each: "Old Reliable" Hardee, "Old Straight" Stewart, and "Old Temporary" Lee—since Lee had held such a vast array of different assignments. Unfortunately the three generals did not make a perfect team under Hood, especially since Hardee disliked, distrusted, and disagreed with his chief and also showed an incapacity for added responsibilities. Thus they and their army proved inadequate to face the situation that Sherman presented.

After the Battle of Atlanta Sherman moved to cut Hood's railway line of communications to the south. The Federals rapidly extended their right and then swept southward a few miles west of Atlanta. Hood learned of this move and devised a grandiose plan of counteraction. On 28 July Lee's corps would move from its position east of Atlanta, straight through the city to Ezra Church on the Lick Skillet Road, take possession of that road and a critical nearby junction, and entrench, thereby holding the Federals facing him. The next morning Stewart's corps would swing around Lee's left and strike the enemy flank.[5]

The Confederate scheme went awry before it really got started. Lee hastened westward and found the Federals already emplaced behind logs and rails along the same line he had hoped to occupy. Without exchanging messages with Hood, as he should have, to ascertain if this situation necessitated a change in plans, Lee elected to attack. Lee believed that he should act quickly because, as he said, "the enemy's works were slight, and . . . they had scarcely gotten into position when we made the attack." The line that Lee thought "would yield before a vigorous attack" stretched along a wooded ridge overlooking an open slope.[6] Lee hurried so much that he failed at coordinated action. Each division went forward separately, and the corps never fought as a team. They charged "with a terrifying yell," but one assault after another was beaten back. Meanwhile Stewart drifted toward the sound of Lee's guns and, seeing the situation, sent two of his divisions into the fight. The battle went on for hours. Many officers stood bravely, trying to encourage their troops. A lieutenant remembered that "Lee looked like the God of War. I can see his face now, positively radiant. . . . I expected to see him fall every minute."[7] But all this activity proved fruitless.

The spirited battle amounted to nothing but a very poor showing for the Confederates. Hood apparently badly misunderstood what had been going on all day. He never rode to the front personally but finally dispatched General Hardee to leave his own corps and go "to look after matters." Hardee arrived in the early evening and found the fight ended. Over 5,000 dead Confederates lay "in windrows"; Stewart was wounded; and the Federals still held their ground. During the night Lee's and Stewart's men sullenly withdrew to the trenches around Atlanta. President Davis was so

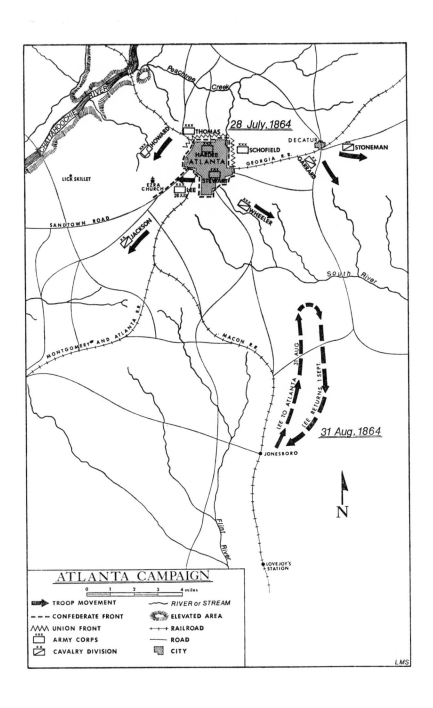

LICK SKILLET

CHATTAHOOCHIE RIVER

Peachtree Creek

28 July, 1864

HOWARD
THOMAS
HARDEE
ATLANTA
SCHOFIELD
DECATUR
STONEMAN
GARRARD
GEORGIA R.R.
EZRA CHURCH
LEE
28 JULY
STEWART
WHEELER
SANDTOWN ROAD
JACKSON

South River

MONTGOMERY AND ATLANTA R.R.
MACON R.R.

31 AUG
LEE TO ATLANTA
LEE RETURNS, 1 SEPT

31 Aug, 1864

JONESBORO

N

Flint River

LOVEJOY'S STATION

ATLANTA CAMPAIGN

0   1   2   3   4 miles

TROOP MOVEMENT

RIVER or STREAM

CONFEDERATE FRONT

ELEVATED AREA

UNION FRONT

RAILROAD

ARMY CORPS

ROAD

CAVALRY DIVISION

CITY

LMS

shocked when he heard about the losses that he urged **Hood** to avoid any further frontal attacks.[8]

Twice in the same fortnight Lee had met defeat in similar assaults. Both times strategic pressures had goaded him into fighting on unfavorable ground against protected defenders, but he was learning—particularly at Ezra Church—the mistake of continuing such an unprofitable series of attacks over so long a period. There had been good reasons for the engagements. Now, with these experiences behind him, Lee had greater discretion.

During the month of August 1864, the struggle for Atlanta became a siege. In the trenches, much to Lee's credit, his men managed to regain some strength and spirit. His corps underwent several changes. Maj. Gen. James Patton Anderson, widely acclaimed as one of the best men the Confederates had in that rank, arrived to replace Brig. Gen. John C. Brown as a division commander. Lee contended with spurious truces arranged between the soldiers and with unofficial agreements not to fire or to refrain from shooting to kill. The Federals launched assaults against his lines from time to time, and all were repulsed.[9]

On the night of 26 August, the enemy disappeared from Lee's and Stewart's fronts. Sherman pushed rapidly around to Jonesboro and secured the Macon Railroad on the thirty-first. The Confederates did not guess Sherman's strategy and at first pushed forward to occupy the Federals' former positions. At sundown on 30 August Hood sent a locomotive to pick up Lee and Hardee, and the three generals held a council of war in Atlanta. Hood made Hardee a sort of deputy army commander and charged him with the direction of both his and Lee's corps. They would move to Jonesboro, attack Sherman's force, and drive it across the Flint River if possible.[10]

The gray column got started just before midnight, but it moved very slowly. Hardee's corps did not get into battle line until 9:00 A.M., and Lee's began to arrive only at 10:00 A.M., requiring another three and one-half hours for all units to come up. By this time the Unionists had entrenched along the crest of an irregular ridge between Jonesboro and the Flint River. Hardee's plan called for Patrick Cleburne, commanding Hardee's corps, to open the battle on the left; then when Lee observed that Cleburne was engaged, he would advance on the right.

Cleburne did not begin his attack until 3:00 P.M., but at 2:20 P.M. Lee heard some heavy skirmish fire, which he mistook for the main assault, and advanced. He earlier had exhorted each brigade: "temporary breastworks can be carried and they must be carried." But the unsupported charge faltered quickly. Some troops just lay down within sixty yards of the enemy's breastworks. "The attack was a feeble one," Lee wrote, "and a failure." It also cost him the services of the capable Patton Anderson who was wounded and had to be relieved by Edward "Old Allegheny" Johnson. Cleburne's efforts, also piecemeal, rendered Hardee unable to effect coordination until late afternoon. By that time Lee's corps, with 1,300 casualties, was too demoralized and exhausted to advance again.[11]

The costly battle of Jonesboro sealed the fate of Atlanta. At 6:00 P.M., hours before Hood learned the outcome, he ordered Lee's corps to return to Atlanta. Lee began the march, but met a courier a few miles from the city with orders for Lee to rejoin Hardee and help cover the evacuation. The Confederates pulled out on 1 September and finally reconcentrated two days later at Lovejoy's Station, about thirty miles southeast of Atlanta.[12]

Hood's army bivouacked at Lovejoy's for two weeks and then moved to Palmetto Station. It suffered numerous difficulties: Hood and Hardee bickered—continuing their longstanding feud, several thousand men had no shoes, food was scant from the loss of commissary stores at Atlanta, ammunition ran dangerously low, and many men deserted. Lee's corps strength lowered to 7,401 effectives —5,500 fewer than when he had first taken command.

On 25 and 26 September Davis visited the army, reviewed the troops, and held long conferences with the generals. Should Hood, or Hardee, be replaced? What operation could the army undertake? Some of the generals felt that Davis ought to put the army under either Johnston or Beauregard, but Lee's opinion is not recorded. Lee did think that the army "should take up the offensive," and Hood asserted later that Lee was one of several generals who negatively assessed Hardee.[13]

Davis eventually decided to accept Hardee's application for a transfer, replacing him with Benjamin F. Cheatham—who had dis-

tinguished himself as a brigade and division commander—and
worked out with Hood an agreement for the army to try to draw
Sherman back northwestward that essentially gave Hood a free
hand thereafter. After failing to entice Sherman rearward, Hood
was gradually attracted to the wistful plan of a long offensive thrust
through Tennessee to the Ohio River. On 29 September Lee's corps
crossed the Chattahoochee River and pushed into Alabama, fighting skirmishes at Resaca on 12 October and at Snake Creek Gap on
15 October. Picking up supplies along the way, they reached Gadsden on 21 October, pushed on, and forced a crossing of the Tennessee River at Florence on the night of 29 October. Easily brush-
ing aside a small Federal garrison, they occupied the town and
remained there for the next three weeks.

The delay proved costly because it dulled the shock effect of
Hood's bold plan, but even the aggressive Lee admitted that it was
required for assembling "necessary clothing, ammunition, and provisions." Many men secured needed shirts, shoes, boots, socks, and
—quite importantly—both some rest and their first good leisurely
meals in months. Lee urged men who could not get shoes or boots
to fashion moccasins out of fresh beef hides, tied on with the hairy
side turned in. He had several small groups detailed to construct
samples. Lee wrote that he considered "the spirit of the army . . .
much improved," but even this new morale and the supplies that
trickled in were insufficient to steel the men for what was ahead
that winter.[14]

Hood's scheme had a slight chance for success if he moved his
army fast enough and executed his plans effectively. The Federal
forces in Tennessee were not united, being scattered instead all
over the middle part of the state, and vulnerable while divided.
But while the Southerners gathered their strength the Federals
also took action. Before Sherman launched his troops on the famous
"March to the Sea," he dispatched Maj. Gen. George H. Thomas,
the Union hero who had prevented a total rout at Chickamauga
and who had been one of S. D. Lee's West Point instructors, into
Tennessee to take charge of the northern army being built up there.

The opposing armies that clashed in Tennessee ultimately were
mismatched by a better than two to one advantage in favor of the
North. Thomas eventually amassed about 55,000 men; but before
they all united, the principal Federal force numbered only 22,000

under scholarly and underrated John M. Schofield at Columbia, Tennessee. When Hood began the campaign, he had about 30,000 infantry and 8,000 cavalry troops. The Confederate army moved toward Schofield, having a golden opportunity to strike at a fraction of the northern enemy with the full mass of the southern army.

The three corps of the Army of Tennessee, one each under Lee, Cheatham, and Steward, began marching on 19 November. After they finally got started, the Southerners managed to move with remarkable speed, considering the unfavorable weather and the poor condition of the roads. Lee's corps marched ten miles the first day and within a week neared Columbia. The army moved along in a cold rain which soon turned into snow and sleet. Where the ground did not freeze, it became a quagmire.[15]

Hood's men made contact with Schofield's forces at Columbia on the twenty-seventh. The two armies drew up in line of battle and lay opposite each other throughout the day. They fired artillery barrages and exchanged small arms fire, but neither side made any charges. Lee personally directed some of the cannonading and inspired the men to be brave and steadfast. One admiring observer recalled: "I have seen General Lee under fire probably fifty times. I have stood in his presence when the earth fairly trembled, and every living thing was in danger of immediate death, but no one never [sic] saw him display the slightest emotion nor lose his dignified bearing."[16]

The same observer remembered an incident at Columbia on the twenty-seventh: "One of Captain Walton's caissons . . . exploded . . . [and] hurled fragments of iron and wood high into the air, killing every man and horse immediately about it, and throwing up a mountain of dirt and smoke. When the smoke had cleared away, every man in the party . . . was dismounted, except General Lee, who sat like a marble statue on his frightened steed. D. H. Hill, I think, was the only General who was Lee's equal in composure."[17]

Schofield chose not to fight Hood south of Columbia. During the night the Federals crossed to a new position on the northern side of the Duck River. The two armies continued to fire at each other with artillery and skirmish fire, but that was the only combat for the time being.

Hood meanwhile determined to divide his forces, leaving Lee

with two divisions at Columbia, hoping to fool Schofield into thinking the whole Confederate force still remained in position, while Hood with the rest of the army tried a turning movement to reach the Federal rear near Spring Hill. Cheatham's and Stewart's corps and Edward Johnson's division of Lee's corps commenced the movement on the night of 28 November.

The movement began sluggishly. Hood determined to cross the Duck River on pontoon bridges only about three miles above Columbia, but his infantry did not even begin to cross until daybreak on the twenty-ninth. Yet Lee managed to deceive Schofield completely. The Confederates in Columbia kept up "such a continual and noisy demonstration," as one Unionist recalled, that the Union troops "believed Hood's whole army" still stood in their front.

Schofield held his entire army opposite Columbia until near noon on 29 November, when he began to withdraw slowly to the north. Lee's men saw the first corps moving off, but the others remained in position until dark. So the Federals continued to play into Hood's hands, progressing more and more into the jaws of the pincers, filling the road with crawling wagons.[18] By 3:00 P.M., Hood had gotten his lead troops to a spot overlooking the pike from Columbia to Spring Hill and Franklin. He knew that Lee was busy, drawing Schofield's attention to the rear. The roar of Lee's artillery could be distinctly heard. Hood and his generals got sight of the enemy's wagons; and Hood, according to his own memoirs, ordered Cheatham and Cleburne immediately to "take possession of and hold that pike at or near Spring Hill." Hood later said he also meant that the Confederates should attack the nearby bluecoats and destroy them. Supposedly he sent a courier with an order to Cheatham, after the latter had gotten into the Federals' path, to attack at once. But "through some misunderstanding or physical exhaustion or too much whiskey going the rounds," or something, the order was not executed and probably was not even delivered.[19]

Meanwhile, earlier in the day, Lee not only fired at Schofield's forces across the Duck River; he also attempted to force a pontoon crossing. "I had several batteries of artillery put in position, to drive the skirmishers of the enemy from the vicinity of the river bank," Lee explained. Finally "having succeeded in putting a boat in the river, Pettus' brigade of Stevenson's division was thrown across . . . and made a most gallant charge on the rifle pits of the enemy, driving a much superior force and capturing the pits."[20] Immediately Lee had his men lay a pontoon bridge, and he crossed with the remainder of his command.

A strong Federal force resisted Lee's advance until about 2:30 A.M. then left his front. "Pursuit was made as rapidly as was prudent in the nighttime," Lee declared. He got his advance columns into Spring Hill by 9:00 A.M., and was about ten miles from Columbia. There Lee learned the horrible news: Hood had not attacked, and Schofield's men had slipped safely past toward Franklin. Schofield's lines during the march had strung out for over five miles. The Northerners required all night to get underway, and it was nearly daybreak before the last wagon even left Spring Hill. The Confederates "remained all night in sound of the voices of the men as they retreated," recalled one disgusted southern warrior. Not a shot was fired into the passing trains, though "a few rounds of artillery would have routed the enemy," Lee believed.[21]

Utterly disgusted, Lee later wrote that, "the enemy almost in a panic passed all night along the pike. . . . Our troops were in bivouac not eight hundred yards from the pike, seeing and hearing it all. . . . A simple advance of one division a few hundred yards would have secured the pike." Some blue-clads actually straggled into the Confederate camps "to light their pipes and were captured," Lee claimed. "Some one . . . should be made responsible for the egregious blunder, mistake, or disobedience." But never did Lee publicly accuse any specific person of the blame. In 1903 he wrote, "I do not think the record sifted down will place the blame on either General Hood or General Cheatham, who have borne the blame these many years." On another occasion he said that "at one time I believed General Cheatham at fault; now I do not, and I believe that in his generous nature he shouldered the blame of subordinates which was not justly his own."[22]

At any rate, Lee believed that "the conception of the whole Spring Hill plan was brilliant and well executed, all but the fighting at the critical moment." In 1878 he wrote that "had the army fought at Spring Hill . . . Hood's Tennessee campaign would have been a brilliant success." Hood, equally complimentary of Lee, declared that "had Lieutenant General Lee been in advance at Spring Hill . . . Schofield's army never would have passed that point."[23]

Schofield's men marched easily into Franklin, about twenty-five miles above Columbia and twelve above Spring Hill. Immediately they began entrenching in a strong hillside defensive position. The Army of Tennessee followed in pursuit; Stewart's corps was in the lead, Cheatham's next, and Lee's to the rear. The advance guard made contact with the Federals about three miles south of Franklin, and Stewart began to establish a battle line at approximately 3:30 P.M. The city of Franklin, located in a bend of the Harpeth River, had been surrounded by lines of entrenchments which touched the shore both above and below the main area of settlement. Schofield had fortified these lines and now occupied them with all 22,000 of his men.

Hood, very eager for action, decided not to wait until Lee moved up with his corps, though almost all of the army's artillery was with Lee because of the action at Columbia. Though it was late in the day, Hood thought that an attack should be launched right away. Probably the frustration at Spring Hill caused him to act rashly. He began hurling his men against the Federal lines in piecemeal, uncoordinated, and fruitless attempts to break through.

Lee reached the scene about 4:00 P.M. and went ahead of his corps to report to Hood. The commanding general ordered him to "go forward and in person to communicate with General Cheatham, and if necessary, to put Johnson's division in the fight." Lee found Cheatham at about dark, a little after 5:00 on this late November day. Cheatham replied that he needed assistance at once, and Lee hurried Johnson's division up in line on the left of the Columbia Pike. Hood had ordered Lee's other two divisions moved within supporting distance, to be used if necessary.[24]

Since neither Lee nor any of his staff had time to become familiar with the ground, Lee asked Cheatham for someone to act as a guide for Johnson's division as it advanced. Lee later recalled that Cheatham replied, "he had no one to give him . . . and pointing to the front said, yonder line of fire at the breastworks is where you are needed and wanted at once."[25] Lee started the division moving about one hour after dark. The only light on the pitch-black scene came, Lee recalled, from "the lurid and rapid flashes from the enemy's works."[26] Johnson's men charged furiously against the breastworks. Miraculously they began driving back portions of the well-fortified lines, but the strong position favored the defenders, and the plucky Northerners fought back in desperate hand-to-hand combat.

As soon as the Federals became aware of Lee's advance in support of the main attack, they opened up artillery fire all along the line. There was a second line of entrenchments, in the rear of the main Federal positions; and as Lee's men made progress, these soldiers fired over their own men in the line to the front. Lee remembered the scene as "looking as if the division was moving into the very door of hell, lighted up with its sulphurous flames."[27] In spite of frightful losses, Hood never called off the attacks. The Confederates made violent charges as late as 9:00 P.M., yet Hood did not commit Lee's other two divisions at all; though he did finally get some of the artillery moved up and ordered the guns to fire a hundred rounds each into the Federal works early the next morning, when the troops would then charge again.

Meanwhile, Schofield evacuated Franklin. Sufficient units remained on the battlefield to exchange skirmish fire with the Confederates until about 3:00 A.M., but then the last bluecoats moved out toward the safety of Nashville, twenty-five miles northward. Hood's army had suffered nearly three times the number of casualties as had the enemy and could not pursue because of exhaustion and disorganization.

The Federals had lost 2,326 in killed, wounded, or missing; the Confederates suffered 6,252 casualties, including 5 generals killed, 1 captured, and 6 more wounded. Johnson's division, the only unit of Lee's corps engaged, lost 587 men. The battle amounted to a staggering disaster—the bloodiest of the entire war considering the time that the men were engaged, as Lee pointed out. Though many units displayed great valor, Lee had special praise for Johnson's division; its charge at Franklin was, he said, "the most gallant feat of arms which I witnessed during the war."[28]

Lee did not say that he thought Hood should not have fought the battle, but he did write that the field was "ill chosen."[29] He observed that the army's morale began to decline after that engagement. Still he did not criticize Hood. Apparently he thought that a battle had to be fought and that whoever was responsible for the failure at Spring Hill was also indirectly responsible for Franklin—by making it necessary to fight the enemy on unfavorable ground.

Lee did what he could to restore morale among his men. On the
morning after the battle of Franklin he made a few remarks to each
of the brigades in Johnson's division, commending them for their
heroism. One brigade had suffered so many casualties that a private,
displaying typical pride in his unit, lamented, "General, our old
brigade is gone; its organization can no longer be kept up." Lee
bolstered his spirits by promising that as long as he had anything
to say about it, the unit would remain in existence.[30]

On the same day, in the afternoon of 1 December 1864, the Army
of Tennessee began marching again toward Nashville—this time,
with Lee's corps in the lead. Lee actually thought of the move as a
pursuit, driving against whatever stragglers from Schofield's force
remained on the roads. But the next real fight would be in the
trenches around Nashville, against Thomas' united army of nearly
55,000. Lee's corps reached the environs of the city at about 2:00
P.M. on 2 December. Already the Federals had occupied strongly
entrenched defensive positions. The Confederates strung out about
a mile away from the Northerners' lines and also began entrenching.[31]

For the next two weeks both armies methodically went about
strengthening their emplacements. The Confederate lines stretched
out about five miles long. Lee's corps occupied the center, covering
the Franklin Pike and extending almost to the Granny White Pike,
with Stewart's corps on the left and Cheatham's on the right. Cavalry covered the large area between the left flank and the Tennessee
River, and redoubts were constructed to help protect this and the
other flank as well.

Time passed, but Thomas made no move to come out of the city
and fight. Hood judged his forces not strong enough to charge the
Federal fortifications, so the two armies remained in a temporary
stalemate. The Confederates added to their lines an abatis of whatever fallen timber they could find, supplemented by earthworks.
On 10 December Hood issued a circular order to all his commanders warning of high probability that a battle would be fought
before the year's end. In that event, he ordered, all the wagons except artillery, ordnance and ambulances should be parked in the
vicinity of Brentwood, south of Nashville. Hood also ordered
preparation of a second line of defensive works along the strong
points to the rear of the Confederate position.

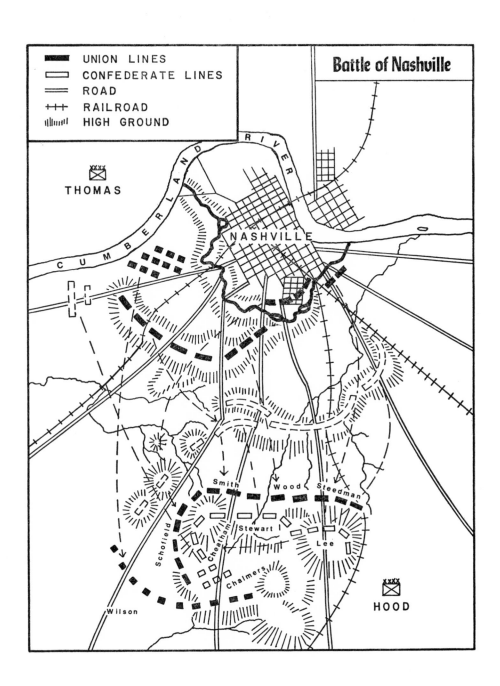

Battle of Nashville

UNION LINES
CONFEDERATE LINES
ROAD
RAILROAD
HIGH GROUND

THOMAS

CUMBERLAND RIVER

NASHVILLE

Smith   Wood   Steedman

Schofield   Cheatham   Stewart   Lee

Chalmers

Wilson

HOOD

The armies fired occasional discharges of artillery at each other, but during the first half of December the troops suffered mostly from the elements and from lack of adequate supplies. Lee and the other officers were able on one occasion to take time out to serve as a military escort in the wedding of Maj. William Clark and Mary Hadley in the Brentwood church.[32]

By the evening of Wednesday 14 December, Thomas felt ready to make his move. Hood foolishly had sent most of Forrest's cavalry to Murfreesboro on an independent operation against a Federal garrison of 8,000 men. Thus the bluecoats could attack the Confederates while the Southerners lacked their "eyes" and their most effective flank protection. Thomas ordered an assault for early the next day.

A dense fog hovered during the early morning of Thursday, 15 December, concealing the northern troop movements. Lucidly recalling the ways of his former tactics instructor, Lee wrote to Stewart that he felt secure but added, "I think you may look out for a demonstration on your left to-day."[33] The enemy movement toward the Confederate lines that Lee predicted already had begun; and even as he wrote, a rattle of gunfire began to the westward.

Thomas' battle plan called for a strong attack upon the Confederate left, a skirmish advance in the center, the mass of the troops withdrawing from the center to join the cavalry for an envelopment of the Confederate left flank, and a feint against the right. In this almost perfectly coordinated maneuver, reminiscent of Frederick the Great, the most serious flaw was that Thomas did not particularly well utilize his artillery. The weather also dulled the shock effect of the plan because the ice had melted and produced mud which slowed troop movements.[34]

Hood at first was deceived as to the direction of Thomas' main attack. The feints met success, and soon the main force hurled heavy blows against the Confederate left with telling effect. Just before noon, Lee realized that he faced no major assault and wrote to Hood that "the main line of enemy in *my* front has apparently but a few men in it." Lee felt able to match Thomas move for move, but Hood remained afraid to use too many of Lee's units for reinforcement on the left, fearing he might need a reserve on the right. But by 1:00 P.M. Hood ordered Lee to send Stewart "all the Brigades you can and keep in constant communication with him."[35]

Lee's lines stretched long and thin, "the greater part of my command being in single rank," he recalled. He could not send an unlimited number of men to Stewart's support, or he would be unable to maintain contact with Cheatham's corps on the right, and the Federals then could break through easily and wreak havoc. Nevertheless, as the day passed, one by one Lee sent Stewart four of his nine brigades—all of Johnson's division. Even with the added strength from Lee's corps, Stewart could not check the blue onslaught. Just before dark Stewart's lines crumbled. The Federals turned his flank and began driving his men back along the Granny White Pike, pushing them southward for about two miles before halting the fighting at nightfall.

Thomas was pleased with his success. With the Confederate flank crushed, he believed that his men easily could finish the job in the morning. Lee analyzed the Federal attack and admitted that "Gen. Thomas's plan of battle was admirable," but added that "his success was due chiefly to a tactical combination of a superior force." Whatever the reason, Lee knew that the Confederates were beaten that day. "Night is all that prevented Stewart's force being cut off entirely," he wrote.[36]

The Confederates did not just rest during the night; they knew renewed attacks would come in the morning. Lee's corps moved straight south and took up a position on the right of Stewart's men. Cheatham shifted his corps around to the far left and occupied that side of Stewart's corps, thus placing the troops which had borne the brunt of the fighting on the fifteenth in the new center. The whole line was only about half as long as the previous one had been. Lee's units now straddled the Franklin pike, which Hood ordered Lee to hold at all costs. The area south of Nashville, mountainous in places and marshy in others, dictated that any retreat would have to be along roads. The Franklin pike might be needed as a lifesaving escape route. Hood's new lines were stronger than those his army had occupied on the fifteenth, but his men were badly dispirited after the all-day fighting.

For several reasons, Lee's corps was in the best shape of any that Hood had. First, Lee's men had not taken part in the worst fighting, except for the brigades of Johnson's division that got over and helped Stewart. Second, the topography added natural strength to Lee's position, since a stone fence to his front that his men strengthened with head logs became a breastworks. Too, "tanglefoot" brush lay about twenty-five paces in front of the works.[37] In addition, Lee's actual presence seems continually to have inspired his men.

The Unionists opened their assault on the sixteenth, beginning about 9:00 A.M., with a two-hour artillery bombardment. Then the main attack hit at Lee's positions. The Federals moved forward in several lines. Lee's men reserved their fire until the enemy moved into easy range and then discharged it with terrific effect. Each time the blue-clads renewed the assault, they were repulsed. Thomas' strategy essentially duplicated the previous day's plan except that the strong frontal assault, the secondary attack, assailed the Confederate right instead of the left. Hence, Lee's corps became much more actively engaged.[38]

"The troops of my entire line were in fine spirits," Lee reported, "and confident of success, so much so that the men could scarcely be prevented from leaving their trenches to follow the enemy." At one point some of them did leave the trenches. A large number of Negro troops assaulted Lee's lines. Judging from the remarks made by some of Lee's men, the Confederates apparently fought even more ferociously against the black troops. When one brigade of colored soldiers made a valiant assault and were halted by the fire of Lee's men, several Southerners leapt out of their defensive works and captured the enemy battle flags. One was inscribed "Presented by the Colored Ladies of Murfreesboro, Tenn." When Lee noticed how elated the men were over capturing it, he had those around him give three cheers and directed that the cheers be passed down the lines—to encourage the Confederates on the left.

Time after time Lee's men threw back assaults. Their morale soared, and Lee spurred them on. He stayed openly with them while the battle raged. Once when he was conferring with a subordinate officer, fire came so close that a bullet passed through the rim of his companion's hat.[39]

But along other portions of the Confederate lines, the defense was not nearly so strong. On the extreme left, the Federals hammered away with advantageously massed artillery. By 3:30 P.M. the blue-coats pinned down the Southerners on the left so that temporarily they could not fire back without being annihilated, massed a division at the base of a mound, and charged suddenly over Confederate entrenchments. After the lines of Stewart's corps were thus pierced, they gave way and broke apart at many points. The men of Lee's corps could see many of Stewart's troops fleeing toward the rear. As soon as the Northerners secured Stewart's old positions, they began moving against Lee's left. Lee shifted some of his troops and checked the enemy advance. The Federals slipped around to Lee's rear while continuing to hammer away at his left. Gradually his corps lines gave way. The Confederates began to pull back, "in some disorder," Lee admitted; but he soon rallied them, and they "presented a good front to the enemy," enough stiff resistance to prevent a rout.[40]

Lee continued to remain at the most threatened points, using his personal presence to the fullest advantage in spurring his men. At one point he seized a flag from a frightened color bearer and encouraged the men to stand fast. They stiffened and held their unsupported lines while the rest of the Confederates were breaking. Federal General Schofield later remarked on the resistance that Lee's men maintained: "I doubt if any soldiers in the world ever needed so much cumulative evidence to convince them they were beaten."[41]

Meanwhile, Stewart's and Cheatham's corps rushed in confusion toward the Franklin pike with Federal soldiers chewing them up in hot pursuit. Lee got Clayton's division formed into a new battle line between Overton Hill and Brentwood. They held this line while the rest of Hood's shattered army streamed over the wooded hills and swarmed onto the Franklin pike. Heavy rain began to fall and slowed both pursuers and retreaters. Lee's men got some help from Chalmers' cavalry, which managed to stave off a charge by Federal Gen. James H. Wilson's mounted men on the Granny White pike.[42]

It was imperative that Lee's men hold long enough to allow the Army of Tennessee to get at least some distance away from the Federals. In this action, Gibson's brigade of Clayton's division rendered significant service. Once when his lines nearly broke, Lee rushed up to one of Gibson's color bearers and tried to take the colors and lead the brigade personally. The color bearer refused to give up his flag saying, "No General, you need not expose yourself in this way, just tell us where you want these colors and that is where we will take them." The rest of the regiment nearby shouted agreement, and Lee cried, "Gibson, these are the best men I ever saw. You take them and check the enemy!"[43] Gibson did exactly that.

At another instant, Lee rushed over to a faltering group and asked if any of them were South Carolinians. He asked them to rally to him, a native of that state. A few men started forward, and the rest followed. Lee then helped unlimber the guns of one artillery section and fired a few shots. Again his lines stiffened, and the bluecoats were checked.[44] A private on Lee's staff recalled Lee's actions throughout the afternoon: "His example was inspiring. I recall his words. . . . They seemed to come from his very soul, as if his heart were breaking. One appeal was: 'Rally, men, rally! For God's sake rally! This is the place for brave men to die!' To those who came in contact with him and under the spell of his presence and personal magnetism the effect was electrical. Men gathered in little knots of four and five, prompted by individual gallantry."[45]

Later in the evening, in a falling mist, the Federals tried once again to force through Lee's thin lines. Lee grabbed a terrified little drummer boy and instructed him to beat the long roll. Again Lee held a battle flag in his hands. Other officers and men brandished so many standards that one veteran remembered it struck him "as a rally of color bearers." Lee's men stood firm; and when the long roll sounded, some of the Unionists actuallly believed that a reserve unit was being launched against them; and they halted their advance.

Shortly before dark Lee received word that the enemy was near Brentwood, to his rear. He rapidly disengaged his men and moved them in that direction. Reaching Brentwood about dark, he found that the other two corps already had passed that point and were temporarily safe. Lee marched his men further south and halted his rear guard about six miles north of Franklin at 10:00 P.M.[46] Thus Lee had succeeded in his efforts to delay the Federals long enough to allow the rest of Hood's men to get started in their retreat.

Lee deserved great credit for his contribution. He was somewhat modest in his accounts of the day, but one of his staff members penned a fitting tribute: "Gen. Lee says his troops were soon rallied. Yes, indeed, they were. But who rallied them? On this point Gen. Lee is silent with his accustomed modesty. He caused them to present a good front to the enemy. Let justice be done. . . . There is not a living man who can deny that Gen. Stephen D. Lee rallied these troops, and to him belongs the credit of saving Hood's army."[47] Even the modest Lee allowed himself to write that the holding action had been "all that saved Hood's army at this critical moment."[48]

The first holding action was by no means the last in the retreat from Nashville. The Northerners maintained one of the most vigorous pursuits of the entire war. Lee believed that "a more persistent effort was never made to rout the rear guard of a retiring column." Nevertheless he knew his men had to have some rest, so he let them go into bivouac at Hollow Tree Gap, just north of Franklin. He kept a small command on watch at the gap in the hills east of where they halted, and he employed a few pickets to keep the road clear of the occasional Federal skirmish lines. The troops snatched whatever rest they could during the uncertain night, their discomfort increased by the freezing rain that began to fall.[49] But Lee's defense lines were strengthened during the night. He had only a part of his corps at this point, Clayton's and Stevenson's divisions, two pieces of artillery, and a small cavalry command under Gen. Abraham Buford.[50]

The Federals launched their first assault against Lee's lines on the seventeenth at 5:00 A.M. Charge after charge hit Lee's stubborn men, but they held. Throughout the morning Northerners occasionally got close enough to capture what eventually amounted to several hundred Confederates; but at the same time, many bluecoats were dragged off their horses and the mounts captured by the Southerners. Gradually Lee fell back into Franklin and made another determined stand in front of the Harpeth River.

Hood's army had been held up at the Big Harpeth because the wooden trestle bridge was burned, forcing the Confederates to lay a pontoon bridge. Lee formed a battle line on a bluff not far from the pontoon bridge. Both flanks were sharply refused—turned back —so that the line formed almost in the shape of a horseshoe, somewhat similar to the classic hollow square.[51]

As the Federals advanced, Lee had his men hold their fire until the last moment. The enemy approached at a trot. A witness recalled the scene: "What a moment of suspense and expectation.

How the brain works in moments like these! But at the last the general, rising in his stirrups as he sat on his grey horse, gave the command in stentorian voice 'Fire!'

"The musketry went off, but the friction primers of both howitzers snapped from the dampness and did not fire.

"Behind the line of battle, where Gen. Lee, his staff, and escort were, was aswarm with carbine bullets, and as alight with flashing sabres as in front, and many of the staff and escort had hand to hand combats in the almost general melee which followed."[52] Lee's plan of delaying fire at the attacking cavalry and in using the modified hollow square formation paid off. In the bitter fight the Confederates withstood the onslaught.

At 1:00 P.M. Lee received a wound from a shell fragment. It shot off his spur and passed through his heel, shattering a few small bones. One of his aides begged him to go to the rear, but he refused to leave the battle. Continuing to direct his men in this successful action, Lee held off the Federals until Hood's last wagons crossed the pontoons. Then he gradually got his own command across and reached the vicinity of Spring Hill at about nightfall, where the army encamped. Lee then turned the command of his corps over to his senior subordinate, Maj. Gen. Carter L. Stevenson.[53]

Lee's services to Hood at Nashville were similar to those of Thomas to Rosecrans at Chickamauga. The Army of Tennessee suffered so severely in the Nashville campaign that it no longer was an effective fighting force. Hood's troops sustained terrible losses, which would have been much greater had Lee been unable to prevent a rout. Lee had the consolation of knowing that at least he and his men had performed well. Hood wrote that "Lee and the corps commanded by him deserves great credit. . . . Lee displayed superior ability as a corps commander whilst in the Army of Tennessee."[54]

A Mobile *Tribune* editor penned a glowing tribute: "The services of this soldier can only be rightfully appreciated when the peculiar circumstances of the retreat are remembered. His heroic valor, his spirited devotion, gleaming like the sun along the field from Nashville to Franklin, have won for him the love and esteem of all his officers and men. . . . He is a soldier, he is a patriot; and next to that great man of the East, who is master of war and prince of the South, stands the worthy, noble, gallant, patriotic, Stephen D. Lee."[55]

Perhaps one of the most touching rewards Lee ever received came years later in recognition of his service in the retreat. R. E. Lee's son Custis presented S. D. with one of his father's spurs, symbolically to replace the one which had been shot away. A newspaper account of the presentation declared that if any officer lived who deserved to wear a spur which belonged to the great commander of the Army of Northern Virginia, it was Stephen D. Lee.[56]

Not one ever to forget the men who enabled him to be a success, Lee took the trouble before he departed to a base hospital to issue personal thanks to the soldiers: "I beg to assure you that I am not only satisfied with your conduct in the recent campaign, but that I shall repose unalterable confidence in you in the future—a future which, despite the clouds which seem to lower around us, will yet be rendered bright. . . ."[57] Those clouds adumbrated defeat, but for Lee a pleasant interlude, a marriage, occurred first.

10

Interlude and War's End

THE DEFEATED Army of Tennessee limped into a position of relative safety at Tupelo, Mississippi. Lee got only as far as Florence, Alabama, where he was hospitalized for several days. Just before Christmas 1864, he wrote to General Beauregard, the department commander and Hood's immediate superior, requesting a conference. Hood had asked Lee to see the Creole and try to explain the events in Tennessee.[1]

Then Lee went to Columbus, Mississippi, to join the girl who soon would become his bride. She was Regina Lilly Harrison, the granddaughter of Thomas C. Blewett, probably the wealthiest man in Columbus.[2] Both the Lee and Blewett families had South Carolina origins, but Stephen Lee apparently did not know Regina until he met her during the Civil War.

Thomas Blewett, born in 1789, moved with his wife to Mississippi in 1832. Always well off financially, the family prospered handsomely until Blewett's death in 1879 and his wife's in 1890. Blewett owned several pieces of property in Columbus, a large farm nearby, and five plantations in Lowndes, Noxubee, and Tallahatchie counties, as well as bank and railroad stock, and five hundred slaves. He used the title, "Major"—apparently even before the Civil War. During the conflict he served as commander of the home guard at Columbus.[3]

Their daughter, Lee's future mother-in-law, was named Regina. In 1840 she married Judge James T. Harrison, a descendant of Benjamin Harrison, one of the signers of the Declaration of Independence. The Judge was born near Pendleton, South Carolina

148

in 1811. A graduate of the University of South Carolina, he studied law under James L. Petigru and became quite well known for his competence and colorful court room technique. One Mississippian said of him: "Although nearsighted, he had a brilliant dancing eye, and what a lawyer he was! He possessed the sarcasm and invective of Voltaire without his venom or infidelity." Harrison moved to Columbus in 1834 and married in 1840. In 1861 he was elected to the convention of southern states which met at Montgomery, Alabama, and established the Confederate government. For the remainder of the Civil War he served as an elected member of the Confederate Congress.[4]

The judge and his wife Regina had five children to survive them: Regina, James, Tam, Allen, and Mary. The oldest child, a daughter, given the same name as her mother, was born on 24 February 1841, in Columbus.[5] Lee apparently met her in 1863 when she was twenty-two and he a major general of twenty-nine or thirty.

Miss Regina, usually called Lilly, was a remarkable young woman. Newspaperman E. A. Pollard remembered her as "a lady known and admired for her intellectual accomplishments as well as for her large portion of the beauty, wit, and amiability belonging to her sex." In 1860 she was described by the New York *Herald:* "In the combination of intellect and beauty Mississippi undoubtedly comes first, and at the head of this sovereign State's representatives stands Miss H———n, of Columbus. Her exquisitely chiselled features, soul flashing eyes, fine taste in dress, and calm and confident self possession at all times and on all occasions, mark something more than the mere transient beauty."[6] Other references indicate that she was widely considered to be truly gifted, accomplished, and charming. Before and during the war she collected friendly letters from an impressive array of notable figures. These included Jefferson Davis, William J. Hardee, Leonidas Polk, and the famous filibusterer—the "gray eyed man of destiny," William Walker.

During the Civil War many military personnel were in Columbus. The town originally had been an arsenal, though most of the arms and equipment was later moved to Selma, Alabama. Following the Battle of Shiloh, Columbus became a hospital center for Confederate forces operating in Mississippi and Tennessee. Lee and other generals maintained headquarters there from time to time.

Lee and Regina each probably considered the other to be a good catch. She had been brought into contact with a wide range of prospective suitors, partially through her work as a nurse in one of the hospitals and partially through her family prominence. Her family's wealth and her own considerable personal charms added to her desirability. Lee on the other hand was good looking and charismatic. To be a lieutenant general at thirty-one was perhaps enough in itself to sweep Regina off her feet, but he had even more. He was a proven battle captain and a wounded war hero. She had been collecting newspaper clippings about him for quite some time; and in May 1864, she accepted his marriage proposal. They finally planned a wedding for 8 February 1865.[7]

One of Regina's disappointed suitors wrote to her: "I commission you to convey my congratulations to General Lee. . . . I have sometimes heard him called a pet of Fortune—but never until now, have realized how favored a child he is of that usually fickle dame." Having, like others, perhaps, noted Lee's characteristic luck—which Lee often actually helped to create himself—he displayed insight into Lilly's character when he continued, "You are much stronger than most of your sex. I have sometimes thought you talk and write with the mind of a man, and the heart of a woman."[8] It was a keen observation about the future Mrs. Lee, who had a strong influence on her husband in the years that followed.

Lee secured the services of several brigadier generals as attendants for the wedding. They included Abraham Buford, Randall L. Gibson, and Lawrence S. Ross. Lee also invited some other generals to attend the wedding, but they could not do so. Forrest on declining indicated that he and his wife "express the hope that the bridegroom in worshipping at the shrine of Venus, will not forget his devotion to Mars."[9] It was rather colorful literary flourish for a man whom many critics considered to be illiterate.

The wedding was a very elaborate affair, performed by the Right Rev. W. M. Green, the Episcopal Bishop of Mississippi. It took place in the Harrison home, a beautiful and interesting building, with a marble mantel supposedly imported from France, and the windows a modification of the French type—with sills that opened as if they were doors. Lee and his bride stood in a huge bay window to exchange vows.

Several of the soldiers present were in less than top physical condition. Lee himself had to stand and walk with the aid of crutches. General Buford was weak from wounds he had recently received, and at one point he fainted. The refreshments were being served, and he had reached over to receive a plate of smoking oyster soup when he collapsed, sloshing the soup all over his companion's dress.[10]

But nothing spoiled Regina's enjoyment of her wedding to the man she called, "the fascinating Gen. Lee." She wore a beautiful gown "in satin with magnificent point lace veil . . . , and she was all aglow with diamonds," a friend remembered. The friend continued: "After supper Lide and I sought an introduction to the General. He was dressed very magnificently and looked very handsome. . . . He received us very gracefully and talked very pleasantly. Everything was so grand and gotten up with as much style as the Confederacy could afford. . . . There was a band of music and we 'tripped the light fantastic toe' during the entire evening. . . . I enjoyed it all wonderfully."[11]

Lee remained with his bride for only a short time before he began thinking of a return to the combat areas. While in Columbus, he established the reputation of being "in social life a modest unassuming unostentatious gentleman." But he received mail from his comrades which turned his thoughts away from society, entertainment, or rest. One letter indicated that, "the corps misses you very much." And another remarkable note came from a fellow officer who also was recuperating from a wound: "I am all this time, the subject of surveillance by the Surgeons, who advise delay etc till the weather becomes less rigorous etc. But I am tired—tired to death of looking out of my door daily, yea almost every hour of the day, and seeing Tom who is 'pretty well,' well enough in fact to be with his regiment if he 'could only get the food there, suitable to his stomach' [sic] or Dick whose wound is 'healed' but 'too tender to withstand the winter of Va. or Tenn.' or Harry who 'really would go' but he does not know how he can possible [sic] reach his command when all the rail roads are cut either by Yankees or freshets! ! ! ! etc. etc. Such spectacles as these superadded to the croaking here, the disaster faction there, and the very general indifference everywhere out of the army, to what I conceive to be the most momentous earthly crisis which men were ever called upon to meet—embitters even the sweets of home to me. . . ."[12]

The words constitute quite an idealistic and patriotic denunciation of the shirkers in any war. This was the kind of friend that Lee cultivated and corresponded with; and this particular man, Patton Anderson—quite a capable general himself—considered Lee well worthy of emulation. He continued, "I rejoice that you and your corps [at Nashville] did all that skill endurance and courage could do and that the country demanded. The enemy themselves admit as much. Then I may be pardoned the vanity in saying that *I am proud to belong to that Corps.*"

Part of the Army of Tennessee already had returned to active service. Forrest's cavalry remained to guard Mississippi. The remainder of the army, including Lee's corps, moved toward Georgia and the Carolinas to unite with other remnants to oppose Sherman's forces. Gen. Carter L. Stevenson remained in temporary command of Lee's Corps, the first unit to leave Tupelo, starting at dawn on 10 January, on the Alabama and Mississippi Rivers Railroad. They encountered so many obstructions and difficulties that Stevenson recommended that all the other units move by way of Mobile. Hence, it was several weeks before effective forces would be moved into the eastern area. The Federals learned that Lee's men were on the way even before they got through Georgia.

Meanwhile, the Confederate Congress refused to confirm Lee's original promotion to lieutenant general. They had never gotten around to considering it; and when at last they did, they decided not to confirm the appointment because he had "been relieved from the discharge of the duties in the command to which he was appointed."[13] Only two weeks after his wedding, however, Lee left on crutches to rejoin his corps. President Davis immediately resubmitted Lee's appointment as lieutenant general and made no mention of the proposed date of rank. The original promotion was dated 23 June 1864; so when the Senate finally acted, on 16 March 1865, the original date stood, and Lee remained the twentieth ranking Confederate general.[14]

Meanwhile, on the recommendation of Robert E. Lee, Davis reappointed Johnston as army commander. Davis rationalized that Johnston was "the only officer of rank superior to that of Lieut. General who was available." Stephen Lee sent congratulations to Johnston and happily noted that Davis also had promised Johnston full support. Johnston glumly replied to Lee, "He will not do it. He has never done it. It is too late now, and he has only put me in command to disgrace me."

At any rate neither Lee nor Johnston had any intention of merely going through the motions of service. They were hard-fighting and determined men. Johnston took the field and ordered Lee temporarily to establish a rendezvous camp at Augusta, Georgia. There the stragglers, returning wounded, and men coming back from furlough were collected and organized. Lee gathered 5,000 soldiers, arranged them in arbitrary nonpermanent brigades, and left Augusta with them on 18 March. They marched through South Carolina, arrived at Rock Hill on 29 March, and there boarded a train bound for Johnston's headquarters at Smithfield, North Carolina.[15]

Meanwhile, Johnston clashed his forces against Sherman's men in the Battle of Bentonville, 19–21 March 1865. Since Lee had not yet arrived, Daniel H. Hill commanded Lee's Corps. Sherman had a large force of approximately 60,000; Johnston had only about 18,000.[16] Nevertheless, the gray-clads almost succeeded in achieving a modicum of victory; and had they been able to do so, it would seriously have hampered Sherman's immediate plans for operations.

One of the Confederates' crucial blunders resulted from confusion in Lee's corps, brought about partly by misunderstanding and lack of teamwork among the generals. But the corps itself fought valiantly and showed some of the spirit Lee had infused in it. "No one who witnessed the inspiring sight can ever forget the charge of S. D. Lee's Corps," one observer remembered.[17]

The battle raged for three days; but after losing their one chance for success, the Southerners were able only to hold their ground in a bloody stalemate. The Federals lost 1,527 in killed, wounded, or captured; the Confederates suffered far worse losses, 2,606.[18] Both proportionately and in actual numbers, the South suffered another disastrous defeat.

Johnston retained his headquarters at Smithfield, about sixteen miles from the Bentonville battle area. There he began to reorganize his badly damaged army. The Confederacy had collected all of its available personnel to bolster this force, and the high command included a number of notable generals, as well as the full generals,

Beauregard and Bragg. When Lee arrived with the reinforcements from Augusta on 31 March and resumed command of his corps, there were four lieutenant generals and twelve major generals.[19]

In the reorganization Johnston divided his army into three corps, one each under Hardee, Stewart, and Lee. The new troops that Lee brought from Augusta raised Johnston's total strength to about 20,400—just over a third of the number that Sherman had. But the Confederates suffered still another disadvantage: many were unarmed. The government did what it could to supply these troops; but even as late as 10 April, the day after Robert E. Lee surrendered in Virginia, more than 1,300 of Johnston's men still had no weapons of any sort.[20]

When Lee had marched through Chester, South Carolina, Mrs. Mary Chesnut noticed how forlorn the men looked. She wrote in her diary: "Today Stephen D. Lee's corps marched through. The camp songs of the men were a heartbreak, so sad and so stirring. I sat down as women have done before and wept. Oh, the bitterness of such weeping! There they go, the gay and gallant few; the last gathering of the flower of Southern manhood."[21] Most of them probably realized that the Civil War was nearly over.

Johnston himself began to suspect that the end was near, and he ordered that all executions be stopped. Meanwhile, much of his troop strength dwindled away as many men deserted. The desertions increased after word reached Johnston's forces of Robert E. Lee's surrender. Finally, on 19 April Johnston announced to his men that he had agreed to a cessation of hostilities while he negotiated with Sherman; and then on 26 April, Johnston surrendered.[22]

For the second time Lee became a prisoner of war, and, as before, he was quickly paroled. He received his release on 1 May 1865, at Greensboro, North Carolina, where the Confederates had been marched to turn in their arms. And there Lee had a friendly visit with his first unit—the old artillery battery from Charleston, South Carolina, that had given him his first chance for field duty in the war.[23]

After their surrender the sad and weary southern soldiers started home. Their short-lived nation was collapsing, and their way of life never would be the same again. During the uncertain years ahead, their society and their whole culture would be altered by the will of a people whom they considered different. Few other Americans ever have had to bear such an experience. Lee's chief engineer, Maj. S. A. Jonas, rather touchingly and pathetically testified to the feeling that many of the men had, when he presented Lee with a Confederate bill on which he had written:

> Representing nothing on God's earth now
> And naught in the water below it.
> As a pledge of a Nation that's dead and gone,
> Keep it, dear friend, and show it.[24]

Lee went home to his wife in Mississippi and never again saw active military service, ending nearly fifteen years of life as a soldier and closing a war career that never has been fully understood or properly appreciated. One of the most professional of soldiers, he was completely devoted to the Confederacy. Nevertheless, many of his contemporaries, and most historians of the period, failed to perceive him as he really was, a man with limitations and great talents mingled together.

As the popular Confederate Gen. John B. Gordon said, Lee was "a brilliant campaigner, . . . one of the most effective commanders on the Confederate side,"[25] and he showed flashes of creativity throughout his career. In retrospect his best performance was at Chickasaw Bayou, but he won credit at every turn: levelheadedness at Sumter, initiative and tenacity in Virginia, self-aided good fortune at Second Manassas, capability of functioning effectively against insuperable odds at Antietam, and executive qualities on many occasions as a general. In brigade command before Vicksburg, he stood out, having no peer; with the Mississippi cavalry division, he accomplished a difficult mission utilizing painfully limited resources, as he also did on a larger scale in departmental command; in the Army of Tennessee, he quickly became the best of its corps commanders.

What then were his limitations? Modesty and inflexibility were his worst characteristics. One might justifiably add his lack of sparkling brilliance; but apparently, his stern professionalism controlled his flair. Then too, for all his good luck, his opportunities for building a big reputation were scant. He did not receive an important command until 1863, and then he led only small bodies of troops in missions that did not attract widespread attention, until he took over a corps almost at the war's end.

Lee himself did not exaggerate his achievements. As newspaperman E. A. Pollard observed, Lee was "shy and reserved except with those he knows well, [and] it is only in such company that he does himself justice."[26] Lee never allowed reporters to travel with him, and he gave very few wartime interviews. Nevertheless, he consciously assumed modesty, believing that such a tactic would give him an even greater reputation when the public finally discovered what he considered the truth and in old age, he revealed deep concern about his place in history.

His personality, and the way he did his job, hindered him from achieving the kind of historical notice he desired. Subdued charisma probably won him many friendly responses and cooperative efforts and made very few enemies. But it also failed to attract much attention. He did his job in a low-keyed manner, always well, and always thoroughly. How ironic that his victories invariably were somewhat less than spectacular, or else he did not receive exclusive credit for them. He lacked the color and the oddity that would have made him more individually memorable.

The final word on Lee the soldier has to be *competent;* no man in the Confederate military exceeded him in this quality. Not a war genius, as possibly Stonewall Jackson and Bedford Forrest were, not a great field marshal as was U. S. Grant, nor an army commander never to be forgotten as was R. E. Lee, S. D. Lee nevertheless made a consummate contribution. Geniuses and field marshalls do not win wars without competent men like Lee to help. The Confederacy desperately needed more S. D. Lees.

During the years that followed, as Lee became variously a planter, insurance executive, politician, educator, and patron and benefactor of the study and writing of history, he continued to show the same degree of competence. His administrative ability, tenacity, attention to detail, and almost uncanny luck enabled him to master a wide variety of situations, as he made a notable mark in the New South, helping and improving the region, while providing his family with an easier, richer, fuller life.

11

A Gentleman in Troubled Times

THE YEARS FROM 1865 through 1877 constituted a quiet period for Stephen Lee. He established his permanent home in Mississippi, and he devoted most of his energies to carving out a new life. Although he did not isolate himself completely from the outside world, he engaged in far fewer and less important public activities than in the decades thereafter. Not quite thirty-two years old at the end of the Civil War, Lee was still a young man. He would outlive most of his Civil War contemporaries, the average age of the other former Confederate leaders who survived the contest being about forty-five.[1]

Compared with many Southerners, Lee and his wife, Regina, had an easy time during Reconstruction. Mrs. Lee's wealthy grandfather, Maj. Thomas C. Blewett, had lost his slaves, but many of them stayed to work on Blewett's lands. Soon after Lee returned from the war, Blewett gave him and his wife a plantation in Noxubee County, two hundred seventy acres, later increased by the purchase of five hundred acres. Blewett called the gift "the York plantation," but the Lees named their holdings "Devereaux." Lee and his wife owned part of their lands jointly, though she retained some in separate ownership—probably most of the portion given by her grandfather. Lee farmed for about ten years, sometimes working in the fields himself, but mostly sharecropping with blacks.[2]

Lee was not a successful farmer; and when he gave up farming, he was disillusioned about the prospects of making a living on the soil. He specifically criticized several conventional agricultural methods then used in the South, and he based many of his ideas to improve these methods upon the lessons he learned in this decade after the war. But more than poor techniques hurt Lee as a farmer. He tried the occupation in a turbulent time. Cotton prices fluctuated erratically, and the labor supply remained undependable.

Lee at first enjoyed good relations with his Negro workers, but the situation changed eventually. Blewett credited Lee's presence with prompting the blacks to remain as long as they did and wrote in 1866 that if Lee "had not been on the place, it is more than likely all my negroes would have left me."[3] But finally many of the workers did leave. Probably this too was partly Lee's fault, as he became convinced that all blacks were lazy. "It is a fact known to those best acquainted with the Negro race since the war," he later wrote, "that more and more of them are becoming idle, and are not giving us as good work as they used to do."[4]

Lee was not militantly "anti-Negro," but he was a stereotype of those of his time and place. He held the paternalistic view of blacks, characteristic of certain aristocratic white Southerners. Race was not usually a big issue to Lee, and he devoted very little attention to the race problem. He rarely touched on it in his public statements and writings. In one of the notable exceptions, he wrote that the Negro, "when left to himself without the strong will and example of the white man, . . . tends to retrograde; when outnumbered by the whites, . . . he assimilates more to the habits of white men, becomes a better laborer and a better citizen."[5]

Lee's only child, a son, was born on 1 March 1867. The baby was named Blewett Harrison Lee—receiving the surnames of his mother's father and her maternal grandfather. Regina's father wrote, "Poor little thing, it little knew what a world it was coming into, or the prospects in the future, or it would not have been in such a hurry in getting into it." Mr. Harrison, a politician and not a military man, looked more pessimistically than Lee did toward the future. Lee loved his boy very much. He sent ex-President Jefferson Davis a bottle of whiskey to drink to the lad's health, and he wrote boasting letters about him to his friends. He was so exuberant and excited that when writing to Wade Hampton he forgot to mention the boy's name. As the child began to grow, Lee spent a lot of time with him. They were warm companions, often reading and studying together, and obviously enjoying each other's company. One woman recalled seeing them frequently out on excursions. Lee's friends generally regarded him as a wise father.[6]

Aside from his happy home life and the financial help of his wife's grandfather, another factor also helped Lee to enjoy peace of mind. Like many other military men, he was resigned to having lost the war. In an application to President Andrew Johnson for a pardon, Lee wrote that he "fought out the war upon fair, and manly principles and according to the modern useages of war." He had surrendered and now considered the contest at an end. He took the amnesty oath and stood "now ready to defend the Constitution and yield obedience of the laws."[7]

While willing to obey, Lee certainly was not happy about the process of Reconstruction after it became more harsh. "The reign of the provisional governors and military officers," he asserted, "was very odious. . . ." He felt special displeasure over the second Freedmen's Bureau Bill: "A more ingenious law to show distrust and alienate the negroes and whites of the South who had to live together, could not have been framed." He believed that the agents were corrupt and claimed that they "cause friction, encourage idleness by raising false hopes of support and obtaining lands from the government, and create the impression that their [Negroes'] rights could only be obtained through them," in order to "prolong the necessity of their offices being continued." He disdained the purpose of the investigative Congressional Committee of Fifteen and declared that "a more one-sided, partisan, unfair, ungenerous investigation was never set on foot against a helpless people." He called Congressional Reconstruction a period of "destruction . . . the greatest trial that the South had to bear, not excepting the terrible ordeal of war."[8]

Lee believed that blacks asserted much unwarranted power during Reconstruction and that the blame chiefly rested with the Carpetbaggers. "The negroes were never very much blamed by the Southern people," he wrote, "for the whites felt that the influences surrounding the negro . . . were irresistible under the circumstances." Quoting another Southerner, Lee asserted that a "splendid picture in general of the carpetbagger during the days of reconstruction" went like this: "His shibboleth is 'the Republican Party.' From that party he sprung as naturally as a maggot from putrefaction. Wherever two or three or four negroes are gathered together, he, like a leprous spot, is seen, and his cry, like the daughter of the horse leech, is always, Give, give me office. Without office he is nothing; with office, he is a pest and a public nuisance. Out of office he is a beggar; in office he grows rich till his eyes stick out with fatness. Out of office he is, hat in hand, the outside ornament of every negro's cabin, a plantation loafer and the nation's lazy-bone; in office he is an adept in 'addition, division and silence.' Out of office he is the orphan ward of the administration and the general sign-post of penury[,] in office he is the complaining suppliant for social equality with Southern gentlemen."[9]

With such feelings about Reconstruction, it is interesting that Lee never became contemptuous of President Ulysses Grant. In fact, Lee always spoke highly of Grant. He respected Grant and deferred to his military victory. Lee's son recalled that "during the whole of the reconstruction period . . . the burden of the defeated South was made more tolerable by the steady kindness and the understanding, one might almost say the sympathy, of General Grant." Obviously the son did not remember hearing Lee speak bitterly of Grant. In fact, Blewett went on to say, "I cannot remember . . . to have heard a harsh word spoken in our own section about General Grant."[10]

Lee also kept aloof from the quarreling that raged occasionally among former Confederates. Thus he never joined with the many Southerners who castigated Jefferson Davis, blaming him for the South's defeat. "I have always been of the impression," Lee declared, "that no other Southern man could have held the Confederacy together as long as did Mr. Davis."[11] In later life Lee remained a warm friend, staunch supporter, and frequent correspondent of the ex-president. Interestingly, unlike typical Davis sympathizers, Lee also consistently honored and respected Robert E. Lee. S. D. was not as close to R. E. Lee as to Davis, but he corresponded with R. E. and always lashed out at any critics of the Virginian. As S. D. Lee aged, he developed a personal philosophy that blended the "lost cause" reverence exhibited by many of Davis' other followers and the "progressive New South with emphasis upon modern education" that R. E. Lee preached.

Although Stephen Lee took part in some extra-legal activities designed to "enforce the peace" during Reconstruction, he did not belong to the Ku Klux Klan. Apparently, however, he did not strongly disapprove of the organization. His son recalled in a 1927 speech that "as a child I have been by my father led to his plantation gate so that I might see the long procession of the Ku Klux riding past, mysterious, silent, and white." Lee wrote sympathetically about the Klan's activities in Noxubee County, Mississippi, where "there were ten negroes to one white person," and Lee felt that "lawlessness and a tendency to riot and override the laws of social life, became so great that a crisis appeared to be near, as shown by abusive language, disorderly meetings, and incendiary proceedings." He said that the Noxubee Klan, by its presence only and not by violence, helped to maintain order.[12]

Lee himself joined—as did many whites during Reconstruction —in night patrolling of Negro areas. His son recalled: "Night after night my mother held me, a babe in her arms, as she watched my father ride away to join the patrol of the roads through the dark hours, so that there might be no reenactments upon the prairies of Mississippi of the terrible deeds done during the race insurrection of the island of San Domingo."[13] Such fears seem unjustified in militarily occupied Mississippi, and possibly Lee actually joined in terrorizing activities against Negroes; but given his character and his other known actions, that probably was not the case. More likely he and his companions genuinely feared outbreaks of unlawful violence—by whites and blacks both—and took steps to prevent such occurrences.

For some years Lee and his wife enjoyed a very happy home life and were able to socialize on occasion. Regina loved to entertain, and one of her friends recalled her as "a queenly woman in appearance and gracious in bearing," possessed of three highly admirable qualities, "beauty of person, cultivation of mind, and loveliness of character." The Lees either hosted or exchanged warm and friendly correspondence with numerous high-ranking military and civil figures of the Confederate period.[14]

Suddenly tragedy struck. Sometime in 1868, when she was twenty-seven, Mrs. Lee's health began to fail. She had hydropsy—an abnormal accumulation of watery fluid in certain body tissues and cavities—which for the rest of her life, another thirty-five years, she suffered with intermittently. Her mind remained sound, and she always helped Lee in many respects; but ultimately she became a semi-invalid. She and Lee took many trips to try mineral springs, or other medical remedies, but nothing helped. As the years passed, she appeared less and less in public.[15]

Lee remained devoted to his wife and tenderly ministered to her. The illness probably provided the catalyst that prompted him to join the Baptist Church. Perhaps he had been contemplating it for a long time; he began to profess a belief in God during the Civil War, but had not belonged to any church. He later recalled that the first serious religious thought he ever had in his life was at the Second Battle of Manassas. Looking out across a vast open field before the Yankee hordes charged over it, he said, "well there is hell to play here, for sure, and . . . nothing but some unseen and superintending power, can tell where this thing is going to end." He was baptized and became active in church affairs, beginning around 1868, soon being made a deacon and known as a "man of prayer."[16]

At about the same time the Lees took up residence in Columbus, Mississippi, where Regina's family lived—the largest town in the area. Thereafter they went only occasionally to the plantation. Their first home in the town was called "Hickory Sticks," a beautiful and large edifice on a hilltop. They lived there until the 1880s, when Lee became the first president of the Mississippi A. & M. College, and then they moved to Starkville.

During his middle period Lee engaged in several activities indicative of his future interests. He joined with other Confederate veterans in various projects—mostly efforts to erect monuments and memorials to those soldiers who fought or died in the war. He also became impressed with the need to preserve the history of the war, at first mostly trying to persuade others to write, but doing some himself, completing his first narrative article in 1876.

At some point during his farming career Lee joined the Patrons of Husbandry, better known as the Grange. The organization originated in 1867 as a nonpolitical, fraternal group dedicated to the self-improvement of farmers. The first Grange in Mississippi formed at Rienzi on 20 May 1871, but it functioned only in the northeastern part of the state. In 1872 a state-wide organization was achieved, and during the next years the Grange spread throughout Mississippi.[17]

The Grange supported some rather far-reaching reforms—which people who harked back to the "Old South" would not find desirable. Lee heartily endorsed these progressive ideas. Soon after he became discouraged with farming, in early 1876, he told a South Carolina newspaper reporter that "the efforts to keep up the systems of large farms which contain thousands of acres . . . have reduced the people to bankruptcy." Lee described the condition of the agriculturalist in Mississippi as "deplorable, and growing worse every year." And he had a solution to suggest: "The only remedy I can conceive of is to reverse the order of affairs under which it is all brought about, reduce the large farms to small ones, introduce citizens from the Northern States by inducing them to come with their capital and buy our surplus lands. The Grange of Mississippi, of which I am a member, is exerting itself to this end. . . . Speedier and better results will follow from the introduction of Northern immigrants into our midst than from any other source."[18]

Lee later would make some real contributions toward bringing these and other progressive goals to fruition; as far as he personally was concerned, he had had enough of farming. "I have been assiduously engaged in farming in Mississippi, with such unsatisfactory results that I became demoralized and have rented my lands," he declared.[19]

Actually Lee had been trying for some years to get a satisfactory position in some business. He began corresponding on the matter with James Longstreet as early as 1866. Longstreet wrote to Mississippi Gov. Benjamin G. Humphreys recommending Lee for the presidency of the Mobile and Ohio Railroad, calling both Lee and another candidate, "very superior men." Lee himself wrote to Humphreys asking for the position of vice-president, but both jobs went to other applicants.[20]

Meanwhile Longstreet tried to find a position for Lee in New Orleans. He wrote Lee, "I think it quite likely that I may have a good opportunity to bring your name forward at a favorable moment for some more pleasant business than your life as a planter." He promised, "I shall look for a good paying and comfortable place for you." And he revealed what Lee had intimated to him as a motive: "I think it a wise conclusion on your part to seek some position that will bring you in contact, more, with the world."[21]

Longstreet continued his efforts to help Lee. In May 1866, he wrote that "there is so little of business now that all enterprise seems to lag. So that I doubt whether anything pleasant for you will open before fall or winter." And when winter came, Longstreet still had nothing for Lee, but he promised that "I have now fixed upon a plan. . . . we can secure your election as Secretary of our insurance company." Longstreet indicated that his real goal was ultimately to make Lee president of that company, Longstreet's own position, because "I have two offers of something else." But ultimately all of Longstreet's effort in Lee's behalf failed.[22]

Lee bided his time, but six years later he still was interested in the insurance business. He corresponded with his old friend Dabney Maury, who also worked in that field. Maury did not offer Lee a position but gave him some instruction concerning the proper conduct of an insurance company.[23] Finally in early 1876, at the age of forty-two, Lee secured the office of superintendent of agencies for the Alabama Gold Life Insurance Company. Headquartered at Mobile, Alabama, the business operated in all of the Deep South states. A New Orleans newspaper noted that "the company is one of the soundest and most prudently managed corporations in the South. . . ."[24] Lee was the only former high military figure among the executive personnel, and presumably the company expected his main contribution to be an illustrious name to bring in new customers.

The job required Lee to travel a great deal, and often in towns where he stopped he was invited to make a speech. He still cut an impressive figure, and audiences considered him to be quite a good speaker. One reporter described him as "tall and commanding in appearance, and with the soldierly bearing and polished address and grace of manner peculiar to the Southerner of the best type, added to a strikingly handsome face and a stalwart physique."[25]

Lee's first business trip took him through Georgia and South Carolina. That year, 1876, was the United States centennial year, so there were many public gatherings and celebrations. Lee usually was invited to attend—and often to participate in an official capacity. In South Carolina his friend Wade Hampton did not "take any stock in the Centennial," but Lee was an enthusiastic partisan in the patriotic proceedings. At Charleston he deeply impressed a reporter, who wrote that Lee "proved what we have so often declared, that those who were first in war would be first in peace—real peace of equality and mutual benefit."[26]

Lee took a long trip through Texas in the summer of 1876. There he worked in conjunction with another Alabama Gold employee, Cornelius Baldwin Hite; and the two men sold a number of policies. This success particularly pleased Hite, since he shared in the profits of policies that Lee helped him write up. Lee's military reputation was a magnet to customers. Hite had been what he himself called only "a high private" in the war; but newspaper reporters writing about his trip with Lee called him "captain," and he wrote his wife that "no one here is below the rank of Captain." Lee's affable manner also helped his salesmanship. Hite wrote that "Lee is a nice gentleman . . . , a successful canvasser of life insurance." In Dallas a number of the "first men" of the city honored Lee at a champagne toasting party which, Hite said, "passed off very happily for all parties concerned."[27]

Though quite successful in the insurance business, Lee soon had to give it up. His wife's illness flared up again, and he feared that his long absences depressed her. Just prior to this latest relapse, Mrs. Lee had been active in various endeavors. She had served as president of the Monumental Association (a Confederate monument erection and preservation society in Columbus), and she had been elected Honorary President of the Daughters of the Confederacy. The New York *Herald* included her in a list of 994 names of "the most beautiful women now on earth." After the relapse Lee returned home to take her on a trip to White Sulfur Springs, West Virginia, but she did not improve. Lee never rejoined the insurance company.[28]

Lee wanted to try something else anyway, and a new period in his life soon began. He entered politics, became a college president and launched a career in public life that continued for another thirty years. Thus, Lee took his place among the Bourbons—the southern Democrats who captured political offices and brought Reconstruction regimes to an end. *Bourbon,* as used in political history, means a politician who clings obstinately to ideas adapted to a past order.

The famous New South historian, C. Vann Woodward, notably in *Origins of the New South,* disapproves of *Bourbon* because he feels it implies a restoration to power of the ante-bellum southern leaders (or men of similar mind). Inasmuch as he sees them as new men with new policies, he prefers *redeemers*[29] and succeeded in convincing many colleagues and followers—but not everyone.

Woodward's issue has two sides. The southern political leaders between 1877 and the 1890s certainly were not clinging to the "Old South Ways of Agrarianism," but they were trying to restore a semblance of the old order as they perceived it. Sometimes they were corrupt, sometimes not; corruption is a red herring as far as the Bourbons are concerned. These men generally were industrialists or would-be industrialists vociferously advocating industrialism. They were entrepreneurs who established new industry and mechanization. They loved to use money—especially other people's money. They wanted to accomplish specific things. They were not Republicans but members of the Democratic Party who had a tinge of Whiggery that distinguished them from both other Democrats and Republicans. Classic conservatives, they resisted radical change and wanted to undo Reconstruction because they disliked what resembled socialist schemes of government and economy. But they did know how to accept change. They chose not to stamp out Negro suffrage, for example, though they did try to control the black vote. They retrenched state budgets, notably in the area of public education at the grade school level. But they made significant contributions to higher education in the South because they needed quality colleges so their children could perpetuate the new regime they were building. And this regime—and the society it generated—is what makes Woodward's argument lose some of its validity. The Bourbons were rebuilding a structured society led by men of status and oriented for their maximum benefit. While some Bourbons had a callous disregard for the masses, others did possess concern—they just happened to be convinced that the kind of society they envisioned would operate best for all. Lee was such a man.

So *Bourbon* is very apt: these men were trying to build a new society, not exactly like the Old South, but very much like it in essence. The real shortcoming in the word results from the attempt of various historians to distill a "typical" Bourbon. The result is a stereotype which can easily be attacked from a number of directions.

Stephen Lee, like most Bourbons, was a special kind of Bourbon—but a Bourbon nonetheless.

Some scholars call the last quarter of the nineteenth century in the South "the Rule of the Brigadier Generals" because so many high-ranking ex-military officials held public office. Since Lee had been so high as lieutenant general, perhaps he had an even easier time in the competition for some of the posts that he wanted. At any rate, he not only was among the youngest but also became one of the most prominent of the fifty former Confederate leaders who made significant contributions to Mississippi's postwar economic and political life.

Lee's thinking fermented and matured in the twelve years after the Civil War ended, and in that period he molded the attitudes that dominated the rest of his life. Altruism and concern for reform became important. He never became involved in questionable deals. He displayed qualities of unselfishness and regard for others. He did what he did in the years that followed because Christian ideals strongly motivated him and because he sought first and foremost to enrich not himself but his region, the South.

12

Southern Bourbon
Strangely Flavored

ONE SCHOLAR WHO studied S. D. Lee's life concluded that "it was inevitable" the general should "sooner or later become involved in politics." Large numbers of ex-Confederate leaders did enter the political arena, particularly in Mississippi, which elected more Civil War veterans to office than any other southern state. Lee never had been strongly attached to any political party, and in 1876 he had told a newspaper reporter: "Excuse me from making allusion to the subject of politics. The extent to which official corruption has been carried is a disgrace to the 19th century, and the very mention of the subject is revolting. The whole subject may be defined as an official attack on the liberties and rights of the people."[1] But by the fall of 1877 Lee had changed his position. The state senate seat in his district became vacant when W. H. Simms was appointed lieutenant governor. Lee decided to seek the Democratic nomination for the office. Although one of Lee's friends proclaimed that the general was "by nature a Democrat," Lee's candidacy did not evoke favor from the regular Democrats of the district. Lee was too liberal to suit the conservative planters who were the Democratic leaders, and his membership in the Grange hurt him, since the organization never was popular with the majority of the influential Bourbons.[2]

The nomination would be decided by the Democratic district convention, representing the senatorial district of Lowndes, Clay, and Oktibbeha counties. This gathering, under the influence of its executive committee, nominated its chairman, W. W. Humphries, of Lowndes County. The disappointed Lee decided to run anyway, as an independent on a separate "Democratic-Conservative" ticket.

He had a chance, because the convention's action had divided the district. The planter class enjoyed strong representation in Lowndes County, and politicians in Clay and Oktibbeha saw the committee's action in pushing Humphries' candidacy as an aristocratic attempt to dictate to the rest of the district. Lee provided a rallying point for anti-Lowndes sentiment though he also lived in Lowndes.

Lee planned his campaign carefully. At one point he announced that he did not wish to run; and although his statement seemed to breathe lofty resignation, it actually was a clever political ploy. Trying to avoid an image as a selfish office seeker, he wanted to explain why he had chosen to crusade against the regular Democratic Party. In a letter to the editors of several newspapers he wrote: "While I would not decline to serve my fellow citizens and be proud of their preference for me, if it be their evident and manifest wish, I will certainly never from desire of office trouble them to provide for me. I submit the whole matter to the judgement and consideration of the people of the District."[3] In result, many letters flowed into the editors' mailboxes warmly supporting Lee. Naturally he did not withdraw from the contest.

The anti-Lee forces finally resorted to the race issue. They charged that on election day the independents planned to bring crowds of Negroes to the polls, in the evening, just before the balloting closed. "Lee's tickets are already in the hands of the negroes," they asserted.[4] In truth, Lee made no bid whatever to the blacks. He did not have to. His strength came from the war veterans and members of the Grange.

Lee won the election. Humphries carried Lowndes, but Lee got a sufficient majority in the other two counties, and thus at the age of forty-five he became a state senator. He received his commission of office on 1 February 1878 and three days later went to Jackson to assume his seat in the recently convened legislature.[5]

Records of his activities in legislative sessions are scant. He made his biggest effort in support of the bill to create an agricultural and mechanical college, but he also supported a bill to organize a department of immigration and agriculture, and he fought one which attempted to reorganize the judicial districts. The few records indicate that when Lee voted he was on the winning side.[6]

Meanwhile, in Columbus, a controversy developed between the defeated regular Democrats and the Lee supporters. A regular

The Report that
Gen. STEPHEN D. LEE

IS NOT BEFORE THE PEOPLE IS A FALSEHOOD BEING CIRCULATED TO DECEIVE VOTERS.

CONTRADICT IT

WHENEVER HEARD AND BE PREPARED FOR THE

DESPERATE TRICKS

Of those who are circulating these reports to decrease his ASSURED MAJORITY. CLAY and OKTIBBEHA have spoken: they are SOLID, and ask LOWNDES to aid in swelling the majority of the PATRIOT AND SOLDIER.

Democratic leader, Bob Banks, reportedly made libelous public statements about Lee, and either he or Lee proposed that they meet in a duel. Lee sent his wife out of town temporarily and went about the business of trying to straighten things out. In an effort to find out what Banks had said, Lee wrote to the newspaper editor who most strongly had opposed his election and to Banks himself. Mrs. Lee's uncle acted as Lee's confidant and messenger. Finally the whole thing blew over. Lee satisfied himself that Banks, although bitterly critical, had not been libelous. Even though no duel took place, the incident illustrates that Mississippi politics were still highly personal.[7]

Lee served only two years in the senate, filling out an unexpired term. In 1880, he left office to accept an appointment as president of the a. & m. college he had labored to create. But he continued to feel the lure of politics, despite his idealism and lack of strong partisanship; and at intervals thereafter he toyed with plans of returning to the political arena. Thus in 1887 Lee considered running for governor. The campaign would not get under way for another two years, but already people were putting forward his name. Various newspapers endorsed him. One editor stated that it was a rarity for the men of talent to attain high office; hence Lee should not be allowed to "languish in obscurity. . . . he is ably fitted to be governor. . . . he is worthy to fill any position in the gift of the people." Another article indicated that Lee should be considered because he "has been prominent of late in building up the waste places of Mississippi."[8]

Obviously much of the support for Lee came from persons aware of Lee's interest in improving farming methods. Some of it came from the new Farmers' Alliance, which had become concerned primarily with scientific agriculture. But the boom for Lee aroused immediate opposition. Some critics sneered that he should not be considered a farmer. Said one: "He is in the college president business . . . and only indulges in a little fancy farming at the expense of the state." And for some he was "too closely connected with the Lowry administration for his own good."[9]

Lee's supporters replied to the critics. One of them said, "We are glad that Gen. Lee is in the college president business, and we believe it to be a fortunate thing for the state . . . , and the farmers of the state especially, have in him an earnest, able and faithful friend." Another declared that "it would be absurd and foolish for us to attempt to convince any well informed man that Gen. Lee is a farmer, because that fact is too well known." The same man continued, "It is however, supremely ridiculous to try to associate him with the Lowry administration . . . ; having nothing whatever to do with politics, Gen. Lee is a pure and good man."[10]

Some observers doubted that Lee had serious interests in running. One of them, Frank Burkitt, who became an arch critic both of Lee and of the college, charged that the general let his name be used only to arouse support for larger monetary appropriations for his school.[11] This thought probably did enter Lee's mind, but in all likelihood he really did want to be governor. He could have stopped discussion of his candidacy by asking the newspapers not to print letters advocating it. Instead he remained silent, and during the next two years the letters continued to appear. The authors were persons evidently representing all classes.

By and large these letters were laudatory of Lee. A typical comment ran, "He has all the elements fitting him for the post of Governor—learning, ability, integrity, and far seeing statesmanship." One of the most remarkable letters came from an anonymous "farmer," who said: "Gen. Lee has been an untiring worker since he surrendered epaulets in 1865 for everything calculated to develop the material interests of our State. He was one of the few men who pointed our people into the prosperity of this day. To him the farmers, and all classes of the State, owe the profoundest acknowledgements for his able and patriotic direction. . . ."[12] The farmers generally seemed to be swinging to Lee, and apparently the Farmers' Alliance backed his candidacy. Lee was not a member of the Alliance, but at first he exhorted others to become members. Later in the 1890s when it went into politics as the Populist Party, he broke with it completely.

By early 1889 the Lee boom reached its height. Lee's supporters announced him as "a man who would be regarded by every Sheriff and tax receiver and Supervisor in every county in the State as ever present with them, overlooking and revising their work." A statement like that perhaps did not win over many sheriffs or tax collectors, but it was popular with the people. Finally in April Lee himself openly announced his candidacy. Since he felt an obligation to his work at the Mississippi A. & M. College, he declared that he "could not, under any circumstances consent to . . . make a canvass of the State," but he would run.[13]

His announcement struck a theme that he consistently returned to: "I would be the Governor of the whole people, and use my utmost endeavors to unite all classes of our citizens in one progressive industrial movement." Then on 15 June 1889, he spoke at the courthouse in Columbus. In his speech, he revealed several tenets of his basic political philosophy. He first dispensed with race: "The question of white supremacy is no issue. That battle has been fought some time ago and won, that the white people should rule, not this State alone but the whole South. . . . But united as the white people are upon the subject, still there are divisions among them, and divisions among them mean division in the ranks of democracy. . . ." Then he touched upon his economic ideas: "Other Southern States are forging ahead to greater wealth and greater importance than we, and we must exert ourselves not to be outstripped by them.

"Enormous fortunes have been amassed, the rich have grown richer, the poor poorer, and the lines have been drawn between these two classes very strongly, and to the advantage of the rich. . . .

"Nine-tenths of the people are engaged in agriculture in this State, and yet most of the laws that have been passed have been for the benefit, directly or indirectly, of capitalists. This is not as it should be."

But he hastened to add that as governor he would not favor the agrarian class over any other. Rather, it "should advance equally with any other branch of industry. If farmers are not making money, then no part of the State can be prosperous. . . ."

On the subject of public education, he again showed himself to be nearly unique among the Bourbon leaders: "Our colleges, high schools, and common schools should be thoroughly taken care of."

Finally came the crux of his platform: "The thing we need most and above all others is white immigration. . . . Not the promiscuous immigration from foreign countries, but men who are already accustomed to the laws of this country. The people in the western and northwestern States . . ."[14] were preferable. The program was remarkable in spite of its leaven of racism and nativism. It squared with most of what his supporters claimed for him, that he was "an advanced thinker—a man of progress—abreast with the needs of the times—patriotic—sagacious . . . ," but it is rather difficult to see how the same supporters could in all honesty then conclude with their one final attribute: that Lee was "conservative," by which they apparently meant standpatist.[15]

Lee said that he would enter the campaign in earnest; and following commencement exercises at his college, he would make appointments for speeches all over the state. But two days later he received a letter from four members of the college board of trustees, imploring him not to run, but to remain at his job as president. Reluctantly, Lee agreed to withdraw.[16] The whole reason for Lee's decision not to continue with the campaign is very difficult to assess. Perhaps he sensed an insufficiency of support, though that is doubtful. It appears that he genuinely loved his work at the college, as he claimed, and that he became convinced that he could serve the people of Mississippi better as college president than as governor. Moreover, his flirtation with politics greatly improved his position for securing what he wanted at the college. Within three months he received a fifty percent increase in salary, and in the years that followed he achieved success in his battles with the school's critics and with those in the legislature who wished to decrease its appropriations.[17]

One year after withdrawing from the gubernatorial race, Lee won election to another political position. Oktibbeha County chose him as its representative at the 1890 Mississippi Constitutional Convention. In Oktibbeha County was located the a. & m. college, and local pride in the general-educator explains the choice of Lee. Also, his known views on white supremacy made him popular with the white voters. During the preceding decade, the 1880s, the county's Caucasian population had increased by only 650 as compared with an increase of 2,630 Negroes.[18] By sheer numbers the blacks posed an increasing problem for those whites who considered it essential to remain in some way superior to the blacks.

At the convention, Lee—the supposed conservative—sided with the supporters of various reform measures. Earlier he had become interested in the "Ocala Platform" advocated by the Farmers' Alliance, and he served as chairman of a committee urging the Constitutional Convention to oppose educational or property qualifications for voting, to favor an elective judiciary, to limit the terms of certain offices, to make railroad commissioners elective, to maintain a system of public schools, and to equalize taxation. The convention chose Lee as chairman of its education committee, and that group succeeded in establishing a renewed and larger system of free public schools—a step forward after the post-Reconstruction regression that took place in many Mississippi Districts.[19] And Lee made his most sensational contribution by suggesting remarkable innovations in women's rights, particularly female suffrage. Many opposed the proposal, including a number of newspaper editors, but Lee made a strong argument; "Women are entering all the professional and business spheres . . . ; women pay taxes. Some say that we do not wish to bring women into the mire and filth of politics. If politics are so corrupt, let us inject something that will purify it."[20]

Lee sincerely believed in women's rights. He often made speeches urging equal pay for women doing the same grade and character of work as men; and on one occasion he proclaimed, "Let us recognize the fact that our wives and daughters are our equals intellectually. . . ." Throughout his life Lee's attitude exceeded the typical upper-class Southern reverence for womanhood. He was quoted, aptly but probably apocryphally, as having proclaimed during the Civil War that the Confederates would not give up "because the women of the South would never agree to it." In later life, more than just good politics prompted him to say things like, "a coward would have had a hard time with the Yankees before him and the women behind."[21]

Yet an ulterior motive also partially motivated Lee in his crusade for women suffrage: he believed it to be a better means to secure white supremacy than by attempting to deny Negroes a vote. He was an unusually practical white supremacist: "We must retain our representation in Congress and the electoral college. We must either submit to negro rule, adopt the shotgun policy, or change our franchise laws." Thus Lee thought more subtly than most convention delegates. He believed that Congress ultimately would insist that Negroes be allowed to vote; and more important, he knew that the blacks wanted to vote. "Let us not fool ourselves. We know that the negro appreciates, and is proud of, his right to vote. He will undertake more trouble, and go further, to exercise this privilege than the white man."[22] So Lee's solution was not to deny the black man a vote but to assure that the whites always could outvote him by enfranchising the *taxpaying* women as well as the men.

Lee worked very hard at his arguments, making many speeches in favor of his proposal. In one, he displayed naiveté: "It is objected to as virtually giving plural voting to the husband. That need not be the case, for they can have separate polling places." In all the discussions, he advocated his scheme as a good one for everyone concerned. "If we be just and prudent there is no reason why the whites and blacks may not live together in all times in perfect peace and harmony."[23]

But in the end Lee could not persuade enough delegates. The convention disenfranchised Negroes, imposing a complex series of measures that included residence requirements, prior payment of a poll tax, literacy tests or the alternative of "understanding" the Constitution, and evidence of registration. In addition, numerous crimes became grounds for disqualification as a voter.[24] Although Lee did not support these provisions, he became convinced that the 1890 Mississippi Constitution was essentially a good document, one to be proud of. He lost out on his big issue, woman suffrage, but he gained some of his goals—and perhaps he saw a greater need to insure white supremacy than to institute other desirable reforms.

The urge for office tugged at Lee once again in the mid-1890s. He permitted, or perhaps himself launched, another newspaper campaign for the governor's chair. Again his motives were complex. The a. & m. college critics once more were threatening to cut appropriations, and Lee's candidacy provided a sounding board for fighting these men. But as before, he had a genuine thirst for the job; and as before, his boom collapsed.[25]

At about the same time, some of his supporters began to talk him up as a candidate for the United States Congress. Sixty-two years old, Lee seemed to relish his renewed popular image, and he travelled about the state making speeches and expressing opinions on various important issues. In particular, he advocated resuming celebration of 4 July in Mississippi (the state had not observed that date with any reverence since the fall of Vicksburg). "Politics will be better for [it] . . . ," he said, because "the Civil War and its issues are things of the past, and . . . the duty of patriotic citizens of every part of our common country is to strive with the citizens of every other section, in promoting the progress and glory of our grand country. . . ." He also took a significant stand in support of a stronger and better national guard—primarily because he expected lawlessness to increase in the growing cities—and he wanted state troops rather than federal forces to deal with the problem.[26]

But Lee was not destined to hold any more elective offices. The tragically failing health of his wife prompted him to withdraw his candidacy. Several years later, during the Spanish-American War, there was considerable talk—obviously politically motivated—that Lee would receive an appointment to some high position. Still later, in 1904, some editors spoke of him as available for the Democratic vice presidential nomination.[27] These were graceful tributes to the aged warrior, but they went no further than mere mention. Lee had finished his political career, which was always overshadowed by his contributions to higher education, themselves enhanced by the added influence that his political lustre conferred.

13

"Gen. Lee Runs the College . . ."

BY THE LATE 1870s Lee desired some sort of position in the field of education. Jefferson Davis recommended him, probably at Lee's request, for the vacant presidency of the University of Alabama. Lee maneuvered while a state senator to become head of the planned Mississippi A. & M. College, which the legislature established during his term in office. Soon afterwards the board of trustees began holding meetings, and construction of buildings got underway. But not until 1880 was the school opened and the president selected. By then a considerable amount of popular sentiment had developed in favor of Lee for the post. On 1 April 1880, the board met and elected him. Various factors weighed in his favor—he was well known and popular with the people, he was a champion of progressive agricultural methods, and he had established himself as a friend of the farmer.[1]

He began his career as an educator with an open mind and a willingness to learn, but most important, with determination to be successful. During the spring of 1880, just after his election to the presidency, he and his wife toured colleges in Michigan and Iowa, gathering ideas and suggestions. He recruited a number of the first Mississippi A. & M. faculty from these northern schools, and thus both he and the board commendably showed that they cared more for a successful establishment of their institution than about any sectional bias.

In spite of disappointing delays, Lee pushed doggedly ahead. The date for opening the college had to be changed several times, but it finally was set for 6 October 1880. The dormitory and president's home were not yet complete, so Lee turned for help to the Starkville residents and asked them temporarily to supply rooms and board. When the dormitory finally was finished Lee lived in it with the boys. The college operated for men only at first, but by 1886 five female day students were admitted, starting a coeducational tradition that never ceased. This policy alone caused the college to stand out among southern institutions, which generally did not make provision for female students until much later. Lee learned this and many other innovative methods on his midwestern tour, and he was prepared to go quite far in their implementation.[2]

In his inaugural address, Lee spoke of industrial education as a necessity. Stressing the money value of an education, he indicated that a great many people earned their living in agriculture. But, he continued, the farming class lived at a disadvantage when contrasted with other workers. Therefore the farmers and mechanics had a right to have a college especially dedicated to training them to be better in their callings. He predicted that the South was on the verge of a great industrial development, and he enjoined all those present to recognize and take advantage of it. A reporter on the scene described the speech as "eminently practical" and well received by the crowd.[3]

Many persons interested in the college argued whether or not Lee had a plan to develop the institution. Unquestionably he did have a plan, indeed many plans, and he found it necessary occasionally to change them as situations developed. He had, by his middle age, greatly intensified his capacity for flexible response. Always pragmatic, he more clearly realized that desired goals often can be approached from several different directions. But regardless of plan, he certainly had a clear purpose. It was to make the college an excellent agricultural school, and then, if possible, a mechanical school—but never anything but practical. Lee carefully thought out every step that he took and probably discussed each with his remarkably bright wife. A favorite joke among campus wags was: "General Lee runs the college, and Mrs. Lee runs General Lee."[4]

One of the teachers described Lee as he looked during his presidency: "Physically robust, . . . head shapely and set forward firmly on broad shoulders, gaze searching and somewhat restless, countenance clear, kindly and serious, stride military, with toes outward and hands to the front. . . . Resolution and nobility were stamped upon his mein and bearing. By the toss of his head and the jerk of his arms alone, the students learned to read the signs of the times at his headquarters."[5] And these headquarters were busy indeed. Lee never functioned as a figurehead; he involved himself directly and enthusiastically in every phase of the college operation.

The first curriculum, a single one to be followed by all students, was designed to give a sound but agriculturally oriented education, culminating with a bachelor of science degree after four years of work. The subjects included mathematics, zoology, bookkeeping, history, drawing, English, horticulture, chemical physics, physiology, entomology, psychology, political economy, geology, civil engineering, agricultural chemistry, and meterology.[6] Always ready to adjust beneficially, Lee allowed several changes by the end of the first year, with different offerings of mathematics, English, and bookkeeping. Despite the rigors of the classes, and the woeful inadequacy of preparation that many students had received in Mississippi's spotty public school system, the college drew a large enrollment. A total of 354 matriculated during the first year alone, although of course a good number of these quickly fell by the wayside.

In addition to "book study," both dormitory and day students were required to do manual labor for two or three hours, five days a week, and more if they wished to earn extra money. Lee, who devised the plan in cooperation with one of the teachers, took great pride in the labor system and, in June 1881, proclaimed that the students "were as earnest in work as in their studies. . . . The youth of Mississippi are capable of anything where they are properly guided. If this college does not succeed, it is not their fault." While the work system was not unique, some of its aspects were. Not only did the students complete many desirable projects for the college and earn most of their way—Lee estimated the extra cost of an entire year at no greater than seventy-five to one hundred dollars— but the work system also had a democratizing effect. With everyone required to do something, the students gained respect for labor and laborers. "Bold," said Lee, "is the youngster who will make a slighting remark about work."[7] With Lee almost in the role of a general, the professorial staff responded to his effective leadership and developed the system into a potent part of the program.

Another requirement that all men students at the college had to endure was military training. Although the Morrill Act required only that military instruction be offered, not that all students had to take it, mandatory military participation was part of the plan from the first, and the initial regulations came from those in force at the Alabama Military Institute. In 1880 the trustees petitioned Congress for muskets, artillery, ammunition, and other military accouterments as well as for a regular army officer to be detailed to serve as commandant. Lee greatly admired the West Point curriculum, which he quickly adopted and which indeed some observers felt that he took over intact, though in reality it was not the letter but the spirit of the West Point system that he copied. He tried to mold the program with a singleness of purpose. Much to his credit, he looked upon military training at the college as a means to instill an attitude of mind, and not as something that had to be tolerated if ever it led to meaningless regimentation. As he said, the military should furnish only "the machinery of discipline, besides giving the boys a manly bearing."[8]

Lee made certain that he would have the last word in matters concerning the military system. The school's first commandant, 1st Lt. Edwin B. Bolton, quickly ran afoul of General Lee over an interpretation of his duties. Apparently Bolton's ideas of discipline did not adapt well from the battlefield to the college campus, and Lee had to censure him for issuing demerits which punished nonmilitary offenses. Bolton stood his ground, gathered his share of supporters, and caused a bitter controversy. The "clash of jurisdiction" required a meeting of the board of trustees for settlement, and the result was that the school requested Bolton's recall by the war department. Lee got along better with the subsequent commandants, but his ideas about discipline continued to prevail. Lee was not, however, an "easy" disciplinarian. He described his policy as "mild but firm," and his letterbook indicates that he expelled any students who committed serious breaches of rules or normal decorum.

Lee took pride in the large number of the school's graduates who went into the regular army or the militia. In 1894 he observed with satisfaction that over twenty per cent of the officers in the Mississippi national guard were former students of the college. But military men were never the primary product; "We breathe the atmosphere of agricultural advancement," Lee wrote, and the military feature served to enhance this goal. "Why do graduates of

West Point make good soldiers?" Lee asked. "It is because they are educated to be soldiers . . . [and see] nothing that is not military. . . ; [thus] when a man goes to an agricultural college, agriculture should be presented in its most attractive style." Lee built a school that made "agriculture attractive in every way so that when the boy wakes in the morning he will see beauties in the farm."[9]

As president, Lee became involved in numerous matters which seem small today, such as the installation of urinals and toilets.[10] But in establishing a new institution someone has to take care of even these details, and nineteenth century presidents of small colleges often did this sort of thing. Lee's distinction resulted from his pervasive interest in everything concerning the college. And his support was important because unless a project became one of his pet interests, in less capable or less dedicated hands it often floundered.

The library, for example, made a rather poor start under Lee; he gave it only scant attention at first. Inadequate funds delayed progress on many of the early goals. Most of the initial library items were gifts; and after five years of operation, Lee reported that the total expenditure for books had been only $2,200. He then began encouraging both the board and the legislature to spend more on books for the college, and two years later he criticized them both for being "penny wise and pound foolish." Finally, in 1893, the board yielded to his insistence and thereafter allocated a matriculation fee of five dollars for library use.

In the early years of the school, however, most of the students had less need for a reference library than for a better academic background. Free public education was still quite new in Mississippi, and many secondary school graduates discovered, to their chagrin, that they were not adequately prepared to do college work. Lee was soon lamenting in the press the deficiencies of the free public school system, but improvements could not be accomplished instantaneously. In the meantime, the a. & m. college established a preparatory department, which became a major part of the institution. Lee hoped to abolish the department eventually, but it remained a necessity during his entire administration.[11]

One of the first academic problems that Lee faced was a controversy between advocates of traditional college curriculum and those favoring radical "practical" innovations. For example, Lee wished to omit teaching Latin and Greek. "We ignore the classics," he explained, "so as not to antagonize, and to make our institution more technical and practical. We aim for a good English education." Much to his amazement, he found opposition from many parents and even a large number of the faculty. A sort of compromise was reached during the school's first year by offering the classics but making them elective. But Lee was firm in his opinion: "You cannot ride two horses—you must either be the ordinary classical and literary college, or you must be the industrial and practical and put on no 'airs.' They won't mix." In the end, he won out. The Department of Ancient Languages ultimately perished from a combined lack of funds and interest.[12]

The issue over the classics had been only the most significant of several struggles between the traditionalists and the innovators. Controversy on other subjects continued until 1882. Actually, a number of matters came to a head about that time; and during the academic year which began in the fall, Lee changed nearly the whole faculty. Pleased with the results, he finally obtained a group of men who shared his opinions. "It is an able Faculty," he boasted; "there is not a discordant element in it. . . . They believe in industrial education."[13] Actually the industrial aspects of the curriculum continued for some years to be secondary to the evolving agricultural courses. By "industrial," Lee meant a pragmatic emphasis.

Lee's ideas about agricultural education were progressive. Envisioning vast improvements, he selected worthy goals, searched constantly for means to achieve them, and seized opportunities as they arose. He asserted that successful farmers in the future "have got to bring brains and education to bear upon Agriculture. . . . We have to introduce the improved machinery of the Northwest." Lee became an advocate of the "New South," as preached by men like Henry W. Grady. Revitalization of the region, Lee thought, lay in industrial education for southern youth. Forecasting a "great industrial future just ahead . . . in the Southern states," Lee considered mechanization paramount; as he said, it was vital "to get the greatest amount of work with the smallest amount of labor."[14] His scrapbooks contain many of Grady's printed writings and speeches, frequently with underlining or notes added by Lee, and he used much of this material in his own speeches and presentations to the students, preaching both diversification in farming and scientific agriculture.

Lee encouraged the various experts among his faculty to engage in continuous experiment and determine what crops, livestock, or agricultural practices would be best for the different areas of Mississippi. One project that particularly interested him was educating Mississippi farmers to make the best possible use of poor soil. He desired to determine "the cheapest and most permanent plan of renewing the fertility on worn-out lands." He believed that cotton seed could be the answer, and he persuaded the board of trustees to authorize the purchase of ten thousand bushels of the seed for use as experimental fertilizer. He also took an interest in recuperative crops, and in 1881 the school began tests by sowing large portions of poor land in cow peas. Very pleased with the satisfactory results, Lee advocated cow pea cultivation as something that "every farmer in this State who has not the capital to buy fertilizers can do in improving his lands."[15]

In some instances Lee meddled with faculty projects to a degree that angered some of his otherwise cooperative professorial staff. For example, he differed with the opinions held by the head of the creamery. Lee wished the dairy herd to be larger than his subordinate believed it should be, but Lee finally gave in. Then the two men argued even more over what type of forage crops should be grown. Lee had a keen interest in lespedeza, a grass which he once described as the "compensation for our loss of negro slaves."[16] How that argument turned out is not known, but the general probably insisted that some lespedeza continue to be grown.

Although Lee took too strong a personal interest in certain activities at the college, his zeal fostered increased services and benefits. In 1888 he fired the livestock overseer to hire a better educated man, competent to conduct feeding experiments. He wrote to a new applicant for the job, "Unless you mean business and work you had better not accept."[17]

Lee labored for a long time to establish a department of veterinary science. In 1885 he strongly urged the legislature to make an appropriation for such a chair, and two years later the board of trustees did allocate some money for this purpose; but the inadequate amount failed to attract anyone qualified. Finally, in

1891, the college created a chair of veterinary science, with the aid of federal funds.

Another business activity which Lee hoped to introduce to Mississippi was the silk industry. In 1882, with the department of horticulture newly established, the first orders to the teacher enjoined him to engage in silkworm culture at the college. Lee expected that the project would "open the silk industry to the ladies of the state." But apparently the experiment was abandoned at an early date.[18]

Lee molded the college into an institution dedicated to helping both its students and all the farmers of Mississippi. This practice was not just public relations work. Lee and the trustees who supported him in these endeavors appear to have been convinced that public service was an integral part of the institution's purpose. The Patrons of Husbandry had been influential in helping to get the college started, and Lee never forgot the debt. He maintained warm relations with Put Darden, master of the State Grange, and Darden replied in kind: his annual addresses nearly always included favorable comments about the college. Whenever the state organization met, Lee or some high-ranking representative from the school attended.

One service that the Grange desired was faculty members occasionally to serve as lecturers at local agricultural meetings. Lee encouraged the teachers to do so, and soon the demand grew greater than the college could supply. A periodic farmers' short course began at the campus in 1884, and in the same year another more remarkable and helpful practice commenced. The school organized "farmers' institutes." Six such institutes came to be held each year at various locations throughout the state. Generally a team of two or more teachers, and occasionally some outstanding students, would go to the selected community and present a series of lectures and demonstrations to any organized group of interested persons who needed and requested the service. Response was instantaneous and enthusiastic, and institutes were held regularly until the late eighties when they had to be abandoned for lack of funds. Lee worked continually to revive them; and although it took him almost ten years, they were thriving again in the late nineties.

Still another of Lee's goals for the college was the establishment of an experiment station. Agitation for it began early; but as with so many projects, fruition required a long time. In 1884 Lee still was seeking financial aid through Congressional action, and meanwhile he tried to prove to Mississippians that the college was doing experimental work with or without the desired station. In 1885 he announced through the press that the college had accumulated results on experimental work in "feed crops, grasses, ensilage, cotton seed and meal farming, field tests of fertilizers, feeding, drainage, vegetable and small fruit growing, milk and butter making, and the determination of the value of feed stuffs and fertilizers." The results, he said, were available to any organized body of farmers or newspapers that solicited them.[19]

Finally the Hatch Act, signed by President Grover Cleveland on 2 March 1887, solved the problem. It provided $15,000 annually in federal funds for each state or territory establishing an experiment station. Apparently Lee and others feared that the state legislature might divide the experiment station funds, giving a share to the all-Negro Alcorn A. & M. College. Consequently Lee addressed the legislators, arguing that the experimental station should be a "centralized operation." If any of the lawmakers needed convincing in the first place, Lee succeeded. The Mississippi Agricultural Experiment Station, to be built at Mississippi A. & M. College, was created by legislative act on 26 January 1888.[20]

From the start, Lee played an active role in the station's operation. He hired as director Samuel M. Tracy, an energetic administrator with experience in agricultural experimentation. At first the two men got along well, frequently working closely with one another. Lee advised Tracy to visit the University of Wisconsin, Yale University, and Rutgers, to solicit advice from the specialists in experiment station work. By 1893 Lee had five men, all proven researchers, working full time at the station and reported that several of the other faculty were giving part of their time to the work. One of the first projects that the staff embarked upon was to establish branch stations to conduct specific experiments on the spot in Mississippi's various soil areas. The first such branch began at Holly Springs in 1890, and several others operated later in Lee's administration.[21]

Apparently Lee conceived the original idea for one particular experiment: a plan for a series of irrigation tests designed to "eliminate disasters incident to temporary drouths in portions of the State where rolling or valley lands can readily supply water from creeks or ponds." He hoped that soon even farmers with small areas "will be independent of dry weather. . . ."[22] Although the results did not constitute a panacea, they did show a number of improvements that Mississippi farmers could achieve, and both Lee and the man he chose to conduct the tests expressed considerable enthusiasm.

Lee did not entrust this project to Tracy but gave it instead to the head of the horticulture department. Apparently miffed, Tracy sharply criticized the conduct of the experiment. Another personality clash ensued, and the following year the board requested and received Tracy's resignation.[23]

In spite of his inability to harmonize with some of his subordinates, Lee generally had excellent relations with his faculty. The instances when men had to be summarily dismissed merely indicate that Lee was taking a significant role in many facets of the college operation. It was natural that not everyone could fit into the organization he demanded. He ran a very military and well-disciplined school, considerably more so than was typical of similar institutions, but the few disputes that occurred centered not on objection to this but upon academic and mission related disagreement. The board of trustees always expressed complete confidence in him; and occasionally when he desired personnel change, they were glad to honor his request.

Lee was so committed to improving the agricultural aspects of the curriculum that at first he neglected the mechanical area. He encouraged only enough mechanical training as might be useful to a farmer.[24] In 1882 one of the faculty requested funds to obtain equipment for engineering work, and Lee replied that it was not yet possible to begin developing in that direction. But by 1883 he admitted that popular pressure was growing for an engineering course; and although he never became enthusiastic about it, he began to indicate in the next few years a willingness to go ahead with mechanical training if the legislature granted additional revenues to support it. Public sentiment continued to mount in favor of engineering courses, and in 1889 Lee took a positive stand and attempted to induce the legislature to relent from its continued parsimony. He even went to the trouble of quoting provisions of the Morrill Act and of a state law passed in 1878, both of which required land grant colleges to offer mechanical training. In 1891, when the legislature still had not acted, the trustees took it upon themselves to earmark a portion of some unallocated funds to create a mechanical department.

Organization proceeded quickly thereafter, and in 1892 Lee asked the legislature for $10,000 to finish setting up "the mechanical feature" and got it. Less than a year later a clamor arose for additional technical courses, particularly in electricity, and Lee asked the legislature in his 1893 report for another $10,000 to electrify both the campus and the engineering course. It was "important," he explained, "that the boys of Mississippi be instructed in an electrical laboratory to fit them for the industrial pursuits now just ahead."[25]

Lee did not get the second $10,000, and the campus had to do without electricity for several years more; but he refused to give up. He complained in 1895, that "every State is establishing schools and laboratories for the instruction of its youth, so they can keep up and get employment in all industrial work. . . . Mississippi boys are going out of the State to get this instruction. . . ." By the end of 1896 no progress had been made toward securing electricity, but Lee continued waging his campaign. "Two years ago," he chided, "I urged the legislature as to the importance of this matter, [and] since that time almost every village and town in the State has been lighted by electricity, and the work has been done by men imported from the North and adjoining States."[26] But Lee's arguments fell on deaf ears. Not until 1897 did the board of trustees reallocate revenues from the fertilizer fund and order the establishment of an electrical plant and laboratory.

Lee's single greatest problem as college president for the entire nineteen years of his administration was defending the institution from its enemies and preventing them from choking it to death by getting its appropriations cut. The detractors of the school found their leader in an Alliance and Populist Party political figure, Frank Burkitt.[27] This man came to represent the exact opposite of much that Lee stood for. A colorful spokesman, in public he wore a wool hat and a Confederate uniform, and he pitched an appeal to the common people's baser instincts. Using all his powers as a public figure and as a member of the legislature, he tried to destroy what he called the overly "expensive" and wasteful school for "bookfarmers."

In 1887 Burkitt wrote that "the A. & M. College has been in operation seven years; during which time $392,000 of the people's money has been expended . . . and if [Lee's] salvation depended upon it he cannot name fifteen graduates of his college, who are today engaged in practical agriculture." The essence of Burkitt's philosophy was that "the Mississippi Industrial schools are gigantic frauds."[28] Perhaps he based this contention in part on conviction, but it appears that spite for Lee and a thirst for greater personal power also spurred his actions. Nevertheless Burkitt scored some points, because an alarming number of the graduates did forsake agriculture for other fields, including Lee's own son who graduated in the first senior class and then went off to Harvard to study law. The numerous other early graduates who went into law or medicine caused Lee much embarrassment, and he carried on a perpetual, sometimes almost frantic, search for students who would become agriculturists upon graduation.

The maneuvering that Lee used to fight Burkitt included a careful handling of press releases; frequent checks to assure that the school gave maximum service to the industrial classes for which it was created, particularly the farmers; the compilation of statistics to refute Burkitt's charges of extravagance and waste; and personal appearance before the legislature to defend the school and advertise its accomplishments. Perhaps Burkitt's attack on A. & M. College prompted Lee to flirt with the possibility of running for various offices himself, particularly the governorship. Lee's motives for entering politics always were complex, but they frequently seemed to contain an element of calculation that the action somehow would make the college appropriations more secure. He was on safe ground, because he prompted such comments from admirers of his educational policies as, "We would make him governor, or United States Senator, but we cannot spare him from our college."[29]

During the lean years, when Burkitt was most threatening, many members of the faculty deemed it necessary to leave for better paying positions elsewhere. Lee even saw some of his college's own graduates, whom he utilized as replacement faculty, find higher pay at other schools. However, the institution also had its staunch supporters. Many newspapers, including some very influential ones and especially the agricultural press, rallied to the defense. The list of out-of-state newspapers that wrote complimentary passages about the school grew to impressive length. Certain individuals who were prominent in state and national affairs gave what help they could. But the mass of the common farmers, as represented in the Grange, provided the strongest volume of praise.

Lee employed several methods to enlist the farmers on his side. His most successful tactic was to invite them, and organizations that represented them, to investigate the college and its work. In another effort he tried producing some of his own propaganda. He wrote a lengthy series of popular newspaper articles eventually published together in 1889 as a pamphlet: *The Agricultural and Mechanical College of Mississippi, Its Origin, Object, and Results Discussed in a Series of Papers.*

Although Burkitt replied, "He who excuses himself accuseth himself," and called Lee's "labored newspaper articles . . . a maze of irrelevant matter," Burkitt's forces finally were vanquished during the 1890s. Lee won his battle with the college critics, and legislative appropriations became somewhat more liberal thereafter. John K. Bettersworth in a history of Mississippi State University credits the institution's survival from Burkitt's onslaught to "the resistance of the Mississippi farmer to agitation and to the generalship of Stephen D. Lee."[30]

Lee remained steadfast and loyal to the school in spite of hard and frustrating times and tempting offers from other institutions. Over a period of several years, colleges in Tennessee, Georgia, and South Carolina tried to induce him away, offering considerably higher salaries than he received in Mississippi, but the general would not accept, even refusing in 1890 a most attractive offer from Clemson. Lee had a passion for his job, and he made it his principal mission. He always took pains in his labors, but they seemed to agree with him; "I am in splendid health," he wrote in the late 1890s, "working harder than I ever did in my life."[31]

In 1899, when he finally retired as college president—even after so long a time in office—many persons lamented his leaving. Perhaps they realized that even to this day Lee would be remembered as the man who made the deepest imprint upon the college. Mississippians recognized and hailed his contributions. He received many tributes, including being named in 1900 as a member of the board of trustees, which promptly placed him on its executive committee. Thus his influence continued for the rest of his life, another eight years. Probably H. Dent Minor, a member of the first A. & M. graduating class, wrote the most touching and appropriate compliment: "The man who won fame in fighting for the Confederacy has my admiration. But he is of small importance when compared to the man who has made the A. & M. College."[32]

Not only had Lee indeed "made the A. & M. College," but also he deserved the title that one of his admirers bestowed upon him, "Father of industrial education in the South." With the land grant system in its infancy, Lee had shown the same celerity he had displayed on the battlefield and had developed a first-rate institution from meagre resources. Lee boasted that he had accomplished a veritable revolution in state agriculture. He had done just that, not suddenly—the change was more evolutionary than revolutionary else it might have been only a flash in the pan—but his was a deliberate, careful, and lasting accomplishment.[33]

Many persons—other educators, politicians, newspaper commentators—admired and commented upon Lee's contribution. Responding to Lee's careful cultivation of good will with the Grange, one local group passed a typical resolution recognizing the college as "one of, if not the very best, of its kind in the United States." Later, when Lee occasionally courted further political office, the editors of numerous newspapers urged him to desist because he was needed at the college, and one lamented that his loss would "strike almost a death blow at one of the grandest institutions of the South." The South Carolina statesman, Benjamin R. "Pitchfork Ben" Tillman, proclaimed that Lee was doing more for the farmers of Mississippi "than all the Confederate brigadiers from Virginia to Texas" and asserted an ambition to emulate him and match some of his accomplishments in "agricultural advancement and enlightenment." And, in 1896, Tulane University formally recognized Lee's eminence as an educator and awarded him its fifth honorary Doctor of Laws degree.[34]

Lee's zeal never lessened, and he never became unwilling to grow and improve. Tirelessly he journeyed to Jackson whenever the legislature was in session, "not as a lobbyist," he insisted, "but to look after the interests of my college, and see that it is properly represented before the legislative committees." As early as 1883 he had begun to establish graduate work on the campus, which interestingly included a beneficial leaven of required work in the humanities, and he expanded other programs in the 1890s. During the lean years a number of the graduates remained as members of the faculty, while quite a few others made respectable names for themselves elsewhere.[35] In his twilight Lee could look back upon his college presidency with the warmest of satisfaction.

14

Comrades Who Wore the Gray

MOST CONFEDERATE VETERANS required a number of years after
the close of the Civil War to revere it as a "glorious conflict" or
form organizations to perpetuate its memory. Numerous factors—
the Reconstruction experience most notably—deterred the growth
of large-scale fraternal movements among ex-southern soldiers. But
the South's veterans gradually did drift into communion with one
another. Individual efforts to provide decent burials, care for families left without a breadwinner, and aid the indigent frequently
evolved into group projects. Lee lent support to some of these, the
first being a music festival in 1871 sponsored by the ladies of Nashville, Tennessee, on behalf of a Confederate orphan fund.[1]

Southern women were the first to form "Confederate-oriented"
organizations, and the men quickly joined with them. One such
group established the observance of an annual floral memorial day,
beginning first in Columbus, Mississippi, and they paid for the construction of numerous monuments to the Confederate dead. Another, the Northeast Mississippi Confederate Veteran Association,
founded on 26 April 1866, sponsored some social activities, although its primary purpose was cemetery improvement and maintenance. It continued to have a separate existence, unaffiliated with
other organizations, and was still going strong in 1894, when Lee
served as its commanding officer.[2]

Far more typical were the many organizations that ultimately
merged to form the United Confederate Veterans. Many company
associations organized in areas where whole units had been mustered from a single place. Other veterans soon came to desire the

kind of fellowship and association enjoyed by the company groups, so they began to form veterans' organizations that were based upon geographic divisions. Memphis, Tennessee, had one as early as 1866. Men who lived close to one another enjoyed getting together and did so through convenience without regard to where they had served during the war. County veteran associations proliferated throughout the South during the 1870s and 1880s.[3]

One of the first groups successfully to organize with membership based upon service in a large unit was the Association of the Army of Northern Virginia. It originally had been formed as the [Robert E.] Lee Memorial Association, dedicated to the erection of a suitable monument to their late commander in chief who had died on 12 October 1870. William N. Pendleton served as chairman of the executive committee. John C. Breckinridge was selected as the first president, and each state represented in the organization provided a vice-president. Lee served as the first one from Mississippi. On 4 November 1870, the group met and decided to continue in existence as a fraternal association. In addition to fellowship, it took as its primary goal the collection of historical materials, muster rolls, and any other information relative to the Army of Northern Virginia. Lee continued his membership and served as a prominent orator at a fund-raising ball in 1877, but he did not attend any of the social reunions.[4]

Lee's first purely social affair with a large group of veterans occurred 13–14 February 1888 in New Orleans, Louisiana, at a gathering of ex-Confederate cavalrymen from thirteen states. Instigated by Col. George Moorman, the commander of a Civil War cavalry regiment from Kentucky, the meeting was a huge success. The group unanimously voted to form a permanent organization and elected Lee as president. They also selected a vice-president from each state represented—in almost every case an ex-general of Confederate cavalry. In his acceptance speech Lee explained, "This is the first reunion of Confederates I have ever attended. I have been invited to many, and why I did not go I cannot tell you. When I received the request from Colonel Moorman to come I hesitated, and said, 'Why go now?' but something took hold of me and my coming here was compelled by an irresistible impulse." He received thunderous applause and then continued, frequently referring to the veterans as "comrades"—a term of endearment that quickly came into wide use among the Southerners. "Comrades—I come here because I desired to look one more time in the face of those who shared with me common danger. . . . The tie that binds us together is one welded out of our common misfortunes—yet made up of glorious memories."[5] The time was ripe; the veterans were ready for Lee's words.

The United Confederate Veterans (UCV) was born in 1889 at New Orleans in a meeting of fifty-two delegates from nine separate veterans' organizations. The precise number of members that the UCV had then or later is not known because it never published exact information on its total membership. Official records reveal only the number of local units, called camps. A mere thirty-six camps sent representatives to the second national reunion meeting in 1891 at Jackson, Mississippi, but the number increased to 188 at New Orleans by the following year. The organization grew rapidly throughout the 1890s culminating with 1,555 camps represented at the 1898 reunion. The next few years marked the zenith of UCV membership. About 1903 the veterans began to die off rather rapidly, and the UCV went into a gradual but permanent decline.[6]

By far the largest and most significant of all the Confederate veterans' organizations, the UCV included men from the navy as well as the army. "We need something of this kind," Lee explained, "to keep alive the sacred memories of the War. The patriotic devotion to our beloved country . . . , the ardor with which we rallied around her flag, the indomitable heroism with which we followed it through danger and disaster: when we meet together all those memories come with a rush. We feel a thrill of pride that nothing can alter."[7]

One of the most important factors that gave the United Confederate Veterans growth and stability was the monthly magazine which in 1894 became its official organ, the *Confederate Veteran*. Many veterans, including Lee, penned recollections or articles for publication in it. A highly successful publishing venture, readership always exceeded the circulation because many camps and soldiers' homes received one or two copies to be read by a great many men. An average of between six and seven thousand copies of each issue was printed during the first year of publication, for example; but its editor estimated that fifty thousand people read the twelfth issue. Lee gave a personal testimonial to the magazine's value, saying that "such a means of communication is absolutely necessary."[8]

Of course Lee became a charter member of the UCV, and he played a significant role in it. He mingled his forward-looking ideas and efforts with reverence for the cause for which he had fought in war. Typically, he addressed an 1895 gathering of Union veterans, saying, "We invite you to invade us again, not this time with your bayonets, but with your business." Nevertheless he always added a word in his speeches to southern youth in his audiences, admonishing them "to preserve and defend the record of your forefathers." This, he said "is not in any way incompatible with true and loyal allegiance to our government as the issues of the great war are settled and accepted by all." In fact, Lee contended, "to us the Confederate Veterans is due the resurrection called the New South, which we bequeath as an inheritance to our sons. . . . Reduced from wealth to poverty, overwhelmed with indignities, we have secured our political rights, brought prosperity and order out of chaos, and never forfeited our self-respect."[9]

UCV members at the first annual reunion reelected the original officers by acclamation. Thus started a precedent of keeping any incumbent officer for as long as he would serve. The veterans chose Gen. John B. Gordon as the first commander in chief and two department commanders: William L. Cabell and Edmund Kirby Smith. Lee did not have a high official position at first, but camps were named in his honor.[10]

The UCV, like any proper American organization, felt it had to outline its purposes and structure in a written constitution, and the veterans designed theirs along military lines. Members holding appropriate UCV "ranks" officered and staffed echelons of command from general headquarters at the top to local camps [companies] at the bottom. The whole membership met annually in a general convention and reunion, presided over by the commanding general.[11]

The department level, two at first and later three, corresponded to an army corps. They were headed by a lieutenant general, UCV, and were ultimately named after the various Confederate armies. The department remained primarily an administrative entity and held no functions of its own. On the next lower level were the divisions, commanded by major generals, and they conformed to state lines. These units often held their own annual meetings in addition to the general conventions. Next came the local camps, the real centers of interest for the mass of the veterans. Many camps acquired their own buildings or clubrooms which served as social centers, and most of the significant relief work done by the UCV was accomplished by these local units.

Although the organizational structure of the UCV was mock-military, the group's announced purposes remained emphatically nonmilitary—to foster "social, literary, historical, and benevolent ends." The annual reunions served as aids to the UCV for accomplishing these goals. The affairs continued to be held long after the UCV membership peak had been passed, and gradually they increased in attendance, length, and splendor. Many Southerners considered them to be major social events. Convention cities made elaborate preparations and usually tried to put on bigger spectacles than had the previous hosts. Numerous veterans took their families and friends along too, further swelling the crowds.[12]

In spite of certain benefits that the UCV accepted from the United States government, such aid never became one of its primary goals. In fact one of the most marked differences between the northern and southern veterans' organizations was that the GAR placed first importance upon securing more and better government pensions, while the UCV officially concerned itself with pensions only occasionally. Many Confederate veterans genuinely came to need a pension of some sort as the years passed, but the UCV aimed its appeal on their behalf at the various southern states rather than to the federal government. Most states responded generously.[13]

The UCV was happy with state action, but it did seek federal aid indirectly. For example, it attempted several times to get the United States government to return the cotton tax which had been collected after the war, because the veterans thought that the states would use this money to finance a more liberal pension program. The UCV also urged an increase in the benefits that the federal government paid to veterans of the Mexican War and their survivors. Confederate veterans who were also eligible for Mexican War veterans' benefits did receive them. Once, a group of UCV members attempted to persuade the organization itself to pension maimed or helpless Confederate veterans, but their efforts did not succeed. Thereafter the UCV limited its action in favor of benefits specifically to urging state help and carrying on a public information program to identify areas where more help was needed.[14]

Although the UCV declared itself to be nonpolitical, it did dabble in politics to some extent. Candidates for office quickly realized the potential power of such an organization, and often they sought to win concerted support from the veterans. Of course, a goodly number of the candidates were themselves veterans and could attend UCV functions as members. But the strength of their vote to elect certain candidates was not what primarily interested the veterans. They had specific goals which included state pensions, soldiers' homes, and relief for the needy. They used political tactics and pressure to secure these things, but they rationalized that their goals transcended politics and were humanitarian rather than political in nature.[15]

Lee's role in the UCV continued to become more and more significant. In July 1892, at the age of fifty-seven, he was elected to command the Mississippi Division. Under his administration, which lasted approximately two years, the division grew from sixteen to forty-eight camps. This was the same time as the beginning of the rapid growth of the whole organization, and Lee seems to have increased in prominence concurrently with its progress.

By 1894 many UCV members expressed interest in redividing the UCV into three departments, and wide support in favor of Lee as commander of the new department developed almost immediately. At the reunion that year, the veterans adopted a new constitution that included the change to three departments. Since Edmund Kirby Smith, one of the original department commanders, had died in 1893, two new slots were to be filled. William L. Cabell continued as commander of the trans-Mississippi Department, Fitzhugh Lee was elected to head the Department of the Army of Northern Virginia, and S. D. Lee was elected commander of the Army of Tennessee Department.[16]

Some veterans questioned the desirability of the new constitution as a whole, however, and after the convention adjourned General Gordon refused to promulgate the new document. He ordered that the old constitution remain in effect at least until the next reunion. Among other things this ruling meant retaining the one department east of the Mississippi River, and Gordon had to decide whether Fitzhugh Lee or Stephen Lee would command it. Gordon chose the Mississippian.[17]

Lee's prominence in the organization, which had been rising dramatically for several years—a trend that continued—accounted for the choice. In 1892 Gordon had called upon Lee to preside over the reunion business meeting, Gordon's voice not being strong enough to be heard in the large hall. At the 1894 reunion one observer expressed the feeling that Lee and Gordon "were the lions" of the organization. In 1903 Gordon gave Lee temporary command of the UCV, and at Gordon's death the next year Lee became commander in chief by acclamation. "If there is any feeling against General Lee or *any* opposition to him as the commander of the veterans," one newspaper noted, "there was not the slightest evidence of the fact manifestd in the convention."[18]

The reunions always mingled serious ceremony with jovial and pleasant activities. The old soldiers showed great gusto. A newspaper reporter captured the flavor with his description of a typical veteran at the Charleston reunion in 1899: "His broad shoulders are stooped, his black slouch hat droops over a heavily bearded face, there is plentiful gray in his hair and whiskers, no fashionable tailor cut his plain suit or gray jeans, but the band is playing *Dixie* and the old man steps like an emperor." Gordon presided over the business meetings, wielding a special gavel that had been made for him out of a tree shot down by bullets at Chickamauga. When Lee became chief, the Confederated Southern Memorial Association had a new gavel made for him, using a piece of a gun carriage from Fort Sumter.[19]

As a top leader in the UCV, Lee was a tireless and faithful worker. He cited three significant tasks to which he thought the veterans should apply themselves in the time remaining to them. One was the continued erection of monuments, with more concentration upon dedicating memorials to the private soldiers, for it was they, he said, "who made our leaders immortal." The second was to insure that each veteran lived the remainder of his life proudly, never bringing shame or regret to others who had been Confederate soldiers. The last was to help take care of the veterans who were hard-pressed financially. He gave speeches wherever interested persons listened. Always he added a word urging that more monuments be erected, "first, for the sake of the dead, but most for the sake of the living, for in this busy industrial age these tablets and stones to our soldiers may stand like great interrogation marks to the soul of the beholder."[20]

One of Lee's most ardent and sustained efforts in the UCV was to venerate the memory of Jefferson Davis. The Confederacy's only president died on 6 December 1889. Five days later he was buried temporarily in Metairie Cemetery, New Orleans, in a large tomb belonging to the Association of the Army of Northern Virginia— which continued its existence even after formation of the UCV. Lee served as one of the honorary pallbearers. That night, at the hall of the Washington Artillery, he attended a UCV sponsored meeting of numerous veterans who had come to New Orleans for the funeral. There Lee made one of the principal speeches and offered a resolution "that we mourn the death of our leader as children for a father, and desire to say that we loved him living and revere him dead as one of the bravest soldiers, ablest statesmen, most peerless orators, truest patriot and most stainless Christian gentleman that the world ever saw."[21]

It took a rather long time to settle all the details concerning Davis's final burial, but at last in 1893 he literally had a second funeral. The body was removed from Metairie and, after lying in state at the New Orleans Confederate Memorial Hall, was transported by train to Richmond, Virginia. At numerous stops in important cities, and all along the way, hundreds of thousands of people turned out to pay homage. Lee took part in the ceremonies in both New Orleans and Richmond, traveling on the funeral train as one of the official UCV representatives.[22]

Lee became a leading force in efforts to help Mrs. Davis financially and to erect a suitable memorial to Jefferson Davis, but he achieved relatively little in tangible aid for the widow. In 1892 the UCV passed a resolution pensioning Mrs. Davis for life, but then failed to provide the funds. In 1897 the veterans officially endorsed Mrs. Davis's book, *Jefferson Davis, Ex-President of the Confederate States of America; a Memoir by his Wife,* and Lee sent out printed circulars urging its purchase. He had more luck with the monument. In 1894 the Confederate National Memorial Association was formed and announced that it hoped to raise $200,000 for a monument. The project succeeded, and the cornerstone was laid in 1896 during the UCV reunion.[23]

Lee, because of his vigorous and significant support for the effort, was given the honor of delivering the principal address. Friends considered the oration to be one of the best speeches he ever made. One account said it "portrayed in chaste style and eloquent words the character, public services and personal virtues of the great President of the Confederate States." "Varina [Mrs. Davis] wept as Lee spoke of her husband," one observer remembered. The widow wrote to Lee and said, "You alone of all my husband's friends recalled the wide range of his powers and capacity. . . ."[24]

After being introduced as "one whose help and courage in time of war has only been surpassed by his devotion to the South in time of peace, and whose special fitness for the position as orator on this occasion is best attested by the distinguished services which he has given in the preservation of the history of the South," Lee received loud cheers then and sporadically throughout the delivery. "When the mists of passion and prejudice have passed away the calm light of justice gives the right niche to each figure in history," Lee said. At times eulogistic—"The descendants of the men who to-day look on Jefferson Davis with unkind expressions will see him as we do— the stainless gentleman, the gallant soldier, the devoted patriot, the pure and gifted statesman"—Lee also touched upon the forward-looking aspects of his philosophy: "Suffice it to say . . . that the war has settled that secession is impracticable. . . . The Southern people have fully accepted the results—they accept the present, and loyally commit themselves to the future." He dwelled upon the positive virtues of Davis and the other Confederate leaders, spoke of the tragedies of the war, and observed that history offers lessons not only in stories about great successes but also in the experiences of men who fail and causes that are lost. It was indeed one of the more noble of his many speaking efforts.[25]

After living to see the monument completed in the last year of his life, Lee left a legacy of impetus for still another Davis memorial. In years past there had been a bridge across the Potomac River, with a plaque honoring Davis for his services as secretary of war under President Pierce. But during the Civil War the plaque had been removed. A crusade began to restore the plaque, and Lee gave it his personal endorsement at the 1907 reunion. By 1909, the year after Lee's death, the goal was reached; and the plaque was put back in place.[26]

Some Union and Confederate veterans urged from time to time that their two organizations, the UCV and GAR, hold a joint meeting. As far as the national UCV was concerned, the movement began in June 1900, at the Louisville reunion. The UCV had received "a greeting" from a high GAR official, probably pertaining to the "blue and gray" reunion that took place the next July in Atlanta. One UCV member offered a resolution that the northern and southern organizations exchange expressions of fraternal feeling, but Joseph H. Shepherd, a Virginia veteran, strongly opposed it. Both Lee and Gordon made rousing speeches in its behalf, however, after which, the UCV Minutes say, "the veterans stood and cheered and screamed and beat their canes and crutches on the seats . . . . the resolution was carried amidst throat-splitting yells." The only recorded negative vote was Shepherd's, and he tried to speak again but was forced to sit down.[27]

Despite this beginning toward reconciliation between the veterans, matters quickly became strained. One enraged UCV member wrote to the *Confederate Veteran* that he and thousands of the comrades were ashamed of the action taken at Louisville. The magazine's editor seemed to agree and indicated that "such proceedings made it appear that Confederates regarded themselves as people of doubtful standing in this country, and were eagerly appropriating signs of recognition. . . ." Then an unpleasant incident occurred at the Atlanta "blue and gray" reunion in July. The GAR commander in chief berated the Southerners there assembled for "the keeping alive of sectional teachings as to the justice . . . of the cause of the South, in the hearts of the children," which he said was "all out of order, unwise, unjust, and utterly opposed" to the terms of the surrender. Gordon immediately took the floor and angrily replied that he would never teach his children that what he fought for was wrong.[28]

The whole affair showed Lee that any future joint meetings obviously would have to be well planned; and when similar efforts arose after he became UCV chief, he insisted upon approaching the matter with caution. In 1904 a group of northern and southern veterans began working toward a joint convention for the next year and reported in its publicity releases that Lee had given his approval. Many rumors concerning Lee's opinion, some mingled with considerable inaccuracy, circulated throughout the UCV. Lee finally requested the *Confederate Veteran* editor to publish his statement that "such a reunion should only be brought about through the appointment of committees by the two commanders of the GAR and UCV, after the matter had been presented to, and discussed by the two bodies, at their annual meetings, and their full approval given." He said that he personally favored "all efforts tending to perfect reconciliation," but that "unfortunately, . . . I have been present at many of these Reunions, when some unwise or inconsiderate person said or did something which marred the occasion. . . ."

Although Lee closed the 1904 deliberations by saying, "I feel we had best consider the matter more maturely before acting in haste, unadvised, and possibly injudiciously" and, in June 1905, "I am sorry to say that it presents practical difficulties that will prevent its fulfillment for another decade," he did continue personal efforts to foster better feeling between the northern and southern veterans. In 1906 Lee and numerous Southerners attended a "Union and Confederate camp fire" in Chicago. Lee diplomatically made a complimentary speech about Lincoln and Illinois and the reunited country. Two years later, at Lee's death, the Chicago GAR post sent an official tribute to Lee, citing the "sweet fraternalizing spirit he exhibited." Numerous successful blue and gray meetings took place thereafter, culminating in a great gathering at Gettysburg in 1913, commemorating the battle's fiftieth anniversary. The veterans continued to recall Lee's contributions and gave him much credit for having laid the foundations for such meetings.[29]

Lee loved both the UCV and the blue-gray reunions, and once he tried to explain why the veterans continued to gather each year: "We come together because we love the past, because our lives have been linked together by a great experience. With us now, all passion and bitterness have passed away. We are holding only to all that is sweetest and best and tenderest in living." Both Union and Confederate veterans often spoke this way about Civil War memories. The war had been their greatest experience. No matter what happened to them afterwards, it remained the great moment in their lives. Lee often quoted Henry W. Grady, who said, "Out there at Appomattox, the Lord God Almighty laid upon every ragged gray cap the sword of imperishable knighthood." Lee would have agreed with Oliver Wendell Holmes, Jr. who said: "Through our great good fortune, in our youth our hearts were touched with fire."[30]

As chief of the UCV Lee symbolically became the greatest living Confederate hero; he lived up to the image magnificently. "I wonder sometimes," he said in his inaugural address, "whether . . . the cause we loved will seem as lost as it once seemed to us. It may be that in the province of God and in the development of humanity these fearful sacrifices were necessary for the highest good of this nation and of the World." "Truly in the human experience," he proclaimed, "without the shedding of blood, there is no redemption. . . . the shed blood has brought blessing, honor, glory, power, and incorruptible treasures. . . ." The greatest loss of the South, he went on, was not in burned houses and wasted fields, and ravaged cities, but in the men that the South lost. Yet, "my comrades," what "a comfort to know that the South had such men to lose. . . . What a magnificent race of men! What a splendid type of humanity! What courage! What grandeur of spirit! What patriotism! What self-sacrifice! It was sublime."[31]

A highlight of each reunion was a big parade, with the veterans passing Lee in review. In 1904 he insisted upon sitting on horseback because "that is where the commanding general should be to review his troops." A Louisville newspaper reporter captured the scene: "Proud and erect he sat his charger. His noble old form was held stiff and straight, with military correctness. Down his cheeks coursed tears. . . . Horse and rider were as one. . . . Looking every inch the great leader that he is, [Lee] lifted his hat in courtly salute. 'God bless you, old boys, my comrades,' he said. . . ." In the years that followed, most veterans had to stop participating in parades; but no UCV man who passed Lee ever failed to salute the chief. Lee always had to devote many hours to receiving the thousands of "grizzled wearers of the gray who came up to kiss the hand of their great leader."[32]

Lee tried to accommodate and please the veterans in small matters as well as the more important ones—for example, in supporting a resolution that the UCV give notice that it would not expect from future host cities the "splendid and lavish hospitality" which the veterans had been receiving. He said, "We do not want to impose burdens which would make other cities hesitate to invite us."[33] He also obviously thought of the advancing age and declining financial security of most veterans, both of which made it more and more difficult for them to continue spending very much money at the reunions.

Some veterans also complained about all the young girls who always were present at reunions. The girls served as "sponsors," but the veterans objected that they received all the comforts and attention instead of the old soldiers. Lee announced that he would discontinue the practice of choosing a general sponsor at the national level, but he pointed out that the various sub-echelons should decide for themselves. With this change, and by limiting the entertainment provided for the sponsors to that supplied by each individual escort, the matter was amicably settled.[34]

Probably the biggest welcome given Lee at a convention city was at Richmond in 1907, the last he attended. A tremendous crowd gathered because the meeting was scheduled to coincide with the unveiling of the Jefferson Davis monument. Hundreds of people met Lee at the railroad station and remained about him for nearly two hours, singing and cheering, until he retired to his apartment. Outside his window a band played "Dixie," and a crowd estimated at over one thousand cheered as he spoke to them. Looking "vigorous, hearty and hale, in spite of his seventy-six years," an observer wrote, Lee "smiled with pleasure."

In great modesty Lee once spoke of his high standing in the UCV and declared, "I am only chief because my comrades have gone before me."[35] Truly, he had been a worthy leader of the veterans, as at the same time he had been a significant contributor to the postwar welfare of the southern people. In this respect, one of Lee's most significant activities was his service in behalf of history and the impetus he added to the UCV in its historical work.

15

In Pursuit of Clio

LEE SHOWED LITTLE concern for the study or production of historical writing during his early years, but after his interest kindled he became more and more serious in the pursuit of Clio. "A people who do not cherish their past," he said in 1904, "will never have a future worth recording." By the standards of his day, he established a solid scholarly reputation, not only as an educator but also as an historian. Someone once introduced Lee by saying that "the true soldier must have the virtues of the true scholar, and the true scholar must have the virtues of the true soldier—General Lee has both."[1] Through the years Lee gradually had come to deserve such an accolade.

At the same time he also developed something of a philosophy of history. Staunchly empirical, he believed that sticking closely to factual sources was a requirement for valid writing. Lee believed that if the historian stuck to the records—and if enough records were available—history inevitably would yield the "truth." Yet, Lee contended, "there is lots of history about the War, that will not be true history," because of biased northern historians and certain inept or misguided southern ones. Lee urged that Southerners, particularly Confederate veterans, gather historical data and prepare writings for publication. "I think if we did more of that," he mused, "it would be better for us and the country." Such history, "should be brief, and state facts boldly, and cite authorities." That procedure would, Lee believed, lead to certain conclusions: recognition of Stephen D. Lee as a great soldier; the realization that the South lost the Civil War because of "superior numbers and resources, under the wisdom of an overruling Providence"; admission that the courage of the southern soldiers had been "sublime"; and acceptance of the idea that the war had not been a struggle between a "united North contending with a united South" but a "united North contending against a divided South."[2]

Lee valued the opinions and recollections of participants in historical events. In fact his first historical activities after the Civil War involved giving his own opinions and recollections to numerous veterans, the first being John B. Hood in late 1865. The two exchanged letters frequently, and Hood included some of them in his memoirs, *Advance and Retreat*.[3] In 1866 Lee corresponded with Daniel Harvey Hill, who was editing a magazine—*The Land We Love*—and who solicited Lee's contributions.

Also in 1866 editor Hill received a manuscript sketch of Lee, written by W. H. Brand of Columbia, Missouri. Hill desired that Lee or a friend look over the material and polish some of the details before publication. "Brand is a beautiful writer," Hill wrote, but, "he is greatly at a loss about dates and sometimes about facts." Furthermore, Hill perceptively argued, "I think your fame as a general officer in history will rest chiefly upon the defense of Vicksburg, and retreat from Nashville. Brand does not bring these out sufficiently." Interestingly, Hill also objected that Brand "likes to give that poor jerk Pemberton a side lick occasionally."[4]

Certainly Lee was not a man who wanted to see Pemberton given any kind of "lick." Lee and Pemberton exchanged warm letters and mutual praise for their soldierly abilities. Through the years after Pemberton's death, Lee often spoke in the latter's defense—and had quite a few opportunities because Southerners resisted forgiving Pemberton for the loss of Vicksburg. To the end of his own life, Lee wrote statements such as "I have always felt great injustice was done General Pemberton," and "General Pemberton did all he could in the campaign and defense of Vicksburg"; and Lee tried hard to prove his opinion with data from the official war records.[5]

For the most part Lee refused to denigrate any prominent ex-Confederate, though there were a few occasional exceptions. For example, although Lee respected Joseph E. Johnston and assisted him once or twice in preparing his memoirs, *Narrative of Military Operations*, in which Johnston spoke of Lee only in laudatory terms, Lee nevertheless did feel constrained to criticize Johnston's military ability. In Lee's opinion, Johnston had been too cautious to fight unless he had equal strength; he lacked the courage to gamble on fighting for total victory. Lee also could bring himself to speak somewhat harshly about any southern veteran who criticized either Stephen Lee or any of Lee's personal heroes—especially Robert E. Lee and Jefferson Davis. Thus Lee and James Longstreet had a cool and strained relationship in their later years despite Longstreet's earlier efforts to help Lee in business.[6]

Lee's two most significant contributions of material for other people's books were in 1868 for George Denison, an English student of cavalry, and, beginning in 1878, for James F. H. Claiborne, author of a massive and broadscoped history of Mississippi. Lee gave Denison an incisive and analytical commentary on the effect that new Civil War weaponry had had on cavalry tactics. For Claiborne—with whom he also exchanged numerous letters—Lee penned many pages of narrative about military activities in Mississippi. Unfortunately Claiborne published only the first of two projected volumes, and the manuscript for the second, as well as some of the documents upon which it was based, were burned in a fire that consumed Claiborne's home in 1884.[7] But some of Lee's notes survived—and, more important, he had begun serious historical work himself. Once he began he never quit.

In preparing letters to Claiborne, Lee had thought out and expressed many historical evaluations and opinions. These include: Lee's confession of what he really thought had happened at Tupelo; that Grant was always unwisely underrated by the South, both as a general and as a politician; that the Spring Hill incident "was a criminal affair of somebody's and necessitated the fight at Franklin"; that his corps saved what was left of Hood's army after Nashville; and that for the whole 1864 Tennessee campaign "Hood is not free from blame, he could have personally directed the movement when he saw delay—My opinion is, that Hood with his leg off at his hip, and maimed arm, was physically exhausted . . . [and] it is a matter of doubt as to whether any soldier so maimed, should have such an important command."[8]

It is interesting that so many of Lee's subjective statements bear upon operations that he participated in with Hood. No doubt Lee felt he had received inadequate credit for his wartime exploits, and perhaps he harbored some jealousy for not having gotten command of the Army of Tennessee himself. One thing is certain; Hood's friendship meant much less to Lee than making sure that Hood said nothing detrimental about Lee in *Advance and Retreat*. It is hard to see what prompted Lee's apprehension, though he did construe certain questionable implications in some of Hood's public statements. Lee wrote to Claiborne that Hood "had best be careful in theorizing, not to reflect on me. . . . I have fairly put him on his guard, and he had best not make a mistake." One wonders what Lee would have done. Of course nothing ever became necessary because Hood never intended to criticize Lee. Nevertheless, despite Lee's final satisfaction on this point, he never particularly liked Hood's book and gave it an unfavorable review.[9]

More pleasant by far were Lee's historical dealings with Jefferson Davis. In 1873 Lee wrote Davis asking for advice on what to do with a body of official war papers that he had retained, "hoping some depository would be indicated for them where they could be useful." Davis suggested a place for the papers and at the same time asked Lee for reminiscences to help with writing his own memoirs. The exchange began a lengthy correspondence between Lee, Davis, and Davis' literary helper, William T. Walthall. Lee visited Davis at least once to talk over the project and later provided Walthall with a considerable amount of material.[10]

Lee's most active period of labors in behalf of history began at the same time that he became interested in organized veterans' affairs, and many of his efforts were associated with UCV endeavors. This factor, and the appearance of the federal government's publication (1880–1901) of the official records of both Union and Confederate armies, account for Lee's writing. Lee and the UCV members believed that the ready accessibility of so large a body of factual material would result in accurate writing about the Civil War and would provide a convenient means of checking and proving errors. Even before certain volumes appeared that Lee desired to use, he secured copied excerpts through the cooperation of Gen. Marcus J. Wright, the agent for collection of Confederate records, and Col. R. N. Scott, one of the editors. After the series was completed, Lee led the UCV in public expressions of thanks and praise for the excellent job he thought had been done in putting the set together and making it available for use.[11]

Likewise, in 1904. when the UCV discussed the U. S. government project to publish rosters of the Confederate and Union armies, the veterans decided to express public thanks to those federal officials involved and to aid the work by contributing as many pertinent old records as they could find in southern hands. After some investigation, many members discovered that some rosters had been lost or destroyed, and they began an effort to supply the missing rolls from memory. When Lee learned of these attempts, he issued a stern admonition that only official and original manuscripts be used. Attempts to pad the existing rolls continued, and Lee requested that the press give wide publicity to his UCV order against supplying undocumented information.[12]

Lee occasionally gave endorsements to monographs or picture books. Several themes stand out in the endorsements: his laudation of southern women, his valuation of truth in history, and his view of history as a means whereby posterity may avoid pitfalls of the past. "No women were ever truer, braver, or more devoted to a cause and displayed more fortitude and sacrifice than the women of the South," he said in one typical advertisement. On another study, that had to do with the mistreatment of prisoners during the war, Lee wrote that "although it is not pleasant to recall what you have so faithfully recorded, yet it is history and should be truthfully recorded." And in a tribute to Gaul's *Portfolio of Pictures,* Lee said that "The 'Portofolio' should be not only in every Southern but in every American family. These paintings, with their pathos, their tragedy, and the great sorrow of the great war period, will perform a duty in directing the younger generation to avoid getting into channels which might provoke a like repetition to that of our great Civil War."[13]

Some of Lee's most notable work in history was done as part of his official duties within the United Confederate Veterans. The veterans revealed early that they had a strong interest in history, and especially in the compilation of a certain kind of history. During its 1892 reunion, the UCV created a "permanent committee of seven comrades, skilled and experienced in such matters," and gave it a broad charge: "That said committee select and designate such proper and truthful history of the United States, to be used in both public and private schools of the South, and that said committee shall, as soon as possible, put the seal of their condemnation upon such as are not truthful histories of the United States."[14]

Four months after the reunion, Commanding Gen. John B. Gordon appointed the first historical committee. He obviously had tried to select educated men, known and respected for their scholarly accomplishments. Edmund Kirby Smith, appointed chairman, had received his early training at Benjamin Hallowell's preparatory school and at West Point. After the Civil War he had become a teacher and had established a short-lived military academy in Kentucky which he served briefly as president. In 1870 he became chancellor of the University of Nashville, but within a few years he moved to the University of the South, Sewanee, Tennessee; and by the time of his appointment, he was a distinguished professor of mathematics there. Also interested in history, he had contributed an article on "The Defense of the Red River" to *Century Magazine*—later reprinted in *Battles and Leaders*.[15]

Most of the other members also displayed impressive qualifications. Lee was one of two college presidents on the committee. The other was James W. Nicholson of Louisiana State University. An eminent mathematician, Nicholson authored at least eleven textbooks, but he enjoyed history and would publish *Stories of Dixie* in 1915. Ellison Capers, the son of a Methodist Bishop, attended the South Carolina Military Academy and served as an assistant professor there from 1850 to 1860. After the Civil War he became an Episcopal minister, and in 1894 he would be named Bishop of South Carolina. He wrote profusely, was an energetic member of the Southern Historical Association, and championed higher education as a function of both church and state. In 1904 he would become chancellor of the University of the South.[16] Two members were professors: Alonzo Hill, at the Tuscaloosa Female Institute, and James N. Stubbs of Woods' Crossroads, Virginia, whose school has not been identified. A final member was Henry L. Bentley of Abilene, Texas, a graduate of the University of Tennessee Law School.

Kirby Smith, as one of his first official acts, tried to secure information and advice on how to identify good historical writing. He called a meeting of his committee to gather in New Orleans in March of 1893. Joining him there were Lee, Bentley, Nicholson, and the president of Tulane University, William Preston Johnston (Confederate General Albert Sidney Johnston's son), who was allowed to participate fully even though he was not officially a member of the committee. During the two days of deliberations Kirby Smith told a *Times-Democrat* reporter, "The matter is one that must of necessity proceed slowly. Why, I recon [sic] there are fifty different histories of the U. S., and every day we have fellows coming into our houses telling us what magnificent histories they have got."[17] This thoroughness with which the committee approached its task reflected the members' cool-headed attitude toward a subject of somewhat uncertain proportions.

Lee admitted that he himself did not know a great deal about how to judge works in history. "I must confess," he wrote to Kirby Smith, "that I hardly know how to start—I have never taught history and am not a student in that line." Lee suggested that the committee seek the help of unbiased experts. "To select those which are partisan to the South," he explained, "would be as objectionable as [selecting] those which are partisan to the North." The committee approved of his idea, and the chairman assigned each member several histories, to read and prepare written reports on them, and in every case to seek competent assistance in doing so. They also agreed that the chairman should correspond with and seek the aid of "the best informed historical experts in the country."[18]

Later in 1893, before the committee made much progress, Kirby Smith and Hill both died. After a thorough search for replacements, Commander in Chief Gordon selected Clement A. Evans and William Robertson Garrett, and he appointed Lee as chairman. Even as a young man Evans had shown amazing intellectual ability. He was educated at the Georgia Law School in Augusta, licensed to practice before he was nineteen, and became a judge at twenty-two. After the Civil War he entered the Methodist Episcopal South ministry, but retired in 1892 to devote the rest of his life to writing, editing, and the affairs of the UCV. Garrett was a graduate of Williamsburg Military Academy, William and Mary College, and the University of Virginia, where he was elected to Phi Beta Kappa in 1858. The University of Nashville in 1891 granted him an honorary doctorate. In Tennessee he served as president of Giles College, principal of Cornersville Academy, and superintendent of public schools for Giles County. Later he would become a professor and a dean at Peabody Normal College, write several books, and edit a scholarly journal, *The American Historical Magazine and Tennessee Historical Quarterly*. Lee later admitted that he had relied upon Garrett's judgment to a surprising degree. "I leaned on my friend in all historical matters," Lee said, "and felt what he wrote I could sign without hesitation!"[19]

Lee approached his chairmanship with zeal. He took advantage of his position as president of the Mississippi Agricultural & Mechanical College and secured aid and advice from various faculty members, especially the English and history professor, Dabney Lipscomb. Lee also collected and studied writings of prominent American historians, and in the process he became quite a writer and patron of history.[20]

He contributed a number of articles to various publications, principally newspapers, the *Confederate Veteran,* and the *Southern Historical Society Papers.* He had intended to do a full-scale military history of Mississippi, and friends urged him to complete it; but he abandoned that project "on account of too much work." Many modern Mississippians correctly consider Lee's articles "boring." In addition to outdated scholarship, the pieces are simple straightforward narratives and are disappointing because of the paucity of Lee's own recollections and insights; although he did stir two major controversies: one with Forrest partisans concerning the Battle of Tupelo and another with P. G. T. Beauregard as to who specifically had fired the first shot at Fort Sumter.[21] Lee later collected and revised almost all of his major articles and reprinted them, eight appearing between 1900 and 1904, in the *Publications of the Mississippi Historical Society*—an organization that he served for ten years as president.

The Mississippi Historical Society, which Lee helped to reactivate from a defunct earlier group, performed important services in behalf of history. Lee and Franklin L. Riley—history professor at the University of Mississippi, Oxford—provided it with dynamic leadership. In addition to persuading the legislature to provide funds for its *Publications,* they later spearheaded the drive that resulted in establishment of the Mississippi Department of Archives and History. Lee became a member of the Archives' first board of trustees and, from 1902 and 1908, was elected its president.[22]

Although the UCV held no reunion in 1893, because the host city, Birmingham, Alabama, requested a postponement, the historical committee continued its work and made a lengthy report in 1894. It declared that "justice to the South imperatively demands a different presentation" of history. Lee later explained that the feeling chiefly was that the South had produced no competent historians of its own since the Civil War. Consequently, the committee believed, "Northern men . . . have . . . given undue prominence to what was done by their section to the omission and corresponding fair statement of what was done by the South." As Lee said in a public speech, "to the South, more than to any other section, is this union indebted for the genius, wisdom, enterprise, patriotism and valor that have given it so proud an eminence among the nations of the earth. . . . The South has suffered much at the hands of school histories." The veterans declared impartiality to be the essence of history, and they charged that many books were "so unfair, so sectional and untrue," that the South could not permit the record to stand as it did.[23]

The committee classified history books intended for use in schools into three groups. The first listed those books issued in the first ten or fifteen years following the close of the Civil War, "dictated by prejudice and prompted by the evil passions that time had not then softened." They deemed all of these books unacceptable. The second category was a catch-all grouping of books which generally were unacceptable, but which contained "many excellent features." The category included histories by northern authors that apparently were fair, made so either through a revision of an earlier edition or a censoring, in an "effort to curry favor with the textbook patrons of both sections"; those histories with separate editions for North and South; and those histories "written and published in the North in which an honest effort is made to do justice to the South," but which failed to emphasize the distinctive features of the South or to emphasize its place in the history of the country as a whole. The third category consisted of books which the committee itself had examined and found acceptable. Eight textbooks and one supplemental reader appeared on the first list of approved works.[24]

In explaining how it reached its decisions, the committee listed its criteria for judgment. Many of the measuring scales had to do with a book's practicality or with its physical features and appearance, but some were specific points of interpretation. No one could disparage the first question the committee asked: "Is the historic value impaired by inaccuracy?" But acceptable books also had to indicate that the southern people were motivated only by a desire for independence and self-government and that the resulting war was "a conflict between the states," not a "rebellion," and due notice had to be given to "the unparallel [sic] patriotism manifested by the Southern people in accepting its results."[25] Naturally, all the books which met these standards happened to have been written in the South by Southerners.

But a higher and more objective tone also appeared in the report: "We need a 'renaissance' of history throughout the South." The committee proclaimed that one of the veterans' most important tasks was to "stimulate historical research; create historical taste; produce not only one work, but many works; employ not only one mind, but many minds." The veterans were interested not only in school histories, "but also State histories, magazine articles, historical essays, popular sketches, local history, etc." And the committee gave an additional boost to state and local history by saying, "here is a mine rich in unexplored history and poetry. We need workers in the field. . . . We need a separate history for each State."[26]

Lee's committee also had laudable suggestions about achieving these goals: "There is but one agency which can compass all the purposes, and can add to these another of great value—that agency is our leading Southern universities. They have the means, the prestige, the appliances, the undying life. They could put work into immediate operation, and continue it forever. We therefore suggest . . . every university in the South to establish a chair of American history; that this chair be not overloaded with additional work, but its occupant be allowed leisure and be provided with appliances for historical investigation and authorship; that the occupant of this chair be selected with special reference to his fitness for historical authorship, and also for inspiring students with a spirit of original historical investigation. . . ." Finally, the committee advised that the association petition the legislature of each southern state to require that public schools teach state history for one year and United States history for one year, and it urged that the same goals be recommended to all private schools and academies.[27]

The veterans heartily approved of the report and adopted its provisions unanimously. Exactly what was to be done at levels below national headquarters remained vague; the historical committee suggested "that the association provide the proper organization" for carrying the program into effect. In practice this method became whatever state and local groups and individuals chose to do. A provision in the adopted committee report authorized the association at lower echelons to "appoint suitable committees to memorialize the several Legislatures and authorities of universities and schools and to request the cooperation of state historical societies, state literary societies, the press, etc."[28]

Just one year after the historical committee made its first report, it happily noted some progress resulting from its efforts in behalf of history in the universities. In both Virginia and Tennessee the UCV state divisions established rapport with the State Teachers' Associations and some other interested organizations. In Tennessee the legislature responded favorably to lobbying operations of these groups and appropriated money for a chair of American history at Peabody Normal College. And shortly thereafter, the college also began publication of the scholarly quarterly mentioned earlier (edited by committee member Garrett), the *American Historical Magazine and Tennessee Historical Quarterly*.[29]

Although Lee's committee expressed confidence that all other southern states would follow the example set by Tennessee, no other colleges received chairs as a direct result of UCV efforts. The committee regretfully acknowledged this failure by 1899, but it also proclaimed a partial victory.[30] The veterans realized they had played a part in generating much new interest in history throughout the South, and successive progress reports told of their pleasure over it.

Regardless of how small or large the impetus the UCV provided, a definite change for the better did take place in southern colleges over the same period when the Confederate Veterans carried on their crusade. Of course not all southern colleges had been without history course offerings before these years, but very few matched the standards advocated by the UCV. History was still considered to be an academic subject of secondary importance in the late nineteenth century, and usually a professor in some other discipline taught it as a sideline. The South probably had no full-time teachers of history in 1880 or 1885, and only about a half-dozen by 1895. The college over which Lee presided, Mississippi A. & M., got its first chair of history in 1892. By 1903 history was being taught in every southern college, and Frederick W. Moore, in a study made that year, observed that in one-half of them the instructors were "ambitious young men, of special training, graduated from the best universities of the land."[31]

The committee endorsed two more books in its second report (1895), but it also registered some strong complaints. Too much material still appeared, the committee said, written by authors who had a "lack of catholic sympathy for all sections of the country," and "we cannot too strongly urge upon our people the great importance of avoiding . . . the purchasing and disseminating of books and literature which are unkind and unfair to the South, which belittle our achievement, impugn our motives and malign the character of our illustrious leaders." The committee generally declined to name and condemn specific works, but it did so this time and cited the *Encyclopedia Britannica* as "a work of exceptional merit in many particulars," though one which "abounds in such a distortion of historical facts in reference to the South as could emanate only from ignorance or malignity." The veterans did not publicly identify which parts they disliked, but one can deduce the passages to which they no doubt objected. The edition of the *Britannica* that the veterans saw, the ninth (1875–1889), did contain a number of passages that reflected critically and even insultingly upon the South.[32]

One enraged Southerner, Thaddeus Kosciuszko Oglesby, wrote a series of angry columns for the *Montgomery Advertiser* in 1891, refuting the "lies and calumnies" of the ninth *Britannica*. These articles were later published as a pamphlet, *Some Truths of History: The Britannica Answered and the South Vindicated,* and still later added to and republished in *Some Truths of History: A Vindication of the South against the Encyclopaedia Britannica and Other Maligners.* In spite of his emotionalism, Oglesby discovered a number of factual errors and omissions in the *Britannica*.[33]

For whatever reasons—it must not have been sales, as the ninth *Britannica* sold 50,000 complete sets in the United States, five times the number that were purchased in Great Britain—the section on American literature in the eleventh edition was completely rewritten, and numerous other changes were made in passages that referred to the South.

In spite of the improvements, the UCV never waxed very enthusiastic about any subsequent *Britannica* editions, but they hailed Oglesby's work and rejoiced over the changes that did appear in a subsequent set. Lee wrote to Oglesby in 1894 "to express my great appreciation for the pamphlet" and proclaimed that "*any* writer of history in the future would find your pamphlet invaluable." Then again in 1903, after a new *Britannica* appeared, Lee wrote to Oglesby: "I congratulate you on the fact that you have caused the *Encyclopaedia Britannica* to haul down its colors."[34] To a great degree, it had done just that.

After the *Encyclopaedia Britannica* incident arose, the UCV began to feel the need of a continuous and uniform watch over school book selections. To make this possible, and also to diversify and strengthen the historical committee, they increased its membership to fifteen, so as to include a member from each southern state. Up to this point, only five men had done most of the work: Lee, Stubbs, Garrett, Nicholson, and Bentley.[35]

Five of the eleven new members had some notable scholarly qualifications. John Overton Casler of Oklahoma City, Oklahoma Territory, graduated from Springfield Academy, West Virginia, in 1859 and in 1893 published *Four Years in the Stonewall Brigade.* Basil W. Duke (a Confederate brigadier general and brother-in-law of John Hunt Morgan) was educated at Centre College and Transylvania University Law School and had a distinguished career as a lawyer, legislator, editor and author after the Civil War. His *Reminiscences* and his *History of Morgan's Cavalry* rank high in both charm and reliability. He also became editor of *The Southern Bivouac: A Monthly Literary and Historical Magazine.* Frederick S. Ferguson of Birmingham, Alabama, educated at Florence Wesleyan University, taught school and studied law. Samuel Gibbs French of Pensacola, Florida, was a West Pointer who would publish his very interesting and valuable autobiography, *Two Wars*, in 1901. Winfield Peters of Baltimore, Maryland, was a Latin teacher.[36]

The other new members, most of whom are obscure, included W. P. Campbell of Little Rock, Arkansas; Graham Daves, of Asheville, North Carolina; W. Q. Lowd of Washington, D. C.; Henry A. Newman of Huntsville, Missouri; William Montgomery of Romney, West Virginia; and Dew M. Wisdom of Muskogee, Indian Territory. The veterans considered West Virginia a "Southern state." Montgomery had been a sergeant in the Stonewall Brigade. In 1893 he wrote an endorsement authenticating the claimed war record of John Overton Casler, which was published in the latter's *Four*

Years in the Stonewall Brigade. The last additional member, Wisdom, was a Creek Indian who had served as colonel of the 19th Tennessee Cavalry under Nathan Bedford Forrest.[37]

This enlarged committee chose some worthy goals. The members sincerely believed that the kind of history they advocated would be acceptable to unbiased people in every part of the country. Lee felt that he had "conservative, levelheaded men" serving under him, and he announced that "the South wants no history in her schools that cannot be taught to the Children in every state in the Union." What the committee desired was "to direct the ambition of our Southern youth to explore the mines of historic wealth, which now lie hidden in legends in scattered records, in unpublished manuscripts, and in the memories of a few old pioneers, who still linger amid the institutions they have helped to create." To help achieve this, they compiled a list of sixty-eight approved titles, which included some of the best published works on the Civil War period and many important reminiscences, and they recommended that these works be purchased by public and school libraries throughout the South.[38]

Thus the UCV enjoined its members at the state and local levels to perform two specific duties: to urge widespread purchase of approved historical materials and at the same time to root out and cause the rejection of disapproved matter. The veterans in most states took no official action at all. Indeed, the bulk of the contributions to historical activities by most veterans seems to have been quite innocuous, such as writing their own bits of history, buying copies of acceptable histories, frequently penning congratulatory letters to the authors, and in helping with the accumulation of appropriate records and papers to be placed in new archival repositories. This last effort alone was of major significance. Few if any archives existed in the United States before this period. Establishment of state archives began in the South, just after this period of activity by the UCV's historical committee—at about the turn of the century.[39] The UCV did not work alone, but it certainly is probable that they helped stir some favorable interest; and many of their members worked with other historically minded groups—as was the case, for example, with Lee in Mississippi.

Ultimately the committee decided to launch publishing ventures of its own. In 1885 it selected a prominent member of the UCV,

Clement A. Evans (who would succeed Lee as chairman of the historical committee in 1904), to edit a twelve-volume Confederate Military History. A large number of variously qualified authors, all southern participants in the Civil War, contributed passages. Lee wrote an article on "The South Since the War." Evans edited each chapter and then submitted them to one or more historical committee members for further revision. The committee regarded the set of volumes which appeared in 1899 as the "standard exposition of our cause" and heartily commended them to the southern people.[40]

The ultimate failing of the committee members was in being unable to realize that the kind of history they advocated was not totally objective. It would not gain general acceptance in the northern states nor weather very well the tests of time and later historical scholarship. But the veterans should be thought of in a different light from their most ardent and sometimes overzealous or even warped sympathizers. The kind of history Lee and the other veterans said they favored sounds like the new scientific history being inculcated at Johns Hopkins in the 1890s by Herbert Baxter Adams and others. Individual veterans occasionally insisted upon inclusion of their own peculiar viewpoints, but they never were as narrow-minded as many other groups in the South became.

One immediate result of the UCV efforts was that the veteran elements in both North and South momentarily were driven farther apart, and the two groups waged an embittered literary and verbal war against one another (also generating perhaps some writings of lasting value), as each struggled to see that history books were slanted to favor its section. Of course, each side believed that what it wanted was truth in history, and neither saw that there might be some truth and some error in any interpretation. The late 1890s marked a turning point in this enmity. Mutual animosity reached a peak and began to decline, while at the same time, the thrust of American historiography started to slant toward the body of ideas now called the "nationalistic tradition." The new history stressed that both sides had been right in the Civil War, and it helped to create the so-called "cult of Lincoln and Lee," the widespread giving of tributes to each. Ultimately its concepts became the dominant mood of the era.[41]

The UCV was considerably more pleased with this new historiography than was the GAR. Perhaps the UCV as a whole was less prejudiced. The northern veterans apparently considered pensions and other federal remuneration to be far more important than correct history, and they probably feared that they would receive less for themselves if the UCV continued to gain ground. So in 1897 the Union veterans proposed that a "commisson of distinguished educators" from the ranks of both sides get together and write a history of the Civil War that would satisfy everyone. The UCV historical committee looked upon this proposal with disfavor, and it stated the reasons: "History is not a mere product, and can no more be written by commissions or committees than can . . . dramatic compositions. Such a body would be apt to produce a colorless, compromised work. . . . The only views with which a historian is concerned are those which are the conscientious result of his investigations, free from the color of preconceived opinions. . . ."[42]

The historical committee reported in 1898 that "the renaissance of history throughout the South, referred to in the report of 1895 as a hope, was in some degree fulfilled." The entire field of history, its members thought, was being explored and its neglected facts more carefully gathered and portrayed. Looking back upon the development of the history profession in the United States, and the degree of interest in history shown by people in general, one can say that the UCV was correct in this claim. But for how much were the veterans responsible? The "renaissance" would doubtless have come anyway. Nevertheless, the veterans worked toward a goal that was fulfilled. Surely their efforts helped some and probably a great deal. Furthermore, the UCV restrained some persons from more stringent action. Lee and other judicious UCV historical committee members exerted a moderating influence upon the whole organization.[43]

In the next year the Spanish-American War caused a wave of unified nationalism to sweep the country. The historical committee noted this in its 1899 report and equated it with a new perspective being shown by historians. This happy turn reduced the committee's duties to "little more than to keep watch upon the histories of the day." To this end, the veterans formed a subcommittee with three members from each state to examine regularly each new history text being considered for adoption in the schools, public or private. In 1900 the UCV passed a resolution to raise money to aid the subcommittee's operations.[44]

The committee again enlarged in 1902 with the addition of a second member from each southern state. This new member was to be either the son or a near relative of a Confederate veteran. Partially, this decision indicated what obviously was a growing concern of the veterans for their advancing age. They certainly wanted to perpetuate their watchful guard on school books, but the organization again distinguished itself by selecting an admirable group of men with formidable scholarly qualifications. It included: for Alabama, Thomas M. Owen, director of the state's department of archives and history; for Virginia, Richard H. Dabney, recipient of a Heidelberg Ph.D. in 1885, an author, and the holder of a history professorship at the University of Virginia; for Mississippi, Franklin L. Riley, a Johns Hopkins Ph.D. since 1896, a prolific author, an organizer of the Mississippi Historical Society, a member of Phi Beta Kappa, and a professor at the University of Mississippi; for Louisiana, A. T. Prescott, a history professor at the Louisiana State University; for North Carolina, Daniel Harvey Hill, Jr., a professor at the agricultural and mechanical college of North Carolina; and for Tennessee, Joshua W. Caldwell, a lawyer, holder of an A. M. from the University of Tennessee since 1895, a trustee of that University, an expert on the constitutional history of Tennessee, and a contributor of articles to the *American Historical Review*. The other new members had impressive but lesser qualifications. They included: for Georgia, Ulrich H. McLaws (a leader of the Sons of Veterans) and for Oklahoma, E. L. Giddings, an attorney.[45]

The 1903 report, the last submitted by the committee while Lee was chairman, contained a condemnation of Ella Hines Stratton's *Young People's History of our Country.* The members reported that this book was "generally fair" but was unacceptable because of the author's vitriolic, one-sided account of the Fort Pillow affair. "The Committee is pained at this late date to see such paragraphs, breathing all the bad blood of the bitterest war of the centuries. . . . Until those paragraphs are expunged by the author, your Committee states that the book should not be bought or allowed in the home of any Southern family."[46]

The wrath of the veterans was justified, for exactly what hap-

pened at Fort Pillow still has not been settled to the complete satisfaction of all historians, but Miss Stratton took a staunchly anti-
southern position. "No Indian massacre could rival the scene," she
wrote and added with a cavalier disregard for dispassionate nar-
ration, "Even the sick in the hospitals were murdered. . . . Nor
was this all. The human fiends seemed to delight in dealing out the
most cruel deaths that they could think of. Men were shot in cold
blood, drowned, even crucified, burned alive, and nailed to houses,
which were then set on fire. The Confederates won the victory of
war at Fort Pillow, but Forrest and his men lost the victory of
principle and the respect of a whole world." Lee and the committee
understandably denounced this as "a misrepresentation of history."[47]

Despite glaring exceptions, like the Stratton book, the committee
by this time had become satisfied with the course that historical
writing was taking. In the next few years, the historical committee
reports contained fewer new suggestions. For the most part, the reports came to be reiterations of earlier goals and claims of progress.
Sometimes while Lee was still chairman, and more frequently thereafter, the reports themselves were primarily research papers on
selected subjects about the Civil War or the New South.

After Lee became commander in chief of the UCV in 1904, and
Clement A. Evans succeeded him as chairman of the historical committee, the veterans engaged in much less agitation. The historical
committee reports in this period all tended to be much shorter
than those of earlier years, possibly indicating that Lee had been
the driving force on the committee but more probably that the
committee considered its goals largely realized.

Lee and the UCV benefitted history in the South by publishing
history, encouraging a widespread interest both in writing and reading it, and aiding the preservation of accurate historical data. Ad-
mittedly, he and the organization inculcated some views not
considered objective today and agitated to have those views adopted
as standard. Ironically, as the UCV labored, the fruits of those
labors more and more insured that historical interpretation would
not sway overly far toward the extremes that a few of the veterans
desired. That the United Confederate Veterans had both positive
and negative characteristics cannot be denied. By the same token,
the organization—and Lee's efforts within it—with small exception,
served Clio well.

16

To Preserve for Posterity

IN JANUARY 1908, the last year of his life, Lee wrote to a friend that "while I will remain forever loyal to the tender memories of the past, I hope I will continue to be loyal also to our great country." He had continued steadfastly to display that apparently divided mind and sentiment so characteristic of many leaders in the post-Appomattox South. He never wavered from the New South doctrine which he had embraced, and he always was unswervingly patriotic toward the United States government. Yet he also revered the South of the past and urged Southerners to preserve and honor the memory of the Confederacy and its soldiers. Glorifying the faithful, courageous, and heroic fighting men of the Southland, he said, in no way contradicted allegiance to the reunited country. "In honoring the vanquished we honor also the victor," he told an 1895 Chicago audience at the dedication of a monument to Confederates who had died there in prison.[1]

During his twilight years Lee broadened his enduring interest in monuments and the collection of accurate historical data to include concern for museums—like Battle Abbey in Richmond, Virginia—and military parks. Lee served as a vice-president of the Shiloh Battlefield Association, but he took a more particular interest in the Vicksburg battlefield area. In 1893 he helped commemorate the siege with an oration there that friends considered one of the best speeches he ever made. Most of the talk recounted wartime events, but toward the end Lee became more philosophical. He hailed the private soldier as needing no better monument than his record, extolled the South's untarnished honor, and closed with a flowery tribute to southern women. The speech was widely reprinted, and it focused considerable attention upon Lee.[2] From that time on he was associated with various preservation efforts at Vicksburg.

On 23 October 1895, under the initiative and direction of Capt. John F. Merry—a Union veteran from Dubuque, Iowa—Lee and others organized the Vicksburg National Military Park Association. It elected a slate of officers, with Lee as president, chose a large number of influential persons to serve on its board of directors, and began activities to carry out its purpose. The executive committee ordered a map of the Vicksburg area prepared and drafted for submission to Congress a bill which would create a military park. The committee also secured options on part of the land to be purchased, at an average price of $35 per acre. The bill, introduced in the House of Representatives on 20 January 1896, underwent a long period of consideration but finally passed on 21 February 1899.[3]

Even before the bill's final passage, Lee began maneuvering to secure a place for himself on the park commission. He wanted it, in addition to his genuine interest, so that he could resign as president of the Mississippi A. & M. College and devote more time to Mrs. Lee, whose health he thought was critical. In early February 1899, Lee wrote to several influential senators asking for their support. Meanwhile one of his friends in Washington circulated a petition among the senators urging that they join in supporting Lee's candidacy, and about thirty of them signed recommendations for him. One of Lee's sponsors, Benjamin Ryan Tillman, wrote him, "I hope you will get the position as I know of no one half so worthy to fill it."[4]

Lee's campaign for the job was successful. He became one of the three initial park commissioners, along with Union veterans William T. Rigby and James G. Everest. They held their first meeting on 1 March 1899, in Washington, D. C. and elected Lee their chairman. Thus Lee became the first ex-Confederate to serve as head of a U. S. military park. To add to the irony, he also thereby became a pioneer in federal conservation. The national park movement, then just beginning, eventually would include millions of acres. Majestic expanses of natural beauty and places which are important parts of America's military and cultural heritage now are preserved and enshrined for future generations.

"I got the place all right," Lee wrote to a friend shortly after his appointment, "a better place than I thought it was and duties apparently light." One wonders what Lee meant by "light." He did get to live at home thereafter, in Columbus, Mississippi, but he worked long and hard on park business. He wrote literally thousands of official letters and made numerous long trips, speaking before groups and organizations and the legislatures of nearly every southern state. In trying to generate interest in the park and to raise funds for individual monuments, he presented an impressive figure. "Lion of battles, and knightly gentleman of the olden time," one newspaperman wrote, Lee "makes an appeal . . . which can scarcely be denied."[5]

The commissioners established an office in Vicksburg on 15 March and immediately began work. Rigby set up a residence in the city and served as the chief functionary, the others keeping in touch through frequent visits and letters. The first task was to secure contracts for land purchases. Human nature being what it is, this brought the committee's first major problem: some of the landowners had a grossly exaggerated idea of the value of their property. The committee achieved some success with reasoned persuasion, but it decided to initiate condemnation proceedings against the more unreasonable property owners. When confronted with this threat, most of the people holding out for more money capitulated and accepted a fair appraisal price. Acquisition then proceeded rapidly; and by the end of September 1899, the commission had secured approximately nine hundred and ten acres.[6]

Lee encountered some major problems and some minor ones as chairman of the park commission. He desired that the park acquire a reference library and secured donations whenever possible. The Confederate Publishing Company supplied a set of *Confederate Military History*, and the War Department promised a complete set of the *Official Records*. The commission also wished to purchase two hundred fifty copies of parts 1, 2, and 3 of volume XXIV—that part of the *Official Records* which pertain to the Vicksburg siege— for distribution to the various state commissions and interested groups. Secretary of War Alger balked at this expenditure, but soon yielded to the commission's urging.[7] The replacement of Alger as secretary of war by an even more economy-minded individual, Elihu Root, together with the commission's growing desire for larger appropriations and additional land purchases, precipitated a much more difficult situation.

When Root attempted to curb the commission's expenditures below the amount originally authorized by Congress, Lee suggested that the commission appeal to Congress. Rigby persuaded Lee to be more moderate, but thereafter relations between Root and Lee were strained. Lee took a clever tack in future requests to Root for land purchases by indicating that most of the existing acquisitions were areas where the Confederates had had positions, and he implied that proper commemoration of the United States troops' activities would suffer if funds remained too short. Root mildy slapped Lee's hand for purchasing any land without specific prior approval from the war department for each individual tract. The criterion for past purchases, Root said, "though perhaps not unreasonable, is not in accord with the present views of this Department." (Sufficient money eventually was secured, and the park now has over 1,300 acres, but its development spread out over many years.) [8]

From the first Lee determined to make the park authentic and complete in every possible detail. In instances where the topography had changed since 1863, he insisted that maps and pictures be prepared to show it exactly as it had been. He journeyed to other military parks, such as Chattanooga, Chickamauga, Gettysburg, and Sharpsburg, to study their good points. "What kind of a park are we to have," he asked when the commission encountered difficulties, "one of dignity and quality like Gettysburg and Chickamauga— Chattanooga, or a cheap park which will not satisfy the American people?" [9]

The commission ran into considerable trouble with its work. "The Secretary wants to know, why a continuous roadway? Why so many bridges? I consider them . . . most essential . . . ," Lee wrote. "I believe we should not yield what we consider essential." Also, the initial authorization from Congress did not allow the purchase of any guns for the park. So Lee early began urging that the war department donate guns from stocks of unused weapons. And Lee wanted to restore the water batteries, a project for which he had no money. He argued persuasively, contending that the United States Navy had served key roles in the Vicksburg campaign —even U. S. Grant had said so, Lee pointed out—and the sailors therefore should receive their share of honor and recognition. [10] But years of difficult negotiations were required before these goals could be accomplished. For several reasons, these difficulties being one, Lee meanwhile resigned the chairmanship.

On 20 December 1899, Lee wrote to Secretary of War Root, asking for temporary relief from the chairman's duties because Mrs. Lee continued very sickly. Rigby took over on several occasions and began acting as chairman full time throughout 1901. Lee formally resigned the post, and Rigby succeeded him, on 15 April 1902.[11] Although no longer chairman, Lee remained a member of the commission for the rest of his life. Mrs. Lee's and his own occasional ill health forced him to curtail some of his activities, but he continued over the next six years to exert a strong influence in park business.

Lee began suffering from periodic physical maladies around 1900. His most troublesome and frequently recurring ills were rheumatisms and carbuncles, but sometimes he suffered from severe colds and insomnia. In 1905 he developed both pneumonia and a troublesome cataract. Finally in 1906 his persistent lumbago prompted him to see a specialist who diagnosed that Lee had diabetes, and subsequent treatment brought him much relief. Relatively he remained in good shape for a man in his late sixties and early seventies. "The doctor tells me," he wrote, "that I am in a better fix physically than $3/4$ of the men my age."[12]

Stephen Lee in later life appeared "physically robust," one of his friends observed. His head was "shapely and set forward firmly on broad shoulders," his gaze was "searching and somewhat restless," his face was "clear, kindly and serious," and his stride was "military." But the same man also remembered that "Lee was given to introspection; and, as if reflected from his early life and accentuated by the loneliness incident to much enforced separation from his invalid wife, an almost melancholy cast gradually settled on his countenance and a suggestion of sadness prevailed in tones of his voice."[13]

Lee and his wife eventually acquired ownership of Major Blewett's spacious house in Columbus. The major died in 1871 and willed it to his daughter, Mrs. Mary Blewett Woolridge. But she soon found that she could not keep the place up and sold it to Mrs. Lee's mother, Mrs. James T. Harrison, who willed it equally to her own two daughters: Mrs. Lee and Mary, who never married. Apparently the Lees divided their time before 1899, living both at the president's home on the a. & m. college campus and at the house in Columbus. As Mrs. Lee became less and less able to help herself, Mary Harrison moved in with them.[14]

Mrs. Lee enjoyed few periods of relief, but she was well enough in 1903 for the Lees to host a "delightful family reunion" celebrating the thirty-eighth anniversary of their marriage. She died on 3 October later that year. Mary Harrison continued living with Lee, to keep house for him. Mrs. Lee willed her share of the house to Lee, and thus he and Miss Harrison became co-owners. They each willed their shares to Lee's son, Blewett, who in turn sold it for a very nominal figure to the city of Columbus.[15] The house now is a civic center and museum.

Some of the park troubles that had a part in prompting Lee's resignation as chairman of the commission continued for a lengthy period. The most vexing one was the war department's parsimony and the secretary's persisting tendency to demand that the commission revise its plans along more economical lines. The secretary found an ally—a real thorn in the commissioners' sides—in the park engineer: E. E. Betts, succeeded on 29 September 1899, by his brother R. D. Betts. The brothers Betts recommended less roadway footage and cheaper bridges for the park, exactly what the secretary wanted to hear. The commission also had trouble with the Betts brothers over surveying and mapping in the park.

The secretary of war seemed continually to overrule the commission's desires in favor of the Betts's recommendations. "It is mortifying indeed," Lee exasperatedly wrote in October 1901, "to have carefully matured plans ignored, and turned down. . . ." The commissioners thought R. D. Betts a "young smart aleck" and a "crafty fellow," and "it is a pity," Lee wrote, "that the Secretary cannot see that he is being deceived . . . by Mr. Betts." At first Lee suspected "that there is someone behind the scenes, who is belittling our park and its work" and decided to pull strings in Congress. He wrote to Missouri Sen. Francis Marion Cockrell, with whom he had served in the Army of Tennessee, asking for intervention. But the scheme backfired; and by May 1902, Lee wrote, "it is evident to me now, we are being punished, and our work retarded, because we have worked over the head of the secretary, using political influence." There was nothing left to do but continue with an earlier conclusion to "pocket our mortification, and do the best we can in carrying out the views of the secretary—we are now virtually relieved of responsibility of the policy of development. . . ."[16]

Actually the situation was not so gloomy as Lee and the other commissioners thought, but their work did drag out over a longer period than would have been required with larger appropriations and more cooperation from the war department. In the long run, the commission's seemingly extravagant approach proved to have been the best and most economical means to accomplish what finally was done in the park. Meanwhile, as the commission moved forward, gradually making progress, other problems of a more internal nature developed.

Lee and Rigby engaged in bitter disagreement over several matters. One concerned the texts of the commentaries to be placed upon the various historical markers in the park. Lee insisted upon strict adherence to official records except where interpolation seemed clearly to be called for. Specifically, he took pains to see that "justice" was done to the Confederate side—and to him this meant showing that the Federals greatly outnumbered the southern forces. Rigby at times was willing to interpolate, but rarely was he in agreement with Lee on the matter of numbers. Both men were adamant and stubborn. The last straw for Lee came when Rigby discredited Pemberton's 31 March 1863 troop returns. "I am the more convinced . . . that we will not be able to get together on our points of divergence," Lee wrote, and "I have therefore about decided to submit the facts where we differ to higher authority. . . ." At last they reached a workable compromise, Rigby taking the advice of John S. Kountz—the park historian—putting fewer words on some of the tablets and changing some others. In the end Lee disapproved of only a few tablets, but even these angered and distressed him considerably.[17]

Another major controversy concerned the park's guns. Rigby asked the war department for fewer guns than Lee thought justified. "The other parks got all the guns they wanted," Lee contended, "and ours from the very nature of a siege and defense requires a large number to illustrate the conditions." "We will get more," he continued; "I will certainly press this matter." But they did not get more; they got only one hundred twenty-eight. Then Lee and Rigby began a long feud over where the guns should be placed. Rigby wanted to divide the guns about equally between the Union and Confederate emplacements; Lee insisted upon the exact same ratio as had been the case in 1863 (236: Union; 102: Confederate). Rigby argued that "the Confederate line will always be the line of greatest interest in the park," and Lee countered that "you are looking more to pleasing appearances on the Confederate line, than to showing the actual facts and relative values of the two sides." Once again, however, Lee did not entirely get his way, but he grudgingly accepted the compromise situation in order to push on with the park's other work—which in truth, he dearly loved.[18]

In spite of their hard fights with each other, the commissioners actually were warm friends. Rigby once received a letter from Kountz, the park historian, referring to Lee as one "whom we all love" and another letter from Everest saying "what a noble soul he is." And in 1903 even Lee wrote to Rigby that "my contact with you has inspired me with such faith in your accurate work, that I am almost ready to accept anything you present. . . ." In 1907 Lee's house guest, the Rev. George C. Cates, led a highly successful religious revival in Columbus. Lee also helped lead some of the prayers, "his ringing voice" filling the large auditorium, but he took time out during the revival to write Rigby twice. "I never expected to see a great Pentecostal Day, as described in the Acts," Lee said, "but yesterday, I saw 218 persons converted." "I wish my Dear-Dear Friend I could see your noble heart touched with love to God —with a fire approaching your loyalty and love for the work that is so near to both of our hearts."[19]

As Lee had advanced in age, his religious sentiment grew stronger and stronger. Intensely active in church, he taught a children's class in Sunday school and attained great popularity among the pupils. He collected religious homilies and advice on "how to enjoy life," which he placed in his scrapbooks. Adopting the philosophy and optimism of the First Psalm, his favorite scriptural passage—the Biblical text that says "Blessed is the man that hath walked not in the counsel of the ungodly. . . , his delight is in the law of the Lord; . . . whatsover he doeth, shall prosper"—Lee impressed others with his exemplary churchmanship. "The general is a bona fide Baptist," one admirer proclaimed, "and is equally well skilled in Emanuel's tactics, as those of Hardee or Upton."[20]

Indeed in all that he did, Lee never ceased to display the qualities of a military man. Well prepared and always competent, he approached any task with the managerial skills of a general. In war he rose rapidly to a lofty rank at a young age, an accomplishment exceeded by only a few better commanders in all of history, such as Alexander the Great, Lafayette, and Napoleon. Lee's credit sprang not from transcending the system and leaving it permanently altered but from his complete mastery of it.

This same mastery propelled Lee into the New South, and for forty years after Appomattox he gave unstinting loyalty and service to the United States at the same time that he helped to organize and lead the United Confederate Veterans and engaged in many activities aimed at upbuilding the Southland. He strove to keep his oath of allegiance taken after the war; for "what I swore to I meant," he emphasized, "and it was no empty mockery." Nevertheless no other statement sums up Lee's sentiments more than one he made in 1900, proclaiming that "the New South is the work of the Confederate soldier, as the Old South was the work of his father. The Confederate soldier loves both."[21] Lee's passion was a love for his region.

In later years Lee genuinely favored reconciliation between the northern and southern people. In 1907, engaging in one last controversy, he supported the Daughters of the Confederacy in their effort to erect a monument to Capt. Henry Wirz, the only southern soldier executed after the Civil War for "war crimes." Lee believed Wirz "innocent of the charges on which he was convicted" and felt that the southern version of the matter ought to be told in "enduring form." But the matter stirred considerable debate, and Lee let the project fall into abeyance because further publicity might "defeat any and all plans for raising money for any of the Military Parks in the South." Clinging to his personal opinion, Lee agreed that the Wirz issue was "a very delicate matter" and expressed his wish to avoid reviving any more bitter feeling.[22]

Lee especially favored reconciliation between the veterans of both sides. He willingly delivered speeches in the Vicksburg park to old survivors from North or South. In one of his last, he told a gathering of ex-Federal soldiers: "The Revolution was glorious, but the Civil War was sublime. . . . War is hell indeed, but in times of war the great values of life shine forth and manhood is not counted in terms of money. . . . There is something very inspiring to me in the fact that Union and Confederate soldiers want to meet each other. I don't hear of any Franco-Prussian celebrations, and I fear there will be no Russo-Japanese reunions. . . . But we meet on a different footing; we are fellow-citizens of the great republic. . . . These meetings signify that our country's wounds have knit together again."[23]

Lee's work at Vicksburg symbolized an effort to preserve the past and to promote harmony among the sections so that all might enjoy the reunited country's glorious future. He could not have been more satisfied that his last public appearance was a speech in the park, before the survivors of Union Gen. Michael K. Lawler's brigade. Lee looked out over the surroundings—perhaps to the spot where, just a few months before, he had been informed that a statue of himself would be erected—mused that Vicksburg to him was "the greatest of the parks," and admired "the tough physical surroundings—high hills and deep valleys [which] add to the picturesque appearance."[24]

Stephen D. Lee, a simple hard-working man, reached the end of his complex and active career. He had risen high in defense of the Old South, and then he surpassed all his former efforts in helping to build a New South. He was energetic, tenacious, and proficient, and these characteristics kept him active and dogged in pursuit of success. He stood out among his contemporaries, an example to emulate. A "pet of fortune," he made much of his own luck. He was the best kind of administrator: meticulous, dedicated, and able to infuse high morale. In his youth, a fire had touched his heart.

Notes

Necessary reduction of space for the notes requires use of both parts of the bibliography. Part two is a complete alphabetical list of works cited, except for the items discussed in part one. Part one lists the numerous private collections and miscellanies that could not be placed in an alphabetized bibliography; for reference to this material, a list of abbreviations follows this note. Numerous unidentified newspaper clippings are listed in the notes with as much identification as possible. The list of cited newspapers furnishes information omitted from the notes. References to materials in the National Archives are identified in the notes by use of an abbreviation (NA-) both as a signal and as a citation. Such references are further abbreviated; thus, NA-RG 92, e. 233, for example, means National Archives, Record Group 92, entry 233. "Microcopy" and "reel" are abbreviated as "mic." and "r."

The Confederate Veteran, listed in part two of the bibliography, is a large collection of materials in a combination of newspaper and magazine format, wherein often the only title is merely a headline. Important items are cited with author and title; otherwise, the notes merely list information sufficient for location of the item. The *Southern Historical Society Papers* are similarly handled.

The many collections of private papers regarding S. D. Lee also required special treatment, and the list of abbreviations explains those citations as well as other abbreviated references.

LIST OF ABBREVIATIONS

BL—Scrapbooks of Blewett Lee, in bibliography, part one.

B. & L.—*Battles and Leaders*—Buel and Johnson, eds., *Battles and Leaders of the Civil War*, in bibliography, part two.

CSR—Compiled Service Records of Confederate General and Staff Officers and Nonregimental Enlisted Men, in National Archives.

CV—*Confederate Veteran*, in bibliography, part two.

DAB—*Dictionary of American Biography*.

D-SDL—S. D. Lee's Diary, SDL Papers, in bibliography, part one.

Data-SDL—Data for a sketch of the life of Stephen D. Lee, in bibliography, part one.

GR—Governor's Records, MDAH.

JCB—John Bettersworth's private collection of documents, in bibliography, part one.

MDAH—Mississippi Department of Archives and History.

MSUL—Mississippi State University Archives, Library, Starkville.

NA—National Archives.

NCAB—*National Cyclopedia of American Biography*.

O. R.—*Official Records*—*The War of the Rebellion*, in bibliography, part two.

O. R.-N.—*Official Records of the Navies*—*War of the Rebellion*, bibliography, part two.

PMHS—*Publications of the Mississippi Historical Society*, in bibliography, part two.

PMHS-C—*Publications of the Mississippi Historical Society*, Centenary Series, bibliography, part one.

"SDL"—scrapbooks, in bibliography, part one.

SDL-P—Stephen D. Lee Papers, Southern Historical Collection, University of North Carolina, Chapel Hill, in bibliography, part one.

SHC—Southern Historical Collection, University of North Carolina, Chapel Hill, in bibliography, part one.

SHC (. . .)—Southern Historical Collection, University of North Carolina, Chapel Hill; material on S. D. Lee in, for example, Claiborne or Alexander papers, bibliography, part one.

SHSP—*Southern Historical Society Papers*, in bibliography, part two.

VPC—Vicksburg Park Commission—various collections stored in the headquarters of Vicksburg National Military Park, Vicksburg, Mississippi, bibliography, part one.

List of newspapers abbreviated in the notes

Charleston, S. C. *Sunday News*	New Orleans, La. *Picayune*
Columbus, Miss. *Commercial*	New Orleans, La. *Times-Democrat*
Columbus, Miss. *Dispatch*	Okolona, Miss. *Chickasaw Messenger*
Columbus, Miss. *Independent*	(*Messenger*)
Columbus, Miss. *Index*	Richmond, Va. *Enquirer*
Dallas, Tex. *Herald*	Richmond, Va. *State*
Jackson, Miss. *Clarion-Ledger*	Starkville, Miss. *Oktibbeha Citizen*
Jackson, Miss. *Weekly Clarion*	Starkville, Miss. *Southern Livestock*
Memphis, Tenn. *Appeal Avalanche*	*Journal (SLJ)*
Memphis, Tenn. *Daily Clarion*	Tupelo, Miss. *Lee County Standard*
Mobile, Ala. *Register*	Vicksburg, Miss. *Daily Herald*

NOTES TO CHAPTER 1

1. T. C. Read, *The Descendants of Thomas Lee of Charleston, South Carolina 1710–1769*, pp. xiii, 1 and passim. Judge Thomas Lee died in 1839 when his grandson Stephen was six years old.

2. Read, pp. vii, xiii–iv. Read acknowledges the kinship between R. E. Lee and S. D. Lee; see also BL 2.

3. "SDL" 2, Abbeville, S. C., 15 Jan. 1908. (See list of abbreviations; unless otherwise noted, references to scrapbooks are to newspaper clippings, with all known information given.)

4. Dr. Lee died on 6 Oct. 1870, and his second wife died fifteen years later, 21 June 1885.

5. D. Lipscomb, "General Stephen D. Lee," *PMHS* 10: 15. Lack of affluence may have developed a strong sense of thrift in Stephen. He occasionally made generous contributions to the church or the needy, but he could be remarkably penurious; though he wrote a tremendous number of letters, he almost never used personal stationery. He used letterheads from one organization or another and asked for a new supply when necessary. Buying his own paper seems never to have occurred to him. Once in 1902 he scrawled a letter on a paper towel! (Lee to Rigby, 11 Jan., VPC).

6. Read, pp. 114–5; NA-Military Academy Orders 1814–67, RG 94, e. 219; U. S. Military Academy Cadet Application Papers 1805–66, mic. 688, r. 11. The older Stephen Lee excelled in mathematics and French and taught mathematics at the College of Charleston. During the Civil War, he organized a regiment for the Confederacy and was thereafter known as "Colonel" Stephen Lee. He and nine of his sons fought for southern independence.

7. D. Lipscomb, p. 15; NA-U. S. Military Academy Cadet Application Papers 1805–66, mic. 688, r. 177; G. W. Cullum, ed., *Biographical Register*, 2: 377. Orr's letter (April 1849) states that the fifteen and one-half-year-old Stephen is "five feet six inches high and exempt from physical or marital [sic] defect or blemish."

8. Cullum, 2: 377; W. W. Hassler, ed., *The General to His Lady*, pp. 3–4. "Lieutenant General Stephen D. Lee," in *The Land We Love* 2: 324. The author probably was W. H. Brand of Columbia, Missouri, mentioned as the author of such a sketch in Hill to Lee, 8 Sept. 1866, SDL-P.

9. Hassler, pp. 3–4; W. H. Green, *Recollections and Reflections*, p. 67; O. O. Howard, *My Life and Experiences*, pp. 55–6; B. J. Lossing, *Memoir of Lieut.-Col. John T. Greble*, p. 97.

10. D. S. Freeman, *R. E. Lee*, 1: 319.

11. NA-list of officers, professors, teachers, etc., constituting the academic and military staff of the military academy, 30th September 1850, RG 92, e. 212; E. J. Warner, *Generals in Gray*, pp. 279–81.

12. Green, p. 86; F. McKinney, *Education in Violence*, p. 52. Lee ranked fourth in his graduating class on the final ratings in cavalry tactics (report, June 1854, NA-RG 94, e. 212).

13. Hassler, p. 262; Warner, pp. 233–34.

14. Hassler, p. 3; Freeman, *R. E. Lee*, 1: 346; The other three were Archibald Gracie and J. E. Villepigue for the Confederacy and Henry L. Abbott for the Union.

15. Brewerton to Toten, 9 Nov. 1850; NA-report, 1 July 1850; RG 92, item 5181, e. 212.

16. D. Lipscomb, p. 28. NA-report of the semiannual examinations at West Point, Jan. 1851; report of the Fourth Class according to general merit, June 1851, RG 94, e. 212.

17. NA-conduct rolls, Sept. 1850, Feb. 1851 and for year 1851, RG 94, e. 232.
18. Ibid.
19. Freeman, *R. E. Lee*, 1: 319, 323–26; Green, pp. 87–8.
20. BL 1, Louisiana newspaper quoting speech of S. D. Lee in New Orleans at a celebration of R. E. Lee's birthday.
21. Green, p. 91; Lossing, p. 22.
22. "SDL" 3.
23. Green, p. 74.
24. NA-conduct rolls for 1852–53, RG ibid.
25. Ibid.; NA-merit rolls of the Second Class as determined at the general examination in June 1853, RG ibid. Lee stood nineteenth in chemistry and twenty-fifth in drawing.
26. NA-conduct rolls for 1853–54, RG ibid.
27. NA-report of the semiannual examinations for Jan. 1854; First Class arranged according to merit, June 1854; cadets especially recommended for promotion in the mounted service, June 1854; and First Class according to general merit, June 1854, RG 94, e. 212.
28. Freeman, *R. E. Lee*, 1: 346; NA-RG 94, e. 232. Each class at West Point selected its own ring emblems (Lossing, p. 24).
29. NA-reports of the Academic Board, RG 94, e. 4, p. 507, #38; record of assignments for the class of 1854, RG 94, e. 230; for more on the regiment Lee joined, see F. Downey, *Sound of the Guns*, pp. 43, 86, 101, 110–11 and T. F. Rodenbough and W. L. Haskins, eds., *The Army of the United States*, pp. 351, 356–57.
30. Lee's commission, SDL-P.
31. Downey, p. 119; Rodenbough and Haskins, p. 358; NA-post returns, Ringgold Barracks, mic. 617, r. 1019.
32. Rodenbough and Haskins, pp. 351, 358.
33. NA-post returns, Ringgold.
34. Howard, *Life*, pp. 74–5; Lossing, pp. 25, 36; NA-post returns, Ringgold.
35. Howard, *Life*, pp. 76, 81–2, 88, 94.
36. NA-post returns, Ringgold.
37. Lee's commission and his acknowledgment are in SDL-P; E. A. Pollard, *The Early Life . . . R. E. Lee*, p. 675; Lee to Mrs. Wright, 22 Oct. 1904, SHC (Pemberton).
38. Howard, *Life*, p. 81.
39. Ibid., pp. 89–90; Page to Brown, Page to Lee, 15 June 1857, NA-records, Dept. of Florida, 1856–58, RG 383, e. 4, p. 231.
40. Howard, *Life*, pp. 90–1.
41. Ibid.; Lossing, p. 28.
42. Page to Kilburn, 13 July 1857; Page to Lee, 15 July; Lee to Loomis, 20 July; Page to Lee, 26 July; Lee to Loomis, 28 July, 1 Aug.; Page to Lee, 2 Aug.; Lee to Loomis, 5, 8 Aug.; Page to Lee, 9 Aug.; Lee to Loomis, 16 Aug. 1857, NA-records, Dept of Florida, 1856–58, RG 393, e. 4.
43. Howard, *Life*, pp. 94–5; Page to Cooper, 31 Aug., 30 Sept. 1857, NA-records, Dept. of Florida, 1856–58, RG ibid.
44. NA-post returns, Fort Leavenworth, mic. 616, r. 611.
45. Ibid.; Cooper to Belton, 31 Oct. 1857, SDL-P.
46. NA-post returns, Fort Leavenworth. Lee's whereabouts is unknown except for a government report of a visit to Utah (NA-post returns, Fort Laramie, mic. 617, r. 595).
47. NA-post returns, Fort Randall; no record of his whereabouts.

48. Ibid.; Lee to Craig, 21 July 1860, Lee Family Mss.
49. Pollard, p. 675.
50. NA-post returns, Fort Randall.

NOTES TO CHAPTER 2

1. Data-SDL, SHC (Claiborne); John Coxe, "Recollections of Gen. S. D. Lee," *CV* 32: 95.
2. S. D. Lee, "The First Step," in C. C. Buel and R. W. Johnson, eds., *Battles and Leaders of the Civil War*, 1: 74 (hereafter cited as *B. & L.*).
3. T. H. Williams, *Beauregard*, pp. 51–2; NA-compiled service records of confederate general and staff officers and nonregimental enlisted men, mic. 331, r. 155 (hereafter cited as CSR); *The War of the Rebellion*, ser. 1, 1, p. 274 (hereafter cited as *O. R.*, citations from ser. 1 unless otherwise stated).
4. NA-CSR.
5. The commission is in SDL-P. Lee began signing as acting assistant adjutant general on 16 March, but an official record of appointment to that post has not been found; Coxe, *CV* 32: 95; E. Rowland, *Varina Howell*, 2: 54.
6. D-SDL. A basic load was 140 rounds.
7. Ibid.; M. W. Wellman, *They Took Their Stand*, p. 82.
8. *O. R.*, 1, p. 59; S. W. Crawford, *The Genesis of the Civil War*, p. 422; W. A. Swanberg, *First Blood*, p. 291.
9. E. Rowland, 2: 54.
10. *O. R.*, 1, p. 18; D-SDL.
11. Bruce Catton, *The Coming Fury*, p. 309; D-SDL; *O. R.*, 1, p. 59.
12. Wellman, *Stand*, p. 85.
13. Lee in *B. & L.*, 1: 76; *O. R.*, 1, p. 60; Wellman, *Stand*, p. 85.,
14. Lee in *B. & L.*, 1: 75; Anderson is quoted in Wellman, *Stand*, p. 85; the early shots at Sumter are colorfully discussed in Ashley Halsey, Jr., *Who Fired the First Shot?*
15. Lee in *B. & L.*, 1: 75–6.
16. *O. R.*, 1, p. 60; D-SDL; Lee in *B. & L.*, 1: 76; Catton, *Fury*, pp. 312–13.
17. Catton, *Fury*, p. 313; Lee in *B. & L.*, 1: 76–7; *O. R.*, 1, pp. 60, 77.
18. D-SDL; Williams, pp. 58–9.
19. Williams, p. 59.
20. D-SDL; Lee in *B. & L.*, 1: 77–8.
21. D-SDL.
22. D-SDL.
23. D-SDL; Lee in *B. & L.*, 1: 78; Crawford, p. 441.
24. Lee in *B. & L.*, 1: 78–9; Swanberg, p. 321.
25. Swanberg, p. 321.
26. D-SDL; Lee in *B. & L.*, 1: 79.
27. D-SDL; *The Battle of Fort Sumter*, pp. 23–5.
28. Ibid.; Lee to Claiborne, 8 July 1878, SHC (Claiborne).
29. D-SDL.
30. D-SDL.

NOTES TO CHAPTER 3

1. *O. R.*, 1, p. 35; ser. 4, 1, p. 229.

2. "Enlistment documents," Headquarters Papers, S. C. Hist. Soc., Charleston; Data-SDL.

3. D-SDL; Lee to Miles, 6 May 1861, SHC (Miles).

4. M. W. Wellman, *Giant in Gray*, p. 50.

5. BL 1, *Sunday News*, 1 Aug. 1897; U. R. Brooks, ed., *Stories of the Confederacy*, pp. 246–47; the unit selected 1st Lt. James F. Hart, a Citadel graduate, as second in command.

6. Brooks, p. 247; Data-SDL; Hampton to Beauregard, 10 June 1861, Wade Hampton Papers; D-SDL; *O. R.* 1, p. 291; Pickens to Lee, 1, 5 June 1861, SHC (Law); Myers to Lee, 3 June 1861, SHC (Law); NA-Treasury Dept. doc., CSR.

7. D-SDL; Wellman, *Giant*, p. 52; Brooks, p. 248; W. F. Amann, ed., *Personnel of the Civil War*, 1: 160.

8. The quotation appears in different forms in several sources. The man claiming to have been the person to whom Davis made the statement is J. W. Jones, *The South in the Building of the Nation*, 12: 87. Yet, even Davis fails to mention Lee in his *Rise and Fall of the Confederate Government*.

9. Brooks, p. 248; H. L. Peterson, *Notes on Ordnance*, passim.

10. Brooks, p. 248; six guns formed a battery; presumably the superseded Tredegar guns went to another unit.

11. D-SDL.

12. Brooks, pp. 248–49; D-SDL; Coxe, *CV* 32: 95; BL 1, "A Sketch of Hart's Battery," 1 Aug. 1897.

13. T. F. Thiele, "The Evolution of Cavalry in the American Civil War," p. 157.

14. D-SDL; Brooks, p. 249.

15. BL 1, *Sunday News*, 1 Aug. 1897; D-SDL.

16. Brooks, p. 249.

17. BL 1, *Sunday News*, 1 Aug. 1897.

18. "SDL" 3; the evaluation harmonizes with most contemporary ratings of Lee.

19. Brooks, p. 249; Lee's commission as major, SDL-P; command of Lee's battery passed to the senior 1st Lt. James F. Hart and was for the rest of the War officially Hart's Battery.

20. J. B. Hamilton, ed., *Papers of Randolph Abbott Shotwell*, 1: 114 indicates that Lee directed some of the guns in the duel at Ball's Bluff on 21 Oct., but that is doubtful; Brooks, p. 249.

21. D-SDL.

22. BL 1, "D. C. R.," (Columbia, S. C.) *State*, 18 Aug. 1877.

23. Coxe, *CV* 32: 95.

24. Wellman, *Giant*, p. 67.

25. Coxe, *CV* 30: 461.

26. Hassler, pp. 63, 76–7, 81, 132, 262.

27. D-SDL; Coxe, *CV* 32: 95. Lee's diary ends at this point, though a few entries were made at later dates in this same book.

28. Coxe, *CV* 30: 461–62.

29. M. M. Boatner, comp., *The Civil War Dictionary*, p. 371; Wellman, *Giant*, p. 69; E. P. Alexander, "Confederate Artillery Service," *SHSP* 11: 99; D. S. Freeman, *Lee's Lieutenants* 1: 218.

30. Wellman, *Giant*, pp. 69–70.

31. *O. R.*, 5, pp. 530, 535; Freeman, *Lee's Lieutenants*, 1: 140–43; no one criticized Lee personally, but he became involved by helping to justify the dispositions.

32. V. J. Esposito, ed., *The West Point Atlas of American Wars*, 1: maps 39–47.

33. *O. R.*, 12, pt. 1, pp. 627, 629.

34. Hood, *Advance and Retreat*, pp. 21–2.

35. *O. R.*, 12, pt. 1, p. 633; Lee's commission as lt. col., SDL-P; Hassler, p. 143. The plaudit obviously came from admirers; Col. W. N. Pendleton remained army chief of artillery.

36. Hood, pp. 22–3; Brooks, p. 250.

37. *O. R.*, 12, pt. 3, p. 686; J. M. Stuckey, Jr., "A History of the Battalion Washington Artillery," p. 16; W. M. Owen, *In Camp and Battle With the Washington Artillery of New Orleans*, p. 84; Hassler, p. 153.

38. *O. R.*, 12, pt. 3, pp. 600, 607; Stuckey, p. 16.

39. *O. R.*, 12, pt. 3, pp. 686–88.

40. Ibid., p. 607.

41. J. C. Wise, *The Long Arm of Lee*, 1: 201; Alexander, "Confederate Artillery Service," *SHSP* 11: 100–03; *O. R.*, 12, pt. 3, pp. 686–87.

42. Esposito, 1: maps 44–46; *O. R.*, 11, pt. 2, p. 746.

43. C. Dowdey, *Seven Days*, pp. 168–69; *O. R.*, 11, pt. 2, pp. 525, 542, 546, 548; Data-SDL.

44. *O. R.*, 11, pt. 2, p. 543.

45. Ibid., p. 746.

46. Stuckey, pp. 17–8; J. Longstreet, *From Manassas to Appomattox*, p. 143; *O. R.*, 11, pt. 2, p. 746; Owen, p. 92; Dowdey, *Seven Days*, pp. 267–69.

47. *O. R.*, 11, pt. 2, pp. 539, 644, 673; Magruder to Randolph, 7 July 1862 and Lee's service record, NA-mic. 331, r. 155.

48. Data-SDL; *O. R.*, 11, pt. 2, p. 924.

49. *O. R.*, 11, pt. 3, p. 745; 12, pt. 2, p. 119; Data-SDL.

50. *O. R.*, 12, pt. 2, pp. 521, 924–25.

51. Lee quoted in G. T. Denison, Jr., *Modern Cavalry*, pp. 424, 433.

52. *O. R.*, 11, pt. 3, p. 653; 12, pt. 2, p. 119; Data-SDL; Lee to Magruder, 8 Aug. 1862, NA-mic. 331, r. 155; Lee to Allen, 2 Aug. 1862, ibid.

53. Magruder to Lee, 3 Aug. 1862, SDL-P.

54. Ibid., 13 Aug. 1862, ibid.

55. *O. R.*, 11, pt. 2, pp. 745–46.

NOTES TO CHAPTER 4

1. Wise, 1: 256–57; *O. R.*, 12, pt. 2, p. 548; pt. 3, p. 933; R. E. and T. N. Dupuy, *Military Heritage of America*, p. 248.

2. *O. R.*, 12, pt. 2, p. 577.

3. D. S. Freeman, ed., *Lee's Dispatches*, p. 58n.

4. Stuckey, p. 86; *O. R.*, 12, pt. 2, p. 577; E. P. Alexander, *Military Memoirs of a Confederate*, p. 212; R. O'Connor, *Hood*, pp. 96–7.

5. *O. R.*, 12, pt. 2, p. 577; G. F. R. Henderson, *Stonewall Jackson*, pp. 466–68; Freeman, *R. E. Lee*, 2: 329.

6. C. A. Evans, ed., *Confederate Military History*, 3: 330; BL 1.

7. *O. R.*, 12, pt. 2, p. 577; Pollard, p. 676.

8. Hamilton, 1: 290.

9. Owen, p. 119.

10. Dowdey, *Lee*, p. 293; R. W. Figg, *"Where Only Men Dare to Go!,"* p. 30.

11. Wise, 1: 271; BL 1; *O. R.*, 12, pt. 2, pp. 577–78.

12. L. Naisawald, *Grape and Canister*, p. 163; F. Vandiver, *Mighty Stonewall*, pp. 370–71.

13. *O. R.*, 12, pt. 2, pp. 577–78; Wise, 1: 273–75, 278; J. W. Ratchford, *Some Reminiscences*, p. 47.

14. Data-SDL; Dowdey, ed., *The Wartime Papers of R. E. Lee,* p. 283.

15. Ample excerpts from Longstreet's report are used in a discussion of the argument in *SHSP* 6: 59–70, 215–17. See also Longstreet, pp. 186–88.

16. See, for example, Data-SDL.

17. Wise 1: 279. Lee's battalion had six batteries; for list, see *O. R.,* 19, pt. 1, p. 806.

18. Owen, pp. 133–34.

19. Ibid., p. 135.

20. *O. R.,* 19, pt. 1, p. 829; for clarification, see Esposito, 1: maps 65, 66.

21. *O. R.,* 19, pt. 1, pp. 830, 844.

22. Longstreet ordered Eubank's battery away from S. D. Lee's battalion southward to support Toombs' brigade at Lower Bridge, where it remained for the battle; *O. R.,* 19, pt. 1, p. 844.

23. Ibid.

24. W. M. Evans, "A Night to be Remembered," *CV* 37: 216 (distinguished from C. A. Evans by citation to *CV*).

25. *O. R.,* 19, pt. 1, pp. 844–45, 1022; Wise, 1: 297.

26. *O. R.,* 19, pt. 1, p. 840; Alexander, *Memoirs,* p. 247; Figg, p. 39.

27. Some material, as here, is based on personal observation; Dowdey, *Lee,* p. 310.

28. *O. R.,* 19, pt. 1, p. 846. This was a serious blow, but it was the only gun Lee's battalion lost. Under these adverse conditions, the performance was laudable.

29. Freeman, *R. E. Lee,* 2: 390; *O. R.,* 19, pt. 1, pp. 896–97.

30. Freeman, *R. E. Lee,* 2: 390 says the sequence of events is indeterminable. I think S. D. and R. E. Lee conferred shortly after 9:00 A.M., because Hood probably sent the message after the third Federal assault started. See also J. P. Dyer, *The Gallant Hood,* pp. 140–41; H. A. White, *Lee and . . . the Southern Confederacy,* p. 218; and S. D. Lee, "Three Personal Incidents," ms., SHC (Herbert).

31. Wise, 1: 303–07; *O. R.,* 19, pt. 1, pp. 845–46; J. G. Walker, in *B. & L.,* 2: 678; see also Esposito, 1: map 68.

32. *O. R.,* 19, pt. 1, p. 846.

33. Wise, 1: 308. Sixty horses, more than half the number Lee had, were disabled in the battle; Figg, pp. 42, 44, 46; Freeman, *Lee's Lieutenants,* 2: 282–83.

34. N. G. Evans in *O. R.,* 19, pt. 1, pp. 939–40; see also p. 847.

35. Downey, p. 138; *CV* 8: 416; see also Evans, *CV* 37: 216–17.

36. Lee personally informed Henderson for use in *Stonewall Jackson,* p. 541; Freeman, *R. E. Lee,* 2: 404 analyses the incident and judges S. D. Lee mistaken; see also Freeman, *Lee's Lieutenants,* 2: 221.

37. Freeman, *R. E. Lee,* 2: 403.

38. Alexander, *Memoirs,* p. 269.

39. See Freeman, *Lee's Lieutenants,* 2: 242–43; Henderson, pp. 541–44; L. Chambers, *Stonewall Jackson,* 2: 229–30; W. L. Goldsmith, "Critical Test for General S. D. Lee," *CV* 3: 136; and Lee, "Three Incidents," SHC (Herbert).

40. Longstreet, p. 243; *O. R.,* 19, pt. 1, pp. 897, 899; Wise, 1: 310; Freeman, *Lee's Lieutenants,* 2: 279.

41. *O. R.,* 19, pt. 1, p. 846; F. Tilberg, *Antietam National Battlefield Site: Maryland,* pp. 1, 47; Wise, 1: 328; W. L. Pickard, "SDL" 3; Alexander, *Memoirs,* p. 247.

NOTES TO CHAPTER 5

1. R. W. Winston, *Robert E. Lee*, p. 189; Hassler, p. 186.

2. *O. R.*, 19, pt. 2, p. 697; W. L. Goldsmith, *CV* 2: 70 says that when Davis made the request R. E. Lee already had recommended S. D. Lee to be brigadier general and intended to make him the Army of Northern Virginia's chief of artillery. Records make the claim dubious, though possible, since nothing is known of Lee's plans for William N. Pendleton, who had the position; see also Lee's service record in NA-mic. 331, r. 155.

3. Dowdey, *Lee*, p. 325; T. H. Williams, Introduction to Alexander, *Memoirs*, pp. xxv–vi; *O. R.*, 19, pt. 2, pp. 697, 703.

4. Freeman, *Lee's Dispatches*, pp. 116–17.

5. Pollard, p. 679.

6. Data-SDL, *State* (clipping).

7. Lee to Alexander, 30 Nov. 1862, SHC (Alexander).

8. Vicksburg, 17 Dec. 1862, scrapbook, M. J. Solomons Papers.

9. I determined the numbers of troops by substracting the number of reinforcements from the totals given in the "Return of Effective Troops in Major General Smith's Command, January 3, 1863," in *O. R.*, 17, pt. 2, p. 825. See also W. Hall, *The Story of the 26th Louisiana Infantry*, pp. 33–4; and a useful synopsis based on the *Official Records* showing the composition and losses of both armies, *B. & L.*, 3: 471.

10. Hall, pp. 33–4; W. P. Chambers, "My Journal," *PMHS-C* 5 (1925) : 253; S. D. Lee, "Chickasaw Bayou," ms., SHC (Claiborne).

11. S. D. Lee, "Details of Important Work by Two Confederate Telegraphy Operators," *PMHS* 8: 51–5; Fall to Mickle, 6 Jan. 1905, Confederate Miscellany, IIb.

12. Chambers, p. 254; Hall, p. 38; Lee, Pemberton, and Smith all describe the area in *O. R.*, 17, pt. 1, p. 665; see also pp. 680–81.

13. S. D. Lee, "The Campaign of Generals Grant and Sherman . . . Known as the 'Chickasaw Bayou Campaign,' " *PMHS* 4: 24–6. The confederate congress acted three months later to legalize this widespread practice of impressing slave labor for military use.

14. *O. R.*, 17, pt. 1, pp. 676–79; pt. 2, pp. 805, 824.

15. Ibid., pp. 681–82; Chambers, p. 254; Hall, p. 41.

16. D. Maury, *Recollections of a Virginian*, p. 169; see also A. Jones, "The Vicksburg Campaign," *Journal of Mississippi History* 29 (Feb. 1967) : 12–27.

17. *O. R.*, 17, pt. 1, pp. 681–82; Hall, p. 42.

18. *O. R.*, 17, pt. 1, pp. 681–82.

19. Ibid.; Hall, pp. 43–5.

20. Lee, "Chickasaw Bayou," SHC (Claiborne) ; *O. R.*, 17, pt. 1, p. 682; Hall, pp. 45–6.

21. W. T. Sherman, *Memoirs*, 1: 290–91; *B. & L.* 3: 467.

22. Sherman, 1: 283; Chambers, p. 255.

23. Maury, p. 169; BL 1, Graham to Lee, 2 July 1899 and Frank Johnston to Blewett Lee, 10 June 1908; J. E. Gaskell, *CV* 23: 128; W. T. Moore, *CV* 22: 553.

24. Lee, "Chickasaw Bayou," SHC (Claiborne) ; *B. & L.*, 3: 468.

25. Hall, pp. 46, 48; *O. R.*, 17, pt. 1, p. 683.

26. *O. R.*, 17, pt. 1, pp. 608, 628; Moore, *CV* 22: 553; *B. & L.*, 3: 470.

27. *O. R.*, 17, pt. 1, p. 683; Maury, p. 179; *B. & L.*, 3: 470.

28. *O. R.*, 17, pt. 1, p. 684; Sherman, 1: 293.

29. Lee, "Chickasaw Bayou," SHC (Claiborne); *O. R.*, 17, pt. 1, p. 684; J. A. Burgess, *CV* 12: 200.

30. H. Strode, *Jefferson Davis,* 2: 355.

31. "SDL" 2, S. Carolina, 15 Jan. 1908; H. H. Hockersmith, *CV* 10: 16.

32. *O. R.*, 17, pt. 1, pp. 669, 674–76, 680; Hall, p. 51; Gaskell, *CV* 23: 128.

33. BL 1; Thayer quoted by D. A. Brown, "Battle at Chickasaw Bluffs," *Civil War Times-Illustrated* 9: 46.

34. E. H. Hagerman, "The Evolution of Trench Warfare" feels the way Chickasaw Bayou was fought and won contributed to the "unfortunate ascendence" of trench warfare for the remainder of the War (p. 419). Possibly; but Lee probably won in the only way he could; and who but an idiot would reject entrenchments?

35. Lee, "The Campaign," *PMHS* 4: 35.

36. Pollard, pp. 675, 687.

NOTES TO CHAPTER 6

1. W. Chambers, pp. 257–58; Hassler, pp. 201, 213; Pollard, p. 680.

2. W. H. Tunnard, *A Southern Record,* p. 221.

3. C. W. Short, *CV* 7: 103.

4. J. C. Pemberton, *Pemberton, Defender of Vicksburg,* p. 291.

5. Lee, "The Campaign," *PMHS* 4: 19–20.

6. *War of the Rebellion: A Compilation of the Official Records of the Union and Confederate Navies,* ser. 1, 24, pp. 499–500 (hereafter cited as *O. R.-Navy*); see also Esposito, 1: map 102.

7. W. G. Everhart, *Vicksburg National Military Park,* p. 15.

8. Tunnard, pp. 220–21.

9. W. Chambers, pp. 259–60.

10. Fragment, D-SDL; Everhart, p. 15; J. R. Soley, *Admiral Porter,* p. 294; *O. R.*, 24, pt. 1, pp. 461–64.

11. Fragment, D-SDL; *O. R.*, pt. 1, pp. 456, 499–500.

12. E. C. Bearss, *Decision in Mississippi,* p. 215.

13. Fragment, D-SDL; *O. R.*, 24, pt. 1, pp. 504–05.

14. Everhart, pp. 18–20.

15. *O. R.-Navy,* ser. 1, 24: 631.

16. S. D. Lee, "The Campaign of Vicksburg," *PMHS* 3: 24.

17. "Historical Sketch of the Third Brigade," VPC; C. L. Stevenson specifically requested Lee; see *O. R.*, 24, pt. 3, p. 820; also J. D. Hartwell, *CV* 1: 264 and F. A. Shoup, *CV* 2: 172.

18. See Esposito, 1: map 105.

19. Lee, "The Campaign of Vicksburg," *PMHS* 3: 37; BL 3, Frank Johnston, "Lee at Champion Hill"; Bearss, pp. 246, 250.

20. Pollard, pp. 680–81; *CV* 2: 70.

21. BL 1, W. T. Moore, *Daily Herald,* 5 Oct. 1902; Bearss, p. 270.

22. Lee, "The Campaign of Vicksburg," *PMHS* 3: 42–3, 48–9; Everhart, pp. 26–7, 30.

23. *O. R.*, 24, pt. 1, pp. 318–19.

24. Emma Balfour Diary (May 16–June 2, 1863), kept during the siege of Vicksburg, typescripts at MDAH and VPC, May 21.

25. F. Johnston, "The Vicksburg Campaign," *PMHS* 10: 83; Everhart, pp. 30–1; S. D. Lee, "Report of the Siege of Vicksburg," *SHSP* 4: 14–5.

26. Pollard, p. 681; Balfour Diary, May 21.

27. S. D. Lee, "The Siege of Vicksburg," *PMHS* 3: 55–6, 64. Lee says Vicksburg "was full of sick and wounded men, quarter-master, commissary employees and extra duty men, and hangers on of every kind" (p. 57). Though ineffective fighting men, they were included in the paroled and account for the discrepancy in 29,491 paroles issued, while supposedly some 10,000 fewer took part in the fighting.

28. Everhart, pp. 34–5; Balfour Diary, May 21.

29. *O. R.*, 24, pt. 1, p. 87; Capers, *CV* 35: 23.

30. Balfour Diary, May 19.

31. Lee, "Report of the Siege," *SHSP* 4: 15; S. H. Lockett, in *B. & L.*, 3: 489.

32. Lee, "The Siege," *PMHS* 3: 59.

33. Ibid.

34. Catton (*Grant Moves South*, p. 450) quotes W. E. Strong.

35. Lee, "The Siege," *PMHS* 3: 60; Benjamin LaBree, ed., *Camp Fires of the Confederacy*, pp. 61–2.

36. Lee, "The Siege," *PMHS* 3: 60. Again Lee excelled as an artillerist.

37. Ibid., pp. 61–3; Lee, "Report of the Siege," *SHSP* 4: 15.

38. J. S. Kountz, *Record of the Organizations Engaged in the Campaign, Siege, and Defense of Vicksburg*, p. 48; Everhart, p. 40.

39. "Historical Sketch of the Third Brigade," VPC; *O. R.*, 24, pt. 3, pp. 914–15; Lee, "The Siege," *PMHS* 3: 66–8.

40. Lee, "Report of the Siege," *SHSP* 4: 16; Lee, "The Siege," *PMHS* 3: 63, 68–9; Balfour Diary, May 30.

41. L. C. McAllister, *CV* 12: 473; BL 1, "Memoirs of William D. Kyle," *Daily Herald*, 4 May 1906.

42. Quoted in P. F. Walker, *Vicksburg*, p. 171.

43. *O. R.*, 24, pt. 2, pp. 348, 351.

44. Shoup, *CV* 2: 173–74; Lockett, in *B. & L.*, 3: 492.

45. *O. R.*, 24, pt. 2, p. 353; Lockett, in *B. & L.*, 3: 492.

46. Lee to Mrs. Wright, 22 Oct. 1904, SHC (Pemberton).

47. D. Rowland, *History of Mississippi*, 1: 883; NA-Lee's parole, mic. 331, r. 155.

NOTES TO CHAPTER 7

1. *O. R.*, ser. 2, 6, p. 113; ser. 1, 24, pt. 1, p. 232. Lee and the other general officers captured at Vicksburg were exchanged for Federal prisoners taken at the battle of Chancellorsville, 1–4 May 1863; *O. R.*, 24, pt. 3, pp. 1011, 1048; Lee's commission as a major general, in Stephen D. Lee Museum.

2. J. E. Johnston, *Narrative of Military Operations*, pp. 160, 373; BL 1.

3. *O. R.*, 30, pt. 2, pp. 197–98; pt. 3, p. 197; pt. 4, p. 504. Grant was concerned because some southern newspapers had indicated that the Confederates might not respect the paroles given at Vicksburg.

4. *O. R.*, 30, pt. 3, pp. 224, 228–29; ser. 2, 6, p. 234.

5. Ibid., ser. 2, 6, pp. 247, 273, 296–97, 311–12; ser. 1, 30, pt. 3, pp. 226–27; Hurlbut to Lee, 29 Sept. 1863, SDL-P.

6. *O. R.*, 30, pt. 4, pp. 517, 576–77; Connelly, p. 268 incorrectly numbers Lee's cavalry at 11,000. Lee eventually had that many but surely not in the fall of 1863; Pollard, p. 683; Thiele, pp. 174–75, 459–60.

7. Lee to Pettus, 17 Aug. 1863, GR 61; *O. R.*, 36, pt. 1, pp. 252, 371; 30, pt. 3, p. 696; pt. 4, p. 609.

8. Ibid., 30, pt. 4, pp. 514, 522; S. D. Lee, "The War in Mississippi," *PMHS* 10: 48. Ironically, this article, written around 1876, and probably the first Lee wrote, was the last of his writings to be published, appearing shortly before his death.

9. *O. R.*, 30, pt. 4, pp. 504, 673–74, 687–88.

10. J. E. Johnston, pp. 256–57; *O. R.*, 30, pt. 4, pp. 724–28, 740–41, 764; 31, pt. 1, pp. 25–8, 594; since Lee sincerely believed that the enemy he would face in Tennessee was at least three times his strength—probably more—I think Connelly, pp. 378, 381 is incorrect to say Lee was timid. J. E. Johnston, p. 259 says Lee "very judiciously abandoned the enterprise"; *O. R.*, 30, pt. 4, pp. 747–48; J. P. Dyer, *From Shiloh to San Juan*, pp. 108–09.

11. *O. R.*, 30, pt. 4, p. 763; 31, pt. 1, pp. 27–31, 763–64; pt. 3, p. 700; W. D. Pickett, *CV* 16: 231; F. Moore, ed., *The Rebellion Record*, 7: 65, 573. The Confederates had inadequate clothing and equipment for the chilly October weather. Federals claimed Southerners wore northern uniforms, but they only wore commandeered blue overcoats; V. Blythe, *A History of the Civil War*, p. 196; J. E. Johnston, p. 260; Lewis, p. 314.

12. E. Sheppard, *Bedford Forrest*, p. 137; R. S. Henry, *"First With the Most,"* p. 175; *O. R.*, 21, pt. 3, p. 793; D. Rowland, *Davis*, 6: 93, 130.

13. W. D. McCain, "Nathan Bedford Forrest," *Journal of Mississippi History* 24 (1962) : 209; *O. R.*, 31, pt. 3, p. 646.

14. J. L. Wofford, *CV* 16: 593; A. Lytle, *Bedford Forrest*, p. 245 says, "Lee was the only man who understood the value of his service, and helped him in every way."

15. Sheppard, pp. 137–39; J. A. Wyeth, *Life of General Nathan Bedford Forrest*, pp. 272–76; T. Jordan and J. P. Pryor, *The Campaigns of Lieutenant General N. B. Forrest*, p. 378; *O. R.*, 31, pt. 3, pp. 846, 853–54, 862, 864–65.

16. *O. R.*, 30, pt. 2, p. 789; 31, pt. 3, p. 631.

17. Lee to Wigfall, 4 Nov. 1863, Manuscripts Div., Lib. of Congress; *O. R.*, 31, pt. 3, p. 841.

18. *O. R.*, 32, pt. 2, pp. 622–26; for other complaints about Lee's cavalry troops, see John LeGrant and others to Miss. Gov. Charles Clark, 30 Nov. 1863 and Clark's reply, 6 Dec. 1863, Governor's Correspondence, MDAH.

19. *O. R.*, 31, pt. 3, p. 744; Lee to Johnston and Johnston to Lee, 23 Nov. 1863; Delay to Clark, with indorsements by Johnston, L. W. Hoeb, James R. Chalmers, and Lee, 27 Nov. 1863; Marthy Cragin to Clark, 28 Nov. 1863 and Clark to Johnston, 6 Dec. 1863, GR 65.

20. *O. R.*, 31, pt. 3, pp. 743–44, 836–37; ser. 3, 3, p. 9; Gholson to Pettus, 5 Aug. 1863, GR 61.

21. NA-Lee to Taylor, 7 Sept. 1863; certificate of 8 July 1863, signed by W. H. Johnson, William Elliot, and E. N. Martin; certificate of 7 Aug. 1863, signed by Lee; Holt to Taylor, 9 Sept. 1864; Taylor to Lee, 11 May 1864; certificate of 17 June 1864, signed by William Elliot; and Lee to Taylor, 12 Aug. 1864, mic. 331, r. 155.

22. NA-Lee to Miles, 28 Jan. 1864; Davis to Polk, 18 April 1864, in D. Rowland, *Davis*, 6: 230; NA-Lee to Jackson, 28 March 1864, mic. 331, r. 155; *O. R.*, ser. 2, 6, p. 531; Lee to Kells, 30 Jan. 1864, GR 65; *O. R.*, 31, pt. 1, pp. 588–89; pt. 3, pp. 268, 704–05.

23. *O. R.*, 32, pt. 2, pp. 546–47; J. H. Parks, *General Leonidas Polk*, pp. 355–56.

24. Sherman, pp. 388–89; S. D. Lee, "Sherman's Meridian Expedition," *SHSP* 8: 59–60; Lee to Claiborne, 22 April 1878, SDL-P; Lewis, pp. 333–34.

25. *O. R.*, 32, pt. 1, pp. 357, 365; W. M. Polk, *Leonidas Polk*, 2: 327; Parks, p. 359.

26. *O. R.*, 32, pt. 1, pp. 365–66.

27. Ibid., pp. 358–61, 366–68; pt. 2, pp. 738, 742, 753; pt. 3, p. 603; Parks, pp. 360–62; Wyeth, pp. 322–23.

28. Henry, p. 235; *O. R.*, 32, pt. 1, p. 333; pt. 2, p. 603; pt. 3, pp. 620–21; H. T. Kane, *Spies for the Blue and Gray*, pp. 207–09. Citizens complained about confiscation of wagons and goods involved in trade with the enemy; one got the secretary of war to rule that offenders should be punished by a judicial tribunal and not summarily by the military. In his report, Lee noted bitterly that "the indorsement of the Secretary of War reflects on me. I consider this rather harsh, when as a soldier I was obeying orders." He had loyally followed instructions but afterwards requested specific written orders from Polk.

29. D. Rowland, *Davis*, 6: 514–16; *O. R.*, 32, pt. 3, pp. 780, 822–23; 825; 38, pt. 4, p. 661.

NOTES TO CHAPTER 8

1. *O. R.*, 52, pt. 2, pp. 669–70; 53, p. 988; 39, pt. 2, p. 587.

2. Ibid., 39, pt. 2, p. 591.

3. S. D. Lee, "Battle of Brice's Cross Roads," *PMHS* 6: 28; NA-Lee to Jackson, 9 May 1864, mic. 331, r. 155; *O. R.*, 52, pt. 2, p. 653; 32, pt. 3, pp. 700, 800, 822; pt. 4, pp. 685, 719, 723; 38, pt. 4, p. 691; Henry, pp. 282, 284.

4. This statement is made, for example, on a prominent plaque in downtown Booneville; see also *O. R.*, 39, pt. 2, p. 639.

5. Lee, "Brice's Cross Roads," *PMHS* 6: 31, 37.

6. *O. R.*, 39, pt. 2, p. 660; NA-Cooper to Lee, 23 June 1864, mic. 331, r. 155; Lee's official notification, Lee Museum. "Stephen Dill Lee" in *DAB* indicates confusingly that Lee's appointment "was later reconsidered and confirmed as temporary." Actually all but the top six full generals held temporary rank, e.g., in the "Provisional Army of the Confederate States," to be disbanded after the War (Warner, p. xxiv). All appointments to general rank were made by the president, subject to advice and consent of the senate. No "reconsideration" of Lee occurred; the senate just did not get around to confirming the appointment until 16 March 1865.

7. SDL-P, clipping, *Daily Clarion*, 29 June 1864.

8. SDL-P, clipping.

9. *O. R.-Navy*, ser. 1, 26, p. 234; *O. R.*, 32, pt. 1, pp. 586–88, 599, 601, 606–07.

10. Lee to T. C. Blewett, 11 June 1864, SDL-P; Elliot to Forrest, 12 June 1864 and various orders, 20, 25, 26 May 1864, Forrest Papers.

11. *O. R.*, 39, pt. 2, pp. 627, 656.

12. Ibid., p. 607; ser. 3, 3, p. 478.

13. Ibid., ser. 1, 39, pt. 2, pp. 628–29.

14. S. D. Lee, "The Battle of Tupelo," *PMHS* 6: 39–42; *O. R.*, 39, pt. 1, pp. 246, 688–89; pt. 2, pp. 688–89, 697; 52, pt. 2, pp. 679–80, 685–86; Davis to Adams, 5 July 1864, in D. Rowland, *Davis*, 6: 279; NA-Lee to Walker, 8 July 1864, mic. 331, r. 155; Lee to Kirby Smith, 9 July 1864, SHC (Kirby Smith); J. H. Parks, *General Edmund Kirby Smith, C.S.A.*, pp. 420–21; Easterlang to Clark, 12 July 1864, Lee to Clark, 4, 5 July 1864, GR 64.

15. *O. R.*, 29, pt. 2, pp. 694, 697; Lee, "Tupelo," *PMHS* 6: 42–3; Sheppard, p. 197; Wyeth, p. 437. Some of the Federals later claimed they had no breastworks. Cf. T. G. Carter, *CV* 14: 309–11. Much other testimony indicates that, while the line probably varied, it had strong breastworks.

16. Henry, p. 318; Lee, "Tupelo," *PMHS* 6: 45–51. Lee's account, published thirty-seven years after the events, drew strong protest from Forrest's old subordinates, who resented any intimation that Forrest might have erred even slightly.

17. J. W. Morton, *The Artillery of Nathan Bedford Forrest's Cavalry*, pp. 207–08.

18. Lee, "Tupelo," *PMHS* 6: 44–5; *O. R.*, 29, pt. 1, p. 322; Wyeth, p. 444; Henry, pp. 323–24; J. M. Hubbard, *Notes of a Private*, p. 126.

19. *O. R.*, 29, pt. 1, pp. 322, 326.

20. Ibid., p. 327.

21. Lee to Clark, 14 July 1864, GR 64; Bragg to Lee, 17 July 1864, SDL-P; *O. R.*, 29, pt. 1, pp. 256, 320, 324, 327; pt. 2, p. 184; Henry, p. 322; Lee, "Tupelo," *PMHS* 6: 50.

22. Wyeth, p. 457.

23. T. G. Carter, "The Tupelo Campaign," *PMHS* 10: 109.

24. Lee to Claiborne, 22 April 1878, SHC (Claiborne).

25. Connelly, pp. 391–419; T. R. Hay, "The Davis, Hood, Johnston Controversy," *The Mississippi Valley Historical Review* 11: 76.

26. Ratchford, p. 48.

NOTES TO CHAPTER 9

1. *O. R.*, 38, pt. 5, p. 892; 39, pt. 2, pp. 719–20. Maury took over Lee's department. Hood's other suggestions were Mansfield Lovell and Wade Hampton.

2. Lee quoted in Hood, pp. 38–9, 184.

3. *O. R.*, 38, pt. 5, p. 911; Ratchford, p. 48.

4. *O. R.*, 29, pt. 2, p. 712; 52, p. 713; 38, pt. 3, pp. 663, 680; pt. 5, p. 281; Connelly, pp. 450, 455.

5. See Esposito: map 147c.

6. *O. R.*, 38, pt. 3, p. 763; Cox, *Atlanta*, p. 184.

7. *B. & L.*, 4: 319; E. L. Russell, *CV* 56: 316.

8. Connelly, p. 455; F. Cleaves, *Rock of Chickamauga*, p. 235; O. O. Howard, *Autobiography*, 2: 25.

9. *O. R.*, 28, pt. 5, pp. 936, 950, 960–63; pt. 3, pp. 763–64.

10. Connelly, pp. 458–62; Hood, p. 203.

11. BL 1; Anderson quoted in D. Rowland, *The Official and Statistical Register*, p. 745; *O. R.*, 38, pt. 3, p. 764.

12. *O. R.*, 39, pt. 1, p. 828; Connelly, pp. 470–72.

13. *O. R.*, 29, pt. 1, p. 810; Hood, p. 250.

14. *O. R.*, 29, pt. 1, pp. 810–11; pt. 3, p. 818; Lee, *CV* 16: 257; R. H. Lindsay, *CV* 16: 423; H. K. Nelson, *CV* 15: 508; Lee to Walthall, 20 May 1878, in D. Rowland, *Davis*, 8: 205.

15. Dyer, *Hood*, p. 285; S. F. Horn, *The Decisive Battle*, pp. 3, 11, 14; I. A. Buck, *Cleburne and His Command*, pp. 309–10.

16. BL 1, *Picayune*.

17. Ibid.

18. Hood, p. 282; Lee, *CV* 16: 257; M. F. Steele, *American Campaigns*, p. 276;

Henry Stone, *Campaigns in Kentucky and Tennessee*, p. 451; Lee, *SHSP* 3: 66; Cleaves, p. 251.

19. Hood, p. 284; Cleaves, p. 251.

20. Lee, *SHSP* 3: 66–7.

21. Ibid., p. 67; W. D. Gale, *CV* 2: 4; Lee, *CV* 16: 257.

22. S. D. Lee, "Johnson's Division in the Battle of Franklin," *PMHS* 7: 82; BL 1, *Picayune;* Lee notes too that "a Tennessee author"—probably J. P. Young, with whom Lee corresponded—had, Lee believed, correctly placed the blame. On Spring Hill, Young hedged, sometimes blaming Hood and other times claiming Schofield achieved success "through the sheerest good fortune" (*CV* 16); see also Connelly, pp. 494–502.

23. Lee, *CV* 16: 257; Lee to Walthall, 20 May 1878, in D. Rowland, *Davis*, 8: 205; Hood, p. 295; Connelly, pp. 501–02 points out that since Schofield had three alternate routes to Franklin or Nashville he did not need to pass that point; also that the Confederate opportunity at Spring Hill was overrated by Lee and those sharing his opinions.

24. *O. R.*, 45, pt. 1, pp. 341, 652, 686–91; Hood, p. 293; Lee, "Johnson's Division," *PMHS* 7: 77–8; Lee, *CV* 16: 257.

25. Lee, "Johnson's Division," *PMHS* 7: 78.

26. Lee, *SHSP* 3: 67.

27. Lee, "Johnson's Division," *PMHS* 7: 79.

28. Horn, *Army*, p. 404; Hood, p. 295; Boatner, p. 305; Lee, "Johnson's Division," *PMHS* 7: 80; Lee, *CV* 16: 258–59.

29. Lee to Walthall, 20 May 1878, in D. Rowland, *Davis*, 8: 205.

30. *CV* 16: 258–59.

31. Lee, *SHSP* 3: 68; Horn, *Battle*, p. 71.

32. Emma L. Scott, *CV* 16: 399–400.

33. *O. R.*, 45, pt. 2, p. 691.

34. McKinney, pp. 409–10; Hay, *Tennessee Campaign*, p. 152.

35. Lee to Mason, 11:45 A.M., 15 Dec. 1864, SDL-P; O'Connor, *Thomas*, p. 318; Hood to Lee, 1:00 P.M., 15 Dec. 1864, SDL-P.

36. Lee, *SHSP* 3: 68; Lee, *CV* 12: 269–70.

37. J. A. Dozier, *CV* 16: 192; these were possibly natural obstacles, or Lee may have ordered them moved there.

38. Lee, *SHSP* 3: 68–9; Horn, *Army*, p. 416.

39. Lee, *SHSP* 3: 69; Lindsay, *CV* 8: 311.

40. Hood, in *B. & L.*, 4: 437; Lee, *SHSP*, 3: 70.

41. Horn, *Army*, pp. 416–17; Schofield quoted in *The American Heritage Picture History*, 2: 599.

42. Horn, *Army*, p. 417.

43. Lee, *SHSP* 5: 130–31; Lindsay, *CV* 7: 311.

44. E. W. Smith, *CV* 11: 532.

45. L. F. Garrard, *CV* 11: 350–51.

46. A. D. Rape, *CV* 35: 179–80; Lee, *CV* 12: 351.

47. Garrard, *CV* 12: 351.

48. Lee, *CV* 12: 270.

49. Lee, *SHSP* 3: 71; Lee, *CV* 12: 270; McKinney, pp. 415–17; Garrard, *CV* 12: 351; Smith, *CV* 12: 532.

50. *CV* 12: 271; Blythe, p. 311.

51. R. S. Dee Portes, BL 1.

52. R. H. Lindsay to Blewett Lee, 29 May 1908, BL 3.

53. Hay, *Tennessee Campaign*, p. 171; Ratchford, p. 50.

54. Hood, pp. 139, 332.
55. SDL-P, clipping.
56. SDL-P, clipping.
57. *O. R.*, 45, p. 706.

NOTES TO CHAPTER 10

1. Lee to Beauregard, 23 Dec. 1864, C.S.A. Archives, army, military telegrams; F. Vandiver, ed., *The Civil War Diary of General Josiah Gorgas*, p. 158.
2. "Story of the Blewett-Harrison-Lee Home," from T. C. Read, Charleston, S. C. (hereafter cited as "BHL Home").
3. Family tombstone, Friendship Cemetery, Columbus, Miss.; "BHL Home"; W. Lipscomb, *History of Columbus*, pp. 125–27.
4. "James T. Harrison," *NCAB* 12: 184; J. A. Stevens quoted in *Commercial*, "SDL" 2.
5. "Background Material," SHC (Harrison); "BHL Home"; tombstone.
6. Pollard, p. 687; New York *Herald*, 25 Aug. 1860.
7. D. Lipscomb, pp. 15–6; Roy to Regina Harrison, 28 Jan. 1865, SDL-P; Davis to Regina Harrison, 8 March 1861; Hardee to Regina Harrison, 12 April 1862 and 11 Oct. 1863; Polk to Regina Harrison, 7 May 1864; Walker to Regina Harrison, 20 Feb. 1859, SDL-P; W. Lipscomb, pp. 125–27; editorial, *CV* 11: 514; packet clippings, SDL-P; Lee to Harrison, 27 May 1864, SHC (Harrison).
8. Roy to Regina Harrison, 28 Jan. 1865, SDL-P.
9. Gibson to Lee, Jan. (?), 1865, Forrest to Lee, 7 Feb. 1865, SDL-P.
10. Mary Billups, "Recollections," tape recorded by Columbus and Lowndes County Hist. Soc.; BL 1; the Harrison house is now a manse for the Presbyterian church; Helen Garner, in *War Reminiscences of Columbus, Mississippi*, p. 14.
11. Regina Lee, in *War Reminiscences*, p. 6; Lucy Neilson, *Lucy's Journal*, p. 59.
12. BL 1; Gibson to Lee, Jan. (?), 1865; Anderson to Lee, 26 Jan. 1865, SDL-P.
13. Suzanne Wilson, *Column South*, p. 275; J. D. Richardson, comp., *A Compilation of the Messages and Papers of the Confederacy*, 1: 537.
14. BL 1; Richardson, 1: 537–38; Lee's second notification of promotion to lieutenant general, Lee Museum.
15. D. Rowland, *Davis*, 6: 429; G. Bradford, *Confederate Portraits*, p. 16; [?] to Lee, 3 March 1865, BL 1; Buck, *Cleburne*, p. 355; *O. R.*, 47, pt. 2, p. 1362; 49, pt. 1, p. 1044.
16. B. L. Ridley, *CV* 2: 20; A. D. Kirwan, ed., *Johnny Green of the Orphan Brigade*, p. 181.
17. J. G. Barrett, *Sherman's March*, p. 171; W. Clark, ed., *Histories of the Several Regiments*, 4: 592.
18. J. M. Gibson, *Those 163 Days*, p. 231.
19. Wellman, *Giant*, p. 175; B. L. Ridley, *Battles and Sketches of the Army of Tennessee*, p. 455; *O. R.*, 47, pt. 1, p. 731.
20. Pollard, p. 686; Barrett, p. 201; G. E. Govan and J. W. Livingood, *A Different Valor*, pp. 360–61; J. E. Johnston, pp. 373–74, 394–95.
21. Mary B. Chesnut, *A Diary from Dixie*, pp. 509–10.
22. Govan and Livingood, p. 360; Barrett, pp. 201–02; Anderson to Lee, 19 April 1865, Falconer to Lee, 24 April 1864, G. O. No. 18, 27 April 1865, in Wilson Letters; *O. R.*, 47, pt. 1, pp. 838–41.

23. Lee's parole, 1 May 1865, SDL-P; Wood, *CV* 16: 585.

24. *CV* 3: 4.

25. J. B. Gordon, *Reminiscences of the Civil War,* p. 124.

26. Pollard, p. 686; also W. A. Hewitt, "Funeral Address—" *Baptist Record,* n. s., 10, no. 25 (June 18, 1908) : 7.

NOTES TO CHAPTER 11

1. W. B. Hesseltine and L. Gara, "Mississippi's Confederate Leaders after the War," *Journal of Mississippi History* 13 (1951) : 89; W. B. Hesseltine, *Confederate Leaders,* p. 20.

2. Blewett Lee to Regina Lee, 30 Jan. 1866, SDL-P; J. K. Bettersworth, *People's College,* p. 86 (Unless otherwise noted, all following citations of Bettersworth are to this volume) .

3. Blewett Lee to Regina Lee, 1 Feb. 1869, SDL-P.

4. Lee quoted in A. B. Hart, *The Southern South,* p. 121.

5. S. D. Lee, "The South Since the War," in Evans, 12: 349.

6. Blewett Lee's application for membership in the Sons of the Revolution, SDL-P; Harrison to Regina Lee, 10 March 1867, Davis to Lee, 17 July 1878, Hampton to Lee, 13 May 1867 and other letters on the subject, SDL-P; Georgia P. Young, *CV* 16: 383.

7. Lee to Johnson, 9 July 1865, SDL-P.

8. Lee, "The South," in Evans, 12: 280, 289, 293, 296, 298.

9. Ibid., pp. 312–15.

10. Speech by Blewett Lee at 1927 celebration of Grant's birthday, SDL-P.

11. BL 2.

12. Ibid.; Lee, "The South," in Evans, 12: 311.

13. Speech by Blewett Lee, Grant's birthday.

14. Lucille W. Banks, "Lieutenant General Stephen D. Lee," BL 1; various letters 1865–67, SDL-P.

15. Lee to Green, 14 Jan. 1869, SHC (Green) ; Sarah Neilson to Read, 16 May 1964, Read Collection; Young, *CV* 16: 383.

16. "SDL" 3, Jan. 1908. Lee's family was Anglican, like others of British ancestry, but various members joined the Congregationalists. Lee's grandfather joined before marrying Kezia Miles, a Unitarian, then he joined his wife's group in 1817 and took his family out of the Christian tradition (Read, p. 86) ; Bettersworth, p. 48; D. Lipscomb, pp. 16, 29; SDL-P.

17. Lee quoted in South Carolina newspaper interview, BL 1; Bettersworth, *Mississippi: Yesterday and Today,* p. 246.

18. Lee interview, BL 1.

19. Ibid.

20. Longstreet to Humphreys, 23 Feb. 1866, Lee to Humphreys, 15 March 1866, GR 78.

21. Longstreet to Lee, 27 March, 2 May 1866, SDL-P.

22. Longstreet to Lee, 12 May, 17 Dec. 1866, SDL-P.

23. Maury to Lee, 22, 30 Dec. 1872, SDL-P.

24. BL 1, New Orleans paper.

25. The same description appeared in the *Herald,* the *Register,* and several other newspapers, BL 1, 2.

26. Hampton to Lee, 31 Jan. 1876, SDL-P; BL 1.

27. Hite to Mrs. Hite, 18, 25 June, 1 July 1876, Cornelius B. Hite, Jr. Papers.

28. D. Lipscomb, p. 16; W. Lipscomb, p. 132; BL 1.
29. C. Vann Woodward, *Origins of the New South,* pp. 14, 75n.

NOTES TO CHAPTER 12

1. Betterworth, p. 50; W. White, "Mississippi Confederate Veterans," *Journal of Mississippi History* 20: 155; BL 1, S. Carolina paper.
2. Pickett, *CV* 12: 328; Bettersworth, p. 51.
3. For example, the *Index,* BL 1.
4. BL 1, *Independent,* 26 Jan. 1878.
5. My account of the senatorial election is based on numerous clippings in BL; Lee's commission as state senator, SDL-P.
6. Bettersworth, p. 51; Lee to Mrs. Lee, 14 Feb. 1878, SDL-P.
7. BL 1; Lee to Mrs. Lee, 17 July 1878, SHC (Harrison).
8. BL 2, *Lee County Standard,* 28 May 1887; *Dispatch,* n.d.
9. Bettersworth, p. 165; *Messenger,* 9 June 1887, JCB.
10. BL 2, *Citizen,* 16 June 1887, *Lee County Standard,* 2 July 1887.
11. *Messenger,* 15 Sept. 1887, JCB.
12. BL 2, *Dispatch,* Feb. (?), 1888.
13. BL 2, N. D. Guerry, 3 Jan. 1889 and various clippings, 29 April 1889.
14. *Clarion-Ledger,* 20 June 1889, JCB.
15. Ibid., 13 June 1889.
16. Ibid., 20 June 1889; BL 2, 17 June 1889.
17. Bettersworth, p. 167.
18. T. B. Carroll, *Historical Sketches of Oktibbeha,* p. 166.
19. Report of the Committee Appointed by the State Farmers' Alliance, in Session at Starkville, to Memorialize the Constitutional Convention Concerning Certain Matters, MDAH; handwritten personal memoranda, 15 Aug. 1890, Charles Regan Papers (hereafter cited as memoranda).
20. BL 2.
21. BL 2, *Commercial,* 4 Oct. 1906; memoranda; Ridley, *CV* 4: 106; BL 3, *Appeal Avalanche,* 27 April 1893.
22. Memoranda.
23. Ibid.
24. V. O. Key, Jr., *Southern Politics in the State and Nation,* p. 539.
25. Bettersworth, p. 169; Lee to Power, 1 Sept. 1894, John L. Power Papers.
26. BL 3.
27. Ibid., *Dispatch,* 10 June 1895; clippings, SDL Papers, MDAH.

NOTES TO CHAPTER 13

1. Davis to S. M., 23 June 1879, SLD-P; Minutes of the Board of Trustees, 1 April 1880, College Archives, MSUL (hereafter cited as Minutes).
2. Minutes, 2 April 1880, 16 May 1879, 7 May 1880; Lee to Gordon, 27 Feb. 1886, President's Letterbook, Archives, MSUL (hereafter cited as Letterbook); Lee to Lamar, 25 June 1881, L. Q. C. Lamar Papers.
3. *Southern Livestock Journal,* 7 Oct. 1880, JCB (hereafter cited as *SLJ*).
4. Bettersworth, p. 58.
5. D. Lipscomb, pp. 14, 27.
6. Bettersworth, pp. 75–6.

7. Ibid., pp. 44, 60–62; *Clarion*, 23 Dec. 1880, *Messenger*, 23 Dec. 1880, JCB.
8. Minutes, 7 May 1880; Bettersworth, pp. 65, 67; *Clarion*, 15 Nov. 1882, JCB.
9. Bettersworth, pp. 66–70, 111.
10. Minutes, 29 March, 25 April 1892, 21 Dec. 1894.
11. Bettersworth, pp. 70–1, 73–4; *Messenger*, 23 Dec. 1880, JCB.
12. Lee to Edgar, 23 Jan. 1885, Letterbook; Bettersworth, pp. 77–8.
13. Ibid., pp. 79–80; *Clarion*, 25 Aug. 1881; Board of Trustees, Mississippi A. & M. College, *Biennial Report*, 1883, p. 7, JCB.
14. *Clarion*, 15 Nov. 1882, JCB; *NCAB* 5: 415; Hesseltine, *Confederate Leaders*, p. 81.
15. Bettersworth, pp. 89–91, 93–5.
16. Ibid., p. 99; Welborn to Lee, 20 May 1898, Archives, MSUL.
17. Lee to Barry, 9 Nov. 1888, Letterbook.
18. Bettersworth, pp. 100–01; *SLJ*, 12 Oct. 1882, JSB.
19. Bettersworth, pp. 111–19; *SLJ*, 22 June 1882, JCB.
20. Bettersworth, p. 120; *SLJ*, 29 June 1882, JCB.
21. Bettersworth, pp. 120–23; Minutes, 10 March 1885; Lee to Montgomery, 3 Oct. 1885, Letterbook.
22. Bettersworth, p. 124; Minutes, 22 March, 16 June 1886.
23. Bettersworth, pp. 124–25.
24. Lee to Darden, Nov. (?) , 1882, Letterbook.
25. Bettersworh, pp. 131–33; *SLJ*, 1 May 1884, *Clarion*, 30 Jan., 1 May 1884, JCB.
26. Bettersworth, pp. 138–39; *Clarion*, 15 Dec. 1886, JCB.
27. Bettersworth, pp. 144–75 provides a detailed account of Burkitt's attack.
28. *Messenger*, 15 Sept. 1887, 14 June 1888, JCB.
29. BL, esp. 2; undated material, SDL-P; Bettersworth, pp. 86, 151–53.
30. *Messenger*, 25 April 1889, JCB; Bettersworth, pp. 144–45.
31. Gordon to Lee, 12 Sept. 1888, SDL-P; Minutes, 16 June 1890.
32. Minor to Lee, 25 Feb. 1899, BL 3.
33. D. Lipscomb, p. 22; Bettersworth, pp. 170, 172.
34. Ibid., pp. 161, 166; F. B. Simkins, *Pitchfork Ben Tillman*, p. 96; A. M. Shaw, *William Preston Johnson*, p. 220.
35. Bettersworth, pp. 169, 173.

NOTES TO CHAPTER 14

1. Kirby Smith to Lee, 3 May 1871 and "List of Invited Guests to the Festival," SDL-P.
2. Evans, 12: 512a; P. M. Savery, *CV* 2: 180.
3. W. White, *The Confederate Veteran*, pp. 14–19. This work contains a number of errors and must be used with caution.
4. J. W. Jones, *Army of Northern Virginia Memorial Volume*, pp. 8–10, 44–6; "Lee Memorial Association Circular," Pemberton to Lee, 24 Oct., 5 Nov. 1870, 10 Feb. 1871, SDL-P; *State*, 16 Aug. 1877, *Enquirer*, 19 Aug. 1877, BL 1.
5. BL 2, *Times-Democrat*, 14 Feb. 1888.
6. Evans, 12: 512c–512e; editorial, *CV* 18: 153–56; W. White, *Veteran*, p. 39; *Minutes of the Annual Meeting and Reunion of the United Confederate Veterans*, 3 (13th) ; 72 (hereafter cited as *Minutes U.C.V.*) .
7. BL 2, *Times-Democrat*, 10 April 1892; BL 3, Lee quoted in *Clarion-Ledger*, 14 Dec. 1893.

8. *CV* 1: 91, 97, 353.

9. Hesseltine and Gara, p. 98; BL 2, *Times-Democrat*, 14 Feb. 1888; unidentified clipping; *CV* 3: 176–77.

10. *CV* 18: 153; the first was at Maben, Miss.; another at Anderson, S. C.; see *CV* 1: 251 and Evans, 12: 512c.

11. W. White, *Veteran*, pp. 29–31.

12. Evans, 12: 512b.

13. Mary R. Dearing, *Veterans in Politics*, p. 74 and passim; P. M. DeLeon, *CV* 23: 255.

14. W. White, *Veteran*, p. 89; *Minutes U.C.V.*, 2 (10th): 80; 1 (3rd): 54; editorial, *CV* 18: 154.

15. W. White, *Veteran*, pp. 44, 86–7.

16. Editorial, *CV* 2: 54, 125, 156, 325; *CV* 18: 154.

17. Mickle, *Orders U.C.V.*, 1, G. O. No. 129; editorial, *CV* 18: 154.

18. BL 2, *Times-Democrat*, 10 April 1892 and UCV G. O. No. 299; Gorgas to "Ria" (Maria Gorgas), 3 May 1894, Gorgas Papers.

19. *Minutes U.C.V.*, 2 (9th): 8; *CV* 13: 154, 294.

20. *Minutes U.C.V.*, 3 (16th): 30–32; Lee quoted in *CV* 22: 487.

21. Invitation to be pallbearer, 10 Dec. 1889, SDL-P; Jones, pp. 570–73.

22. The second Davis funeral is recounted interestingly in "Story of the Jefferson Davis Funeral Train," *L & N Magazine*; BL 2, 3.

23. Jones, p. 573; *CV* 18: 153; *CV* 3: 8–9; circular, 12 Oct. 1897, Papers UCV, S. C. Div., Charleston, General & Special Orders 1895–1902, South Caroliniana Lib.

24. D. Lipscomb, p. 17; *CV* 4: 99; Evans, 12: 512f; Ishbel Ross, *First Lady of the South*, p. 388; Mrs. Davis to Lee, 23 Oct. 1896; SDL-P.

25. S. D. Lee, "Speech," *SHSP*, 24: 364, 380.

26. Editorial, *CV* 17: 123, 140.

27. *CV* 8: 11–12, 397; *Minutes U.C.V.*, 2 (10th): 112–13; Dearing, p. 495.

28. *CV* 8: 397; Dearing, p. 495.

29. *CV* 12: 373, 502; 16: 439; 24: 437; BL 1, "With the Confederacy Forty Years Later"; "SDL" 2.

30. *Minutes U.C.V.*, 3 (13th): 85; *CV* 23: 294.

31. *CV* 22: 326.

32. BL 1, 2.

33. *CV* 22: 55.

34. *CV* 25: 7, 152; 16: 205.

35. *Minutes U.C.V.*, 4 (17th): 10–12; *CV* 26: 384.

NOTES TO CHAPTER 15

1. Lee, *SHSP*, 32: 182; BL, unnumbered, Iowa paper.

2. Lee to Munford, 29 Oct. 1906, Munford-Ellis Letters; Lee to Green, 17 Oct. 1904, SHC (Green); Lee to Kountz, 6 Aug. 1907, VPC; *CV* 2: 40; 12: 294–95.

3. Hood to Lee, 29 Nov. 1865 and other dates, SDL-P; see also Hood, pp. 138–39.

4. Hill to Lee, 29 June, 4, 18, 21 Sept., 22 Oct., 20 Nov. 1866, 11 Jan. 1867, SDL-P. Hill apparently revised Brand's article, with Lee's help.

5. Pemberton, pp. 248, 291; Lee to Mrs. Wright, 22 Oct. 1904, SHC (Pemberton); Lee to Mrs. Wright, Dec. (?), 1907 and Lee to Eppa Hunton, 9 Feb. 1906, VPC.

6. Johnston to Lee, 14 Oct. 1867, SDL-P; L. H. Harrison, "How the Southern Generals Rated Their Leaders," *Civil War Times-Illustrated* 5 (July 1965): 29, 33; Colston's Recollections, SHC (Alexander); Lee to Claiborne, 30 July 1878, SHC (Claiborne).

7. Denison, pp. 362–65; W. B. Hamilton and R. Nuermberger, "An Appraisal of J. F. H. Claiborne," *Journal of Mississippi History* 7 (July 1945): 131–34.

8. Lee to Claiborne, 22 April, 17 May, 12 June 1878, SHC (Claiborne).

9. Hood to Lee, 10, 14, 18 April 1879, SDL-P; Lee to Claiborne, 28 April, 12 June 1878, SHC (Claiborne).

10. Lee to Davis, 3 July 1873, Lee to Walthall, 20 May 1878, Maury to Davis, 2 Nov. 1877, in D. Rowland, *Davis*, 7: 347, 8: 39, 204; Davis to Lee, 28 July, 28 Aug., 4 Sept. 1873, 26 Oct. 1874, 28 April 1882, SDL-P; Lee to Walthall, 28 May, 15, 20 July, 1 Aug. 1878, 21 April, 22, 23 Oct., 11 Nov. 1878, 26 April 1882, Walthall Papers; Walthall to Lee, 16 May, 8, 17 Nov. 1878, SDL-P.

11. Lee to Wright, 16 April 1885, Wright to Scott, 22 April 1885, penciled endorsement, SHC (Wright); *CV* 31: 50.

12. *CV* 12: 183–84; *Minutes U.C.V.*, 3 (13th): 76, 83. Rolls constructed from memory are of course less important than authentic documents. If Lee was overzealous, fortunately the two types of rolls were not intermixed.

13. *CV* 13: 378; *CV* 14: 376; *CV* 16: 424.

14. *Minutes U.C.V.*, 1 (3rd): 99.

15. Mickle, *Orders U.C.V.*, 1, G. O. No. 75; Warner, pp. 279–80; *DAB*, 10: 426; *B. & L.*, 4: 369–74.

16. Warner, pp. 43–4; *DAB*, 3: 483.

17. Kirby Smith to Lee, 8 Oct. 1892, SDL-P; *Picayune*, 4 March 1893. In 1878 W. P. Johnston had published a biography of his father: *The Life of Albert Sidney Johnston* (New York: D. Appleton and Co.); *Times-Democrat*, 3 March 1893.

18. Lee to Kirby Smith, 17 Oct. 1892, SHC (Kirby Smith); *Picayune*, 4 March 1893.

19. Mickle, *Orders U.C.V.*, 1, G. O. No. 118; Warner, p. 83; *Who's Who*, 6: 607; 3: 544; *CV* 12: 129.

20. D. Lipscomb, pp. 14, 16–7; BL 3.

21. Lee to French, 6 Aug. 1896, S. G. French Papers; W. J. Love, interview with the author, 16 July 1968; Beauregard to Lee, 12 Nov. 1892, SDL-P; BL 2, 20 Nov. 1892; typewritten excerpt from newspaper article, VPC; *SHSP*, 11: 501–04. Lee and Beauregard were adamant in their contentions though neither saw the firing of the first shot.

22. D. Rowland, *Mississippi: Heart of the South*, 2: 284–85, 319; Green to Lee, 14 May 1906, VPC; H. D. Southwood, "Riley of Mississippi," *Journal of Mississippi History* 3: 193, 197, 199.

23. This report, originally published separately, was included in *Minutes U.C.V.*, 1, following minutes of the 1894 reunion—Hist. Com. Report, pp. 4–6; Lee to French, 21 Jan. 1899, S. G. French Papers; Lee, "The South," in Evans, 12: 4.

24. About 1890, the committee noted a definite favorable change in historical work, an observation supported by Pressly (pp. 145–46), who says books written before that date tended to find a single cause for the War while those written later found the causes complex; *Minutes U.C.V.*, 1, Hist, Com. Report, pp. 9–10; the supplemental reader was Ann E. Snyder, *The Civil War* (by a Tennessean). Approved texts included *Grammar School History of the United*

States (L. A. Field of Georgia) ; *Hansell's Histories* (Professor H. E. Chambers of Louisiana) ; *History of the American People* (J. H. Shinn of Arkansas) ; four books entitled *History of the United States* (one each by Blackburn & McDonald of Maryland; Robert R. Harrison of Virginia; George F. Holmes of Virginia; Alexander H. Stephens of Georgia, and J. T. Terry [Derry] of Georgia) .

25. *Minutes U.C.V.,* 1, Hist. Com. Report, pp. 10–11.

26. Ibid., p. 8.

27. Ibid., pp. 8–9.

28. Ibid., pp. 9, 12.

29. Ibid., 1 (5th) : 18; 1 (6th) : 36–7.

30. Ibid., 2 (9th) : 147.

31. J. J. Mathews, "The Study of History," *Journal of Southern History* 31 (February 1965) : 4; Minutes, 1: 351, 357; 2: 18; F. Moore, "The Status of History in Southern Colleges," *South Atlantic Quarterly* 2 (April 1903) : 169.

32. The endorsed books were both by Virginians: Susan P. Lee, *History of the United States;* Dr. J. L. M. Curry, *The South: Constitution and Resulting Union,* both mentioned in *Minutes U.C.V.,* 1 (5th) : 17, 24; *Minutes U.C.V.,* 1 (5th) ; 15, 23–4; for more information, see Herman Hattaway, "Clio's Southern Soldiers: The United Confederate Veterans and History in the South," *Louisiana History* 12 (Summer 1971) : 213–41.

33. The first pamphlet apparently was published privately between 1891 and 1894. Byrd Publishers of Atlanta issued the second in 1903. Oglesby studied law under both his father and Confederate Vice President Alexander H. Stephens, whom he worked for as secretary. Preferring to write, he never practiced law but supported himself as a newspaperman and book salesman; see T. K. Oglesby Papers; H. Einbinder, *The Myth of the Britannica,* pp. 59–60; H. Kogan, *The Great E. B.,* pp. 63–4.

34. Lee to Oglesby, 6, 22 May 1894, Oglesby Papers.

35. Mickle, *Orders U.C.V.,* 1, G. O., No. 147; Lee to French, 2 May 1896, S. G. French Papers; *Minutes U.C.V.,* 1 (4th) : 12; (5th) : 25.

36. *Who's Who,* 2: 187, 232; Warner, pp. 76–7, 93–4; sources do not indicate where Ferguson studied or taught. He was admitted to the Alabama bar in 1865 and served in the state legislature in 1866 and 1892; I am assuming the William Peters of Maryland, the Latin teacher, mentioned in Evans, *Confederate Military History,* 2: 130 is the same Peters.

37. Mickle, *Well Known Confederate Veterans,* p. xxxviii; *Minutes U.C.V.,* 1 (6th) : 29.

38. Lee to Capers, 14 July 1896, Capers Papers: *CV* 5: 452; *Minutes U.C.V.,* 1 (6th) : 38, 42–3, 46–8.

39. UCV divisions in at least South Carolina and Virginia went farther; see Hattaway, pp. 213–42; Philip C. Brooks, *Research in Archives,* p. 21.

40. *Minutes U.C.V.,* 1 (6th) : 39; 1 (9th) : 153.

41. Bessie Pierce, *Public Opinion and the Teaching of History,* p. 146; Dearing, pp. 420–21, 485; Pressly, pp. 221–23.

42. Dearing, pp. 481, 485. Reconciliation was delayed until the twentieth century. Paul Buck (*The Road to Reunion,* pp. 236–37, 241–43, 246) reveals the difficulty in determining the contributions of the GAR and UCV; *Minutes U.C.V.,* 1 (7th) : 50.

43. Ibid., 1 (8th) : 47; Lee receives proper credit for moderation from Wallace Davies, *Patriotism on Parade,* p. 234.

44. *Minutes U.C.V.,* 2 (9th) : 144–47, 151–52; 2 (10th) : 80–1.

45. Ibid., 2 (12th) : 58; 3 (13th) : 62–3; *Who's Who,* 3: 221, 353, 1246.

46. *Minutes U.C.V.*, 3 (13th) : 64.

47. Ella Stratton, *Young People's History of Our Country* (Philadelphia: American Book and Bible House, 1902), p. 258, also published under several similar titles; *Minutes U.C.V.*, 3 (13th) : 64.

NOTES TO CHAPTER 16

1. Lee to Cunningham, 16 Jan. 1908, Confederate Veteran Papers; Lee quoted in *CV* 3: 176–77.

2. Ibid., pp. 8–9; NA-letter #90, RG 92, e. 175; D. Lipscomb, pp. 17–8.

3. Rigby, *CV* 8: 169; NA-Rigby to sec. of war, 6 Nov. 1909, RG, ibid.

4. Lee to Jonas, 6 March 1899, SDL Papers, Evans Memorial Lib., Aberdeen, Miss.; Lee to Rigby, 24 April 1899, VPC; Mooney to Lee, 17 Feb. 1899, BL 3; Lee to Daniel, 7 March 1899, J. W. Daniel Papers; Tillman to Lee, 17 Feb. 1899, BL 3.

5. Na-Lee's report, 30 Sept. 1899, RG 92, e. 715, box 233; editorial, *CV* 8: 169–70; Lee to Jonas, 6 March 1899, Evans Memorial Lib.; BL 1.

6. NA-Lee to Alger, 16 March, 7 July 1899, Rigby to Lee, 31 March 1899; Lee's report, 30 Sept. 1899, RG, ibid.

7. Confederate Pub. Co. to Lee, 27 July 1899, war dept. to Lee, 7 June 1899; Rigby to Root, 9, 23 Feb. 1900; Rigby to Govt. Prt. Office, 23 March 1900, VPC.

8. Rigby to Lee, 17 March 1900, VPC; NA-Lee's report, 22 May 1899; Root to Lee, 15 Nov. 1899, Rigby to sec. of war, 3 Jan. 1901; RG, ibid.

9. Lee to Rigby, 5, 17, 22 Sept., 25 Oct. 1900, 20 June, 17 Aug. 1901; Kountz to Rigby, 16 Oct. 1900, VPC.

10. Lee to Rigby, 18 July 1901, VPC; NA-Lee's report, 22 May 1899, RG, ibid.

11. Lee to Root, 20 Dec. 1899; Rigby to Root, 10, 13 May 1902, VPC.

12. Lee to Rigby, 1 May 1900, 14 Jan. 1902; 12, 19, 24 Jan., 1 March 1903; 28 July 1904; 18, 26 Dec. 1905; 28 Feb., 6 March, 21 April, 20, 26 Aug. 1906, VPC; Lee to Green, 4 Sept. 1906, SHC (Green) .

13. D. Lipscomb, p. 20.

14. "BHL Home."

15. BL 1; Lee to Rigby, 9 Oct. 1903, VPC; Lucille Banks, "Lieutenant-General Stephen D. Lee," BL 1.

16. Lee to Rigby, 21 June, 13, 17 Aug., 20 Sept., 28 Oct., 13, 16, 28 Nov. 1901; 25 Feb., 4, 25 March, 22 May 1902; Lee to Everest, 13 Sept. 1901; Everest to Rigby, 17 Feb. 1902, VPC; NA-Porter to Gillespie, 28 Jan. 1902, RG, ibid.

17. Lee to Rigby, 23, 30 June, 4, 9, 12, 19, 27, 29, 31 July, 2, 5, 7, 10, 12, 29 Aug., 20, 24 Sept., 8 Oct. 1902, Kountz to Rigby, 15, 28 Aug. 1902, VPC.

18. Lee to Rigby, 11, 19 June, 5, 8, 12, 15, 23 Aug., 22 Dec. 1903; 5, 10, 15, 26 Aug., 5 Sept. 1904, VPC.

19. Kountz to Rigby, 15 Aug. 1902; Everest to Rigby, 3 Nov. 1903; Lee to Rigby, 22, 25 March 1907, VPC; Georgia P. Young, *CV* 16: 384.

20. BL 1; Lipscomb, p. 29.

21. *Minutes, U.C.V.*, 2 (9th) : 164; 2 (10th) : 48; Hesseltine and Gara, p. 98.

22. Lee to Rigby, 29 Aug. 1906; Everest to Rigby, 6 Feb. 1907, Kountz to Rigby, 26 Feb. 1907, Lee to Rigby, 2, 7, 16 March 1907; Kountz to Rigby, 4 April 1908, VPC; Brown to Lee, 14 Jan. 1907, Lee to Brown, 28 Jan. 1907, Lee to Cunningham, 5, 18 March 1907, 4 April 1908, Confederate Veteran Papers; editorial, *CV* 17: 270.

23. Lee, *CV* 16: 9.

24. BL 3; Lee to Alexander, 18 May 1908, SHC (Alexander) .

Bibliography

PART I

BIBLIOGRAPHICAL ESSAY ON MANUSCRIPTS
AND SELECTED PRIMARY SOURCES

The largest and most useful collection of manuscript, typescript, and miscellaneous documents pertinent to this study is The Stephen Dill Lee Papers, in the Southern Historical Collection, University of North Carolina, Chapel Hill. The bulk of the material falls within the period after 1860 and consists mainly of military and personal correspondence. There are no items from the period 1904 to 1908.

Second in value and scope only to the Southern Historical Collection holdings are the pertinent Lee materials at the Mississippi Department of Archives and History, Jackson, Mississippi. The following collections aided this study: Samuel G. French Papers, L. Q. C. Lamar and Edward Mayes Papers, William H. McCardle Papers, John L. Power Papers, Charles K. Regan Papers, Alfred Holt Stone Literary Papers, and William T. Walthall Papers.

Smaller collections, also named The Stephen Dill Lee Papers, are located at the following repositories: Manuscript Department, William R. Perkins Library, Duke University, Durham, North Carolina; Mississippi Department of Archives and History, Jackson; North Carolina State Department of Archives and History, Raleigh; and the South Caroliniana Library, University of South Carolina, Columbia. Another similar collection, the Lee Family Manuscripts, has some S.D. Lee letters and is located at the Alderman Library, University of Virginia, Charlottesville.

The Southern Historical Collection, University of North Carolina has numerous other manuscript sets which contain some useful material. The collections cited in this study include: E. Porter Alexander Papers, Ellison Capers Paper (one item), J. F. H. Claiborne Papers, Confederate Papers (Misc.), Thomas Jefferson Green Papers, James Thomas Harrison Papers, Hillary A. Herbert Papers, E. M. Law Papers, William Porcher Miles Papers, Leonidas Lafayette Polk Papers, John Clifford Pemberton Papers, Edmund Ruffin Papers (microfilm), Edmund Kirby Smith Papers, Harvey Washington Walter Papers, and M. J. Wright Papers.

The Manuscript Department, William R. Perkins Library, Duke University, Durham, North Carolina, also has a rather large number of manuscript sets, each of which contains one or more useful items. These include: George William Brent Papers, William Lowndes Calhoun Papers, Ellison Capers Papers, I. H. Carrington Manuscripts, *Confederate Veteran* 1786–1933 Papers (Military Prison Records Division), C.S.A. Archives Army Military Telegrams (Mississippi), John W. Daniel Papers, R. G. M. Dunovant Papers, Nathan Bedford Forrest Papers, Wade Hampton Papers, Hemphill Manuscripts, Cornelius Baldwin Hite, Jr. Papers, Charles Colcock Jones, Jr. Papers, Charles Edgeworth Jones Papers, Munford-Ellis Papers (Thos. T. Munford Division), Thaddeus Kosciuszko Oglesby Papers, Daniel Ruggles Papers, and the M. J. Solomons Scrapbook 1861–1865.

The South Caroliniana Library at the University of South Carolina, Columbia, has several useful collections, mostly pertaining to the United Confederate Veterans. These include: Matthew Calbraith Butler Papers; Ellison Capers Papers; Joseph B. Kershaw Papers; United Confederate Veterans, S. C. Division, Charleston, General & Special Orders, 1895–1902; and United Confederate Veterans Confederate Survivor's Association, Camp Hampton, Richland County Records.

The Special Collections Department of the Emory University Library, Atlanta, Georgia, has several useful sets of letters which include: Candler Letters, Confederate Miscellany IIb, Miscellaneous Literary Manuscripts, Taylor Letters, and Wilson Letters.

Six repositories have small but useful holdings in Lee or UCV material. These include the University of Alabama Library, Tuscaloosa (Gorgas Family Papers); Manuscripts Division, Library of Congress, Washington, D. C. (Louis T. Wigfall Papers); South Carolina Historical Society, Charleston, South Carolina (Headquarters Papers, 1861–1865, James Gadsden Holmes Collection 1890–1903, and B. H. Teague Collection); The Virginia Historical Society, Richmond, Virginia (Holmes Conrad Papers, 1812–1950, Section 7, and Elizabeth Byrd Nicholas Papers); the Alderman Library, University of Virginia, Charlottesville (Warren H. Biggs Family Papers and the Leigh Robinson Papers); and the E. G. Swem Library, College of William and Mary, Williamsburg, Virginia (Warner T. Jones Papers).

Three collections of Lee items belong to private individuals. The author owns one which consists mainly of correspondence between himself and S. D. Lee's grandson, Mr. John G. Lee of Farmington, Connecticut, and correspondence with other historians regarding their candid opinions of S. D. Lee. The second collection was very kindly loaned by Dr. John K. Bettersworth, vice-president for academic affairs at Mississippi State University. The third belongs to a genealogist who requests that he be cited as "Thomas C. Read, compiler of *The Descendants of Thomas Lee of Charleston, South Carolina 1710–1769*, 37 Broad Street, Charleston, South Carolina."

The department of Archives at Mississippi State University, Starkville, has both the President's Letterbooks, 6 volumes extant, all covering the period when Lee served as president of that institution, and the Board of Trustees Minutes.

A huge unnamed collection of correspondence is at the Vicksburg Military Park Headquarters, Vicksburg, Mississippi. It contains letters to and from members of the Vicksburg Military Park Commission, but Lee and others wrote copiously and sometimes quite freely on a variety of subjects while engaged in park business. The material is notable and well worth preserving. It probably should go to the National Archives.

Of inestimable value are the Scrapbooks of Blewett Lee, 4 volumes, reassembled by Mrs. John G. Lee, 1967 and the Scrapbooks "SDL," 2 volumes extant (there is no volume I, the existing volumes are "II" and "III"), all now at the Stephen D. Lee Museum, Columbus, Mississippi. These large scrapbooks contain varied items, including some letters, but the vast bulk of the material is a myriad of newspaper clippings. Many of the clippings are identified; some unfortunately are not. There are passages about Lee and others written by him. His own scrapbooks also include clippings on various subjects of interest to him, although they do not pertain to him directly. He penned notes next to some of these.

Other scrapbooks of some use include those of Mrs. Florence S. Hazard, 2 volumes (she is director of the Columbus and Lowndes County Historical Society, Columbus, Mississippi), the Micajah Woods Scrapbook at the University of Virginia Library, and some unnamed collections at the Evans Memorial Library, Aberdeen, Mississippi (which also has one Lee letter).

A look at terrain and historical markers can sometimes be of value in reaching a better understanding of a military figure, and the present study is not an exception. Many sites, especially in Georgia, Mississippi, Tennessee, and Virginia were visited. Further, the military parks, particularly those at Antietam, Manassas, and Vicksburg, are rich in information that can be obtained in no other way than by a tour.

Very useful and interesting material on Lee was found in the National Archives, Washington, D. C. Most of this material of course pertains to the period when Lee was at West Point or later in the U. S. Army. The Archives also has a small collection of civil war documents captured at the "Rebel Archives" when Richmond fell, and several Lee items are in the Federal Pension file for Indian War Veterans.

Neither part of this bibliography lists all of the numerous collections, periodicals, and books which I have searched, but from which I have not cited any material. In some cases, such items have been of noteworthy utility: for example, all of Lee's uncited writings and his will. The writings of persons with whom Lee had interactions likewise have been useful: especially those by United Confederate Veterans members, the annual reports of Franklin L. Riley while Lee was associated with the Mississippi Historical Society, and the controversial comments by Nathan Bedford Forrest's partisan supporters, notably those whose works were included in Robert S. Henry, ed., *As They Saw Forrest*. Jackson, Tennessee: McCowat-Mercer Press, 1956.

PART II

LIST OF WORKS CITED

Alexander, Edward Porter. *Military Memoirs of a Confederate*. Edited with an Introduction and Notes by T. Harry Williams. Bloomington: Indiana University Press, 1962.

Amann, William F., ed., *Personnel of the Civil War*. 2 vols. New York & London: Thomas Yoseloff, 1961.

The American Heritage Picture History of the Civil War. 2 vols. New York: The American Heritage Publishing Co., 1960.

Balfour Diary. May 16–June 2, 1863. Typescript of the diary kept by Emma Balfour of Vicksburg during the siege. Copies at Mississippi State Department of Archives and History and at Vicksburg Military Park.

Barrett, John G. *Sherman's March Through the Carolinas*. Chapel Hill: University of North Carolina Press, 1956.

The Battle of Fort Sumter and First Victory of the Southern Troops, April 13th, 1861. New ed. Charleston, S. C.: Shaftesbury Press, 1961.

Bearss, Edwin C. *Decision in Mississippi: Mississippi's Important Role in the War Between the States*. Jackson, Mississippi: Mississippi Commission on the War Between the States, 1962.

Bettersworth, John K. *Mississippi Yesterday and Today*. Austin, Texas: The Steck Co., 1964.

———. *People's College; A History of Mississippi State*. University, Alabama: University of Alabama Press, 1953.

Blythe, Vernon. *A History of the Civil War in the United States*. New York: The Neale Publishing Co., 1914.

Boatner, Mark Mayo, comp., *The Civil War Dictionary*. New York: David McKay Co., 1959.

Bradford, Gamaliel. *Confederate Portraits*. Boston and New York: Houghton Mifflin Co., 1914.

Brooks, Philip. *Research in Archives: The Use of Unpublished Primary Sources*. Chicago and London: University of Chicago Press, 1969.

Brooks, Ulysses R., ed., *Stories of the Confederacy*. Columbia, South Carolina: The State Co., 1912.

Brown, D. Alexander. "Battle at Chickasaw Bluffs." *Civil War Times-Illustrated* 11 (July 1970) : 4–9, 44–48.

Buck, Irving A. *Cleburne and His Command*. New York and Washington: The Neale Publishing Co., 1908.

Buck, Paul H. *The Road to Reunion, 1865–1900*. Boston: Little, Brown and Co., 1947.

Buel, Clarence C. and Johnson, Robert U., eds., *Battles and Leaders of the Civil War*. 4 vols. New York: The Century Co., 1887.

Carroll, Thomas Battle. *Historical Sketches of Oktibbeha County*. Gulfport, Mississippi: The Dixie Press, 1931.

Carter, Theodore G. "The Tupelo Campaign." *Publications of the Mississippi Historical Society* 10 (1909) : 91–113.

Catton, Bruce. *The Coming Fury.* Garden City: Doubleday & Co., 1961.

———. *Grant Moves South.* Boston and Toronto: Little, Brown and Co., 1960.

Chambers, Lenoir. *Stonewall Jackson.* 2 vols. New York: William Morrow & Co., 1959.

Chambers, William Pitt. "My Journal." In *Publications of the Mississippi Historical Society.* Centenary Series, vol. 5. Jackson, Mississippi: Printed for the Society, 1925.

Chesnut, Mary Boykin. *A Diary From Dixie.* New ed. by Ben Ames Williams. Boston: Houghton Mifflin Co., 1949.

Clark, Walter, ed., *Histories of the Several Regiments and Battalions From North Carolina . . . 1861–1865.* 5 vols. Raleigh, N. C.: Published by the State, 1901.

Cleaves, Freeman. *Rock of Chickamauga; The Life of General George H. Thomas.* Norman: University of Oklahoma Press, 1948.

Confederate Veteran. 40 vols. Nashville: [Sumner A. Cunningham, publisher], January 1893–December 1932.

Connelly, Thomas Lawrence. *Autumn of Glory: The Army of Tennessee 1862–1865.* Baton Rouge: Louisiana State University Press, 1971.

Cox, Jacob. D. *Atlanta.* New York: Charles Scribner's Sons, 1909.

Crawford, Samuel W. *The Genesis of the Civil War; The Story of Sumter, 1860–1861.* New York: C. L. Webster & Co., 1887.

Cullum, George W., ed., *Biographical Register of the Officers and Graduates of the U. S. Military Academy at West Point, New York From the Establishment in 1802 to 1890 With the Early History of the United States Military Academy.* 3rd ed. 2 vols. New York: D. Van Nostrand, 1868.

Davies, Wallace Evan. *Patriotism on Parade: The Story of Veterans' and Hereditary Organizations in America.* Cambridge: Harvard University Press, 1955.

Dearing, Mary R. *Veterans in Politics.* Baton Rouge: Louisiana State University Press, 1952.

Denison, George T., Jr. *Modern Cavalry: Its Organization, Armament and Employment in War.* London: Thomas Bosworth, 1868.

Dowdey, Clifford. *Lee.* Boston & Toronto: Little, Brown and Co., 1965.

———. *The Seven Days: The Emergence of Lee.* Boston & Toronto: Little, Brown and Co., 1964.

———, ed., *The Wartime Papers of R. E. Lee.* Boston and Toronto: Little, Brown and Co., for the Virginia Civil War Commission, 1961.

Downey, Fairfax. *Sound of the Guns: The Story of American Artillery From the Ancient and Honorable Company to the Atom Cannon and Guided Missile.* New York: David McKay Co., 1956.

Dupuy, R. Ernest and Dupuy, Trevor N. *Military Heritage of America.* New York: McGraw-Hill, 1956.

Dyer, John P. *From Shiloh to San Juan: The Life of "Fightin' Joe"*

Wheeler. Rev. ed. Baton Rouge: Louisiana State University Press, 1961.
————. *The Gallant Hood.* Indianapolis: Bobbs-Merrill, 1950.
Einbinder, Harvey. *The Myth of the Britannica.* New York: Grove Press, 1964.
Esposito, Vincent J., ed., *The West Point Atlas of American Wars.* 2 vols. New York: Frederick A. Praeger, 1959.
Evans, Clement A., ed., *Confederate Military History: A Library of Confederate States History, in Twelve Volumes, Written by Distinguished Men of the South, and Edited by Gen. Clement A. Evans of Georgia.* Atlanta: Confederate Publishing Co., 1899.
Everhart, William C. *Vicksburg National Military Park, Mississippi.* National Park Service Historical Handbook Series No. 21. Washington, D. C.: Government Printing Office, 1954.
Figg, Royal W. *"Where Men Only Dare To Go!"* or, *The Story of a Boy Company (C.S.A.).* Richmond: Whittet & Shepperson, 1885.
Freeman, Douglas Southall, ed., *Lee's Dispatches: Unpublished Letters of General Robert E. Lee, C.S.A., to Jefferson Davis and the War Department of The Confederate States of America, 1862–65.* New ed. with Additional Dispatches and Foreward by Grady McWhiney. New York: G. P. Putnam's Sons, 1957.
————. *Lee's Lieutenants: A Study in Command.* 3 vols. New York: Charles Scribner's Sons, 1943–47.
————. *R. E. Lee.* 4 vols. New York and London: Charles Scribner's Sons, 1934–35.
Gibson, John M. *Those 163 Days: A Southern Account of Sherman's March From Atlanta to Raleigh.* New York: Coward-McCann, 1961.
Gordon, John B. *Reminiscences of the Civil War.* New York: Charles Scribner's Sons, 1903.
Govan, Gilbert E. and Livingood, James W. *A Different Valor: The Story of General Joseph E. Johnston, CSA.* New York: Bobbs-Merrill, 1956.
Green, Wharton J. *Recollections and Reflections, An Auto of Half a Century and More,* n.p.: Presses of Edwards and Broughton, 1906.
Hagerman, Edward Hayes. "The Evolution of Trench Warfare in the American Civil War." Ph.d. dissertation, Duke University, 1965.
Hall, Winchester. *The Story of the 26th Louisiana Infantry, In the Service of the Confederate States.* n.p.: no pr., [?1890].
Halsey, Ashley, Jr. *Who Fired The First Shot? and Other Stories of the Civil War.* New York: Hawthorn, 1963.
Hamilton, Joseph G. de Roulhac, ed., *Papers of Randolph Abbot Shotwell.* 3 vols. Raleigh: The North Carolina Hist. Com., 1929–36.
Hamilton, William B. and Nuermberger, Ruth K. "An Appraisal of J. F. H. Claiborne, with His Annotated 'Memoranda' (1829–1840)." *The Journal of Mississippi History* 7 (July 1945): 131–55.
Harrison, Lowell H. "How the Southern Generals Rated Their Leaders." *Civil War Times-Illustrated* 5 (July 1965): 29–33.
Hart, Albert B. *The Southern South.* New York and London: D. Appleton and Co., 1910.

Hassler, William W., ed., *The General to His Lady: The Civil War Letters of William Dorsey Pender to Fanny Pender*. Chapel Hill: University of North Carolina Press, 1962.

Hattaway, Herman. "Clio's Southern Soldiers: The United Confederate Veterans and History in the South," *Louisiana History* 12 (Summer 1971) : 213–42.

Hay, Thomas Robson. "The Davis, Hood, Johnston Controversy of 1864." *Mississippi Valley Historical Review* 11 (1924–25) : 58–84.

———. *Hood's Tennessee Campaign*. New York: W. Neale, 1929.

Henderson, George F. R. *Stonewall Jackson and the American Civil War*. 2nd ed. London, New York and Toronto: Longmans, Green and Co., 1936.

Henry, Robert S. *"First With The Most," Forrest*. Indianapolis and New York: The Bobbs-Merrill Co., 1944.

Hesseltine, William B. *Confederate Leaders in the New South*. Baton Rouge: Louisiana State University Press, 1950.

——— and Gara, Larry. "Mississippi's Confederate Leaders After the War." *Journal of Mississippi History* 13 (1951) : 88–100.

Hewitt, W. A. "Funeral Address—General Stephen D. Lee." *Baptist Record*, n. s. 10, no. 25 (June 18, 1908) : 7–8.

Hood, John B. *Advance and Retreat: Personal Experiences in the United States and Confederate States Armies*. New ed. with an Introduction by Richard N. Current. Bloomington: Indiana University Press, 1959.

Horn, Stanley. *The Army of Tennessee; A Military History*. Indianapolis and New York: Bobbs-Merrill, 1941.

———. *The Decisive Battle of Nashville*. Baton Rouge: Louisiana State University Press, 1956.

Howard, Oliver O. *Autobiography of Oliver Otis Howard*. 2 vols. New York: The Baker and Taylor Co., 1908.

———. *My Life and Experiences Among Our Hostile Indians*. Hartford: A. D. Worthington and Co., 1907.

Hubbard, John M. *Notes of A Private*. Memphis: E. H. Clarke & Brother, 1909.

Johnston, Frank. "The Vicksburg Campaign." *Publications of the Mississippi Historical Society* 10 (1909) : 63–90.

Johnston, Joseph E. *Narrative of Military Operations Directed, During the Late War between the States*. New ed. with an Introduction by Frank Vandiver. Bloomington: Indiana University Press, 1959.

Jones, John William. *Army of Northern Virginia Memorial Volume*. Richmond: J. W. Randolph and English, 1880.

Jordan, Thomas and Pryor, J. P. *The Campaigns of Lieutenant General N. B. Forrest and of Forrest's Cavalry*. New Orleans, Memphis and New York: Blelock & Co., 1868.

Kane, Harnett T. *Spies For the Blue and Gray*. Garden City, New York: Hanover House, 1954.

Key, Valdimer O. Jr. *Southern Politics in the State and Nation*. New York: Random House, Vintage Books, 1949.

Kirwan, Albert D., ed., *Johnny Green of the Orphan Brigade.* [Lexington]: University of Kentucky Press, 1956.

Kogan, Herman. *The Great E. B.; The Story of the Encyclopedia Britannica.* Chicago: University of Chicago Press, 1958.

Kountz, John S. *Record of the Organizations Engaged in the Campaign, Siege, and Defense of Vicksburg.* Washington, D. C.: Government Printing Office, 1901.

La Bree, Benjamin, ed., *Camp Fires of the Confederacy.* Louisville: Courier-Journal Job Priting Co., 1898.

The Land We Love: A Monthly Magazine Devoted to Literature, Military History, and Agriculture. 6 vols. Charlotte, N. C.: J. P. Irwin and D. H. Hill et al., May 1866–March 1869.

Lee, Stephen D. *The Agricultural and Mechanical College of Mississippi, Its Origin, Object, Management and Results, Discussed in a Series of Papers.* Jackson, Mississippi: n.p., 1889.

———. "Battle of Brice's Cross Roads or Tishomingo Creek, June 2nd to 12th, 1864." *Publications of the Mississippi Historical Society* 6 (1902): 27–38.

———. "The Battle of Tupelo, or Harrisburg, July 14th, 1864." *Publications of the Mississippi Historical Society* 6 (1902): 39–52.

———. "The Campaign of Generals Grant and Sherman Against Vicksburg in December, 1862, and January 1st and 2nd, 1863, Known as the 'Chickasaw Bayou Campaign.'" *Publications of the Mississippi Historical Society* 4 (1901): 15–36.

———. "The Campaign of Vicksburg, Mississippi, in 1863—From April 15 to and Including The Battle of Champion Hills, or Baker's Creek, May 16, 1863." *Publications of the Mississippi Historical Society* 3 (1900): 21–53.

———. "Details of Important Work by Two Confederate Telegraphy Operators, Christmas Eve, 1862, Which Prevented the Almost Complete Surprise of the Confederate Army at Vicksburg." *Publications of the Mississippi Historical Society* 8 (1904): 51–55.

———. "Johnson's Division in the Battle of Franklin." *Publications of the Mississippi Historical Society* 7 (1903): 75–83.

———. "Sherman's Meridian Expedition and Sooy Smith's Raid to West Point." *Southern Historical Society Papers* 8 (February 1880): 49–57.

———. "The Siege of Vicksburg." *Publications of the Mississippi Historical Society* 3 (1900): 55–71.

———. "The South Since the War." In C. A. Evans, ed., *Confederate Military History*, 12: 267–368.

Lewis, Lloyd. *Sherman: Fighting Prophet.* New ed. with a new Appraisal by Bruce Catton. New York: Harcourt, Brace and Co., 1958.

Liddell Hart, Basil H. *Sherman: Soldier, Realist, American.* New York: Dodd, Mead and Co., 1930.

Lipscomb, Dabney. "General Stephen D. Lee; His Life, Character, and Service." *Publications of the Mississippi Historical Society* 10 (1909): 14–34.

Lipscomb, Dr. William L. *A History of Columbus, Mississippi During the*

19th Century. Birmingham, Alabama: Press of Dispatch Printing Co., 1909.

Longstreet, James. *From Manassas To Appomattox; Memoirs of The Civil War in America.* Philadelphia: J. B. Lippincott, 1896.

Lossing, Benson J. *Memoir of Lieut.-Col. John T. Greble.* Philadelphia: Printed for private circulation, 1870.

Lytle, Andrew N. *Bedford Forrest and His Critter Company.* Rev. ed. New York: McDowell, Obolensky, 1960.

McCain, William D. "Nathan Bedford Forrest: An Evaluation." *The Journal of Mississippi History* 24 (1962) : 203–25.

McKinney, Francis. *Education in Violence, The Life of George H. Thomas and the History of the Army of the Cumberland.* Detroit: Wayne State University Press, 1961.

Mathews, Joseph J. "The Study of History in the South." *The Journal of Southern History* 31 (February 1965) : 3–20.

Maury, Dabney. *Recollections of A Virginian in the Mexican Indian and Civil Wars.* New York: C. Scribner's Sons, 1894.

Mickle, William E., ed., *Orders U.C.V.: General and Special.* 2 vols. New Orleans: United Confederate Veterans, 1911–12.

———, ed., *Well Known Confederate Leaders and Their War Records.* New Orleans: William E. Mickle, 1907.

Minutes of the [number] Annual Meeting and Reunion of the United Confederate Veterans. New Orleans: United Confederate Veterans, 1891–1912. Reissued as *Minutes U.C.V.* 6 vols. New Orleans: United Confederate Veterans, 1907–1913.

Moore, Frank, ed., *The Rebellion Record: A Diary of American Events, with Documents, Narratives, Illustrative Incidents, Poetry, etc.* 11 vols. New York: D. Van Nostrand, 1864–68.

Moore, Frederick W. "The Status of History in Southern Colleges." *South Atlantic Quarterly* 2 (April 1903) : 169–71.

Morton, John W. *The Artillery of Nathan Bedford Forrest's Cavalry; "the wizard of the saddle."* Nashville and Dallas: Publishing House of the M. E. Church South, 1909.

Naisawald, L. Van Loan. *Grape and Canister: The Story of the Field Artillery of the Army of the Potomac, 1861–1865.* New York: Oxford University Press, 1960.

Neilson, Eliza Lucy Irion. *Lucy's Journal.* Greenwood, Mississippi: Baff Printing Corporation, 1967.

O'Connor, Richard. *Hood: Cavalier General.* New York: Prentice-Hall, 1949.

———. *Thomas: The Rock of Chickamauga.* New York: Prentice-Hall, 1949.

Owen, William Miller. *In Camp and Battle with the Washington Artillery of New Orleans.* Boston: Ticknor and Co., 1885.

Parks, Joseph H. *General Edmund Kirby Smith, C.S.A.* Baton Rouge: Louisiana State University Press, 1954.

———. *General Leonidas Polk, C.S.A.; the Fighting Bishop.* Baton Rouge: Louisiana State University Press, 1962.

Pemberton, John C. *Pemberton, Defender of Vicksburg.* Chapel Hill: University of North Carolina Press, 1942.

Peterson, Harold L. *Notes on Ordnance of the American Civil War 1861–1865.* Washington, D. C.: The American Ordnance Association, 1959.

Pierce, Bessie Louise. *Public Opinion and the Teaching of History in the United States.* New York: Alfred A. Knopf, 1926.

Polk, William M. *Leonidas Polk: Bishop and General.* 2 vols. New ed. New York: Longmans, Green and Co., 1915.

Pollard, Edward A. *The Early Life, Campaigns, and Public Services of Robert E. Lee with a Record of the Campaigns and Heroic Deeds of His Companions in Arms.* New York: E. B. Treat & Co., 1871.

Pressly, Thomas J. *Americans Interpret Their Civil War.* New York: Macmillan, The Free Press, 1965.

Publications of the Mississippi Historical Society. 14 vols. Oxford, Miss: Printed for the Society, 1898–1914.

Publications of the Mississippi Historical Society. Centenary Series, vol. 5. Jackson, Mississippi: Printed for the Society, 1925.

Ratchford, J. W. *Some Reminiscences of Persons and Incidents of the Civil War.* Richmond: Whittet & Shepperson, 1909.

Read, Thomas Carpenter. *The Descendants of Thomas Lee of Charleston, South Carolina 1710–1769: A Genealogical-Biographical-Compilation.* Columbia, South Carolina: The R. L. Bryan Co., 1964.

Richardson, James D., comp., *A Compilation of the Messages and Papers of the Confederacy Including the Diplomatic Correspondence 1861–1865.* 2 vols. Nashville: United States Publishing Co., 1966.

Ridley, Bromfield L. *Battles and Sketches of the Army of Tennessee.* Mexico, Missouri: Missouri Printing & Publishing Co., 1906.

Rodenbough, Theophilus F. and Haskins, William L., eds., *The Army of the United States: Historical Sketches of Staff and Line.* New York: Charles E. Merrill Co., 1896.

Ross, Ishbel. *First Lady of the South: The Life of Mrs. Jefferson Davis.* New York: Harper & Brothers, 1958.

Rowland, Dunbar, ed., *Jefferson Davis, Constitutionalist; His Letters, Papers, and Speeches.* 10 vols. Jackson, Miss.: Printed for the Mississippi Department of Archives and History, 1923.

———. *History of Mississippi: The Heart of the South.* 4 vols. Chicago and Jackson: Clarke Publishing Co., 1925.

———. *The Official and Statistical Register of the State of Mississippi.* Nashville: Brandon Printing Co. Press, 1908.

Rowland, Eron. *Varina Howell: Wife of Jefferson Davis.* 2 vols. New York: The Macmillan Co., 1927–31.

Sheppard, Eric William. *Bedford Forrest: The Confederacy's Greatest Cavalryman.* New York: The Dial Press, 1930.

Sherman, William T. *Memoirs of General William T. Sherman by Himself.* 2 vols. New York: D. Appleton and Co., 1875.

Shotwell, Walter G. *The Civil War in America.* 2 vols. New York: Longmans, Green and Co., 1923.

Simkins, Francis Butler. *Pitchfork Ben Tillman: South Carolinian.* Baton Rouge: Louisiana State University Press, 1944.

Soley, James Russell. *Admiral Porter.* New York: D. Appleton & Co., 1903.

The South in the Building of the Nation: A History of the Southern States Designed to Record the South's Part in the Making of the American Nation; to Portray the Character and Genius, to Chronicle the Achievements and Progress and to Illustrate the Life and Traditions of the Southern People. 13 vols. Richmond, Virginia: The Southern Historical Publication Society, 1909–13.

Southern Historical Society Papers. 52 vols. Richmond, Virginia: Southern Historical Society, 1876–1959.

Southwood, Howard D. "Riley of Mississippi." *The Journal of Mississippi History* 13 (1951) : 193–211.

Steele, Matthew F. *American Campaigns.* Washington, D. C.: Combat Forces Press, 1951.

Stone, Henry. *Campaigns In Kentucky and Tennessee Including the Battle of Chickamauga 1862–1864.* Papers of the Military Historical Society of Massachusetts, vol. 8. Boston: Published by the Society, 1908.

Strode, Hudson. *Jefferson Davis.* 3 vols. New York: Harcourt, Brace and Co., 1955–64.

Stuckey, John M. Jr. "A History of the Battalion Washington Artillery, 1861–1865." Master's thesis, Louisiana State University, 1963.

Swanberg, William A. *First Blood; The Story of Fort Sumter.* New York: Scribner's, 1957.

Thiele, Thomas Frederick. "The Evolution of Cavalry in the American Civil War, 1861–1865." Ph.D. dissertation, The University of Michigan, 1951.

Thomas, Edison H. "The Great Chieftain's Last Ride." *L. & N. Magazine* (February 1955) , 3–5. Reprinted as a pamphlet, "Story of the Jefferson Davis Funeral Train." Louisville: Advertising and Publications Department, Louisville and Nashville Railroad Company, n. d.

Tilberg, Frederick. *Antietam National Battlefield Site: Maryland.* National Park Service Historical Handbook Series No. 31. Rev. ed. Washington, D. C.: Government Printing Office, 1961.

Tunnard, William H. *A Southern Record. The History of the Third Regiment Louisiana Infantry.* Baton Rouge: no pr., 1868.

"Tupelo National Battlefield Site." Washington, D. C.: Government Printing Office, 1961.

Vandiver, Frank, ed., *The Civil War Diary of General Josiah Gorgas.* University, Alabama: University of Alabama Press, 1947.

———. *Mighty Stonewall.* New York: McGraw-Hill, 1957.

Walker, Peter F. *Vicksburg; A People At War, 1860–1865.* Chapel Hill: University of North Carolina Press, 1960.

War of the Rebellion: A Compilation of the Official Records of the Union and Confederate Armies. 70 vols. in 128 pts. Washington, D. C.: Government Printing Office, 1880–1901.

War of the Rebellion: A Compilation of the Official Records of the Union and Confederate Navies. 30 vols. Washington, D. C.: Government Printing Office, 1895–1927.

War Reminiscences of Columbus, Mississippi and Elsewhere 1861–1865. Compiled by Columbus Chapter U.D.C. Copyright by Stephen D. Lee Chapter Number 34, U.D.C. West Point, Mississippi: Printed by Sullivan's, 1961.

Warner, Ezra J. *Generals in Gray: Lives of the Confederate Commanders.* Baton Rouge: Louisiana State University Press, 1959.

Wellman, Manley Wade. *Giant in Gray: A Biography of Wade Hampton of South Carolina.* New York and London: Charles Scribner's Sons, 1949.

———. *They Took Their Stand; The Founders of the Confederacy.* New York: Putnam's, 1959.

White, Henry Alexander. *Robert E. Lee and the Southern Confederacy, 1807–1870.* New York: G. P. Putnam's, 1905.

White, William W. *The Confederate Veteran.* Confederate Centennial Studies, No. 22. Tuscaloosa: Confederate Publishing Co., 1962.

———. "Mississippi Confederate Veterans in Public Office, 1875–1900." *Journal of Mississippi History* 20 (1958) : 147–55.

Williams, Thomas Harry. *Beauregard, Napoleon in Gray.* Baton Rouge: Louisiana State University Press, 1955.

Wilson, Suzanne C. *Column South.* Flagstaff, Arizona: J. F. Colton & Co., 1960.

Winston, Robert W. *Robert E. Lee: A Biography.* New York: William Morrow & Co., 1934.

Wise, Jennings C. *The Long Arm of Lee or The History of the Artillery of the Army of Northern Virginia with a Brief Account of the Confederate Bureau of Ordnance.* 2 vols. Lynchburg, Virginia: J. P. Bell Co., 1915.

Woodward, Comer Vann. *Origins of the South.* Baton Rouge: Louisiana State University Press, 1951.

Wyeth, John A. *Life of General Nathan Bedford Forrest.* New York: Harper, 1901.

Index

Abbott, Henry L., 237*n14*
Adams, Herbert Baxter, 220
Advance and Retreat, 207, 209
Alabama Gold Life Insurance Company, 164–65
Alabama Military Institute, 180–81
Alabama, University of, 178
Alcorn A. & M., 186
Alexander, Edward Porter, 60, 62, 65
Alexandria, Virginia, 34
Alger, Russell A., 226
Allison, Caroline. *See* Lee, Caroline Allison
American Historical Magazine and Tennessee Historical Quarterly, 212, 216
Anderson, James Patton: and Battle of Jonesboro, 131; and views on "war shirkers," 151–52; mentioned 239*n14*
Anderson, Richard H.: Federal commander at Fort Sumter, 16–26 passim
Antietam, Battle of: *Map,* 54; and Second Manassas, 51; clash at, 53; Lee at, 155
Antietam Creek, 53, 55, 58
Army of Northern Virginia: R. E. Lee commands, 39; reorganization, 44–45; at Second Manassas, 50; in Antietam campaign, 51–61; at Opequan Creek, 62
Army of Tennessee: Johnston commands, 108; Lee in, 124–25, 155; and Confederate command arrangements as Nashville campaign begins, 133; and Confederate command arrangements in Battle of Franklin, 136; at Battle of Nashville, 138; in retreat from Nashville, 146; to Tupelo, 148;

against Sherman in 1865, 152; *see also* Hood, John B.
artillery: in South Carolina Army, 16; Lee and Confederate Corps of, 19; at Fort Sumter, 23; and the Hampton Legion, 28; with Tredegar Ironworks, 29; increased, 30, 33; and Lee in Virginia, 32; in Peninsular campaign, 37; in Battle of Eltham's Landing, 38; in Seven Days campaign, 39; used by Magruder and Longstreet, 40; at Malvern Hill, 43; at Sharpsburg, 53, 55–56; in Battle of Tupelo, 120–21; at Columbia, Tennessee, 133; in Battle of Nashville, 140; in retreat from Nashville, 145; Lee and, 245*n36*
Ashley River (near Fort Sumter), 26
Association of the Army of Northern Virginia, 194, 200
Atlanta, Battle of: *Map,* 129; mentioned, 128
Atlanta, Georgia: Sherman moves toward, 118–19; and July 1864 Confederate command reorganizations, 124; after Battle of Ezra Church, 128; struggle for became a siege, 130; and Battle of Jonesboro, 131

Bacon Race Church, Virginia, 30, 37
Baker's Creek, Battle of. *See* Champion's Hill, Battle of
Baker's Creek, Mississippi, 88
Baldwin, William E., 89, 97–98
Balfour, Emma, 88–89, 91, 92, 96–97
Ball's Bluff, Battle of, 240*n19*
Baltic (Federal steamer), 19
Baltimore, Maryland, 123–24
Banks, Bob, 171
Banks, Nathaniel P., 67–68

271

erate command, 125; and command after fall of Atlanta, 131; and command at Nashville campaign, 133; and command in Spring Hill campaign, 134–35; and command in Battle of Franklin, 136; and Battle of Nashville, 138, 141, 143

Cherokee Station, Mississippi, 103–04

Chesnut, James, 20–21, 22

Chesnut, Mary, 154

Chickahominy River (Virginia) , 39, 40–41

Chickamauga, Battle of, 146

Chickasaw Bayou, Battle and Campaign of: *Map*, 66; Lee's role in, 62–77, 155; troop strengths, 69; weather conditions, 70; principal assault, 73–74; analysis of, 75–77; effect of on Grant's strategy, 79; and effect on trench warfare, 244n34

Chickasaw Bayou (near Vicksburg) : and Confederate defense, 67; significance of, 68–69

Chickasaw Bluffs, Battle of. *See* Chickasaw Bayou, Battle and Campaign of

Citadel, the, 16

Claiborne, James F. H., 208

Clark, Charles (governor of Mississippi) , 107, 119

Clark, William, 140

Clayton, Henry D., 127, 143, 145

Cleburne, Patrick, 125, 130–31

Cleveland, Grover, 186

Cockpit Point (near Washington, D.C.) , 33

Cockrell, Francis Marion, 229–30

Colchester, Virginia, 33, 36

Columbia, Tennessee: Schofield opposes Hood at, 132; artillery duel at, 133; and Spring Hill campaign, 134–35; and the Battle of Franklin, 136

Columbus, Mississippi: Lee's headquarters at in 1864, 111; and Battle of Brice's Crossroads, 118; as hospital and military headquarters, 149; birthplace of Regina Harrison Lee, 149; and Lee's residence after Civil War, 162

Confederacy: formation of, 16; and Fort Sumter, 17, 22. *See also* Lee,

R. E.; Lee, S. D.; *entries of individual leaders and battles*

Confederate command arrangement: conflicts in, 112–13; departmental system, 112–13, 248n1; after fall of Atlanta, 131; in Battle of Franklin, 136

Confederate Congress: James T. Harrison a member of, 149; and Lee's promotion to lieutenant general, 152, 247n6; and impressment of slave labor, 243n13

Confederate department system. *See* Confederate command arrangement

Confederate Military History: published by UCV, 220. *See bibliography*

Confederate National Memorial Association, 200

Confederate Orphan Fund, 193

Confederate States Army, 17–18

Confederate Veteran (magazine) , 195–96, 202–03. *See bibliography*

Confederate veterans, 193

Confederate War Department, 20

Confederated Southern Memorial Assn., 199

Congressional Committee of Fifteen, 159

Congressional Reconstruction, 159

Connelly, Thomas L.: incorrectly numbers Lee's cavalry, 245n6; and assessment of Lee's daring, 246n10; on Franklin campaign, 249n23

Cooper, Samuel (Confederate adjutant general) , 118

Corinth, Battle of, 70

Cornersville Academy, 212

Cosby, George B., 106

Crossland's Kentuckians, 120–21, 123

Crutchfield, Stapleton, 47

"cult of Lincoln and Lee," 220

Cunningham, Sumner A., 202, 203

Dabney, Richard H., 222

Darden, Putnam, 185

Daughters of the Confederacy, 165

Daves, Graham, 218

Davies, Wallace E., 256n43

Davis, Jefferson: as U. S. Secretary of War signs Lee's U. S. Army commissions, 10, 12; opinion of Lee, 29,

mander, 100–02; withdrawal from Tuscumbia, 103–04; and Forrest, 104–05; supply problems, 105–07, 111; at Moscow, Tennessee, 105; cavalry harasses Mississippi citizens, 106–07, 246n18, 247n28; clash with Sherman, 108–09; and cavalry command in Polk's department, 109–10; and Meridian expedition, 110–11; on Fort Pillow affair, 111, 116–17

——, as department commander: assumes command, 111–12; and Battle of Brice's Crossroads, 114–18; promotion, 115, 152, 247n6; opinion of Negro Union troops, 116–17; supply problems, 117–18, 247n28; relieved by Maury, 248n1

——, and Battle of Tupelo, 119–21; analysis of fight, 124, 248n16

——, in Atlanta campaign: assumes corps command, 124–26; and entrenchments, 126–27; in Battle of Ezra Church, 128; in Battle of Jonesboro, 130

——, in Nashville campaign: and Spring Hill, 134, 135, 137, 249n22, 249n23; in Battle of Franklin, 136–37, 141–46; gets R. E. Lee's spur, 147; criticizes J. B. Hood, 208–09; breastworks, 249n37

——, and Reconstruction Era: paroled, 154; and son, 158–59; applies for pardon, 159; as farmer, 157–58, 163; and Grange, 162–63; views on Reconstruction, 159–61; opinion of Grant as President, 160; opinion of U. S. Centennial, 165; and business dealings with Longstreet, 163–64, 208; as agent for Alabama Gold Life, 164–65

——, in politics: as reformer, 167; as candidate for state senate, 168–69; controversy over election of, 169–71; as state senator, 169, 171; campaign for governor, 171–74; breaks with Populists, 172; as Bourbon, 173; candidate for governor in 1887, 173–74; representative to 1890 Constitutional Convention, 174; and female suffrage, 175–76; and second candidacy for governorship, 189–90

——, as President of Mississippi A. &

M.: activities and endeavors, 178–192 passim; and industrial education, 179, 182–84; and land improvement, 183–84; and philosophy of education, 181–82; controversy over curriculum, 182–83

——, and United Confederate Veterans, 162, 193–205 passim; views on joint reunions, 202–03, 232–33; as commander, 198; as commander in chief, 204, 210–15; at funeral of Jefferson Davis, 200; and Lost Cause, 204, 224–25; and history committee, 205, 210–15, 222–23; and *Encyclopedia Britannica*, 218

——, as historian: debate with Longstreet, 50–51, 208; urges writing, 206; assesses southern defeat, 206–07; opinions on War events, 207–08; published works of, 209, 213, 220, 246n8, 254n4; controversy and assessment of works, 213, 221; view of women in history, 210; views on good history, 210, 212; as president of Mississippi Historical Society, 213

——, and Vicksburg Military Park: on parks, 224–25, 227–28; as commissioner, 225–26; efforts to get library, 226; controversy over construction, 227–30; resigns as commission chairman, 228

——, assessment: place in history, xi; as a military leader, xi–xiii, 6–7, 34, 64, 75–77, 88, 100–102, 111, 113–14, 155–56, 240n31, 240n18; conduct under fire, 49, 128, 133, 144; compared with others, 96, 104, 156, 232; attacks recklessly, 130; Gordon's analysis of, 155; military career, 155–56; daring, 246n10

——, ability with troops, 29, 33, 55–56, 73–74, 78–79, 96; conduct under fire, 49, 128, 133, 144; compared with others, 96, 104, 156, 232; attacks recklessly, 130; Gordon's analysis of, 155; military career, 155–56; daring 246n10

Lee, Thomas (ancestor of S. D. Lee), 3

Lee, Judge Thomas, Sr. (grandfather of S. D. Lee), 3, 237n1

Stewart, Alexander P.: and command organizations, 125, 127; at Ezra Church, 128; and Battle of Jonesboro, 130; in Spring Hill Campaign, 134; in Battle of Franklin, 136; and Nashville Campaign, 133, 138, 140–43
Stono River, 26
Stories of Dixie, 211
Stratton, Ella Hines, 222–23
Stuart, James E. B., 5, 6, 42, 43
Stubbs, James N., 211
Stubbs, James, 218
Sturgis, Samuel D., 114–15
Sunflower River, 80

Taft, William Howard (President of the United States), xiii
Tennessee, 68, 132; *see also* Memphis
Tennessee River, 132, 138
Thayer, John Milton, 76
Thiele, Frederick, 100–01
3rd Louisiana Infantry, 80
30th Alabama Regiment, 85, 94
31st Alabama Regiment, 85
31st Louisiana Infantry, 74
Thomas, George H.: as West Point professor, 5; dispatched by Sherman to oppose Hood, 132; and Battle of Nashville, 138, 140, 141, 142
Thoroughfare Gap (significant in Second Manassas campaign), 45, 46
Tillman, Benjamin R., 191, 225
Toombs, Robert, 242n22
Tracy, Edward D., 85
Tracy, Samuel M., 186–87
Tredegar Ironworks, 29
Tulane University, 191
Tupelo, Battle of (also called Battle of Harrisburg): *Map,* 122; troop movements, 120, 123; described, 120–24; claim by Federals that they had no breastworks at, 248n15. *See also* Harrisburg, Mississippi
Turner's Gap, 53
Tuscumbia, Alabama, 102–04
20th Alabama Regiment, 85
28th Louisiana Infantry: at Chickasaw Bayou, 70–71; at Steele's Bayou, 80
22nd Louisiana Infantry, 80
26th Louisiana Infantry, 70–71, 73
23rd Alabama Regiment, 85, 89

Union navy: at Vicksburg, 79–80; in Steele's Bayou expedition, 80; cuts Confederate supply lines, 92; Confederates sink gunboats of, 95
United States Centennial, 165
United Confederate Veterans: origins, organization, activities, 193–200; joint reunions with northern veterans, 202–03; reunions, 195–97, 199–200, 204–05, 213; compared with Grand Army of the Republic, 197; and aid to Mrs. Jefferson Davis, 200; and image of Jefferson Davis, 201; Lee as commander in chief of, 204, 223; sponsors, 205; and *Official Records,* 209–10; and muster rolls, 255n12. *See also* United Confederate Veterans history committee
United Confederate veterans history committee: purpose and goals, 210–11, 215, 219; activity, 210–12, 223; publishing efforts, 219–20; members of 211–12, 218, 221–22; Lee active on 210–12ff.; assessment of histories, 211–15, 222–23; controversy over *Encyclopedia Britannica,* 217–18; list of approved textbooks, 217, 219, 255n25, 256n32; results of work assessed, 216–17, 220–21
United States Army: and Lee's career, xii, 10, 16, 17, 19; *see also individual leaders, battles*
University of Nashville, 211, 212
University of Tennessee Law School, 211
University of the South, Sewanee, 211
University of Virginia, 212

Valley Road (near Vicksburg), 67, 69
Vernon, Mississippi, 102
Vicksburg and Jackson Railroad, 90
Vicksburg Battlefield: Lee makes speech at, 224–25. *See also* Vicksburg Military Park Association
Vicksburg, Battle and Siege of: *Map,* 81; preliminary actions, 82–83, 84; siege, 90–98; caves used for shelter, 92; role of supply assessed, 94–95; role of naval strength assessed, 95; Pemberton calls council to consider surrender of, 97; Lee opposes surrender of, 97–98; paroles, 98, 245n1;